Surimono from

the Chester Beatty Collection

ROGER S. KEYES

with an introduction by
WILFRED LOCKWOOD

INTERNATIONAL EXHIBITIONS FOUNDATION

ALEXANDRIA, VIRGINIA

1987

The catalogue is underwritten in part by funds from
The Andrew W. Mellon Foundation

Library of Congress Catalogue Card Number 87-081105
ISBN 0-88397-093-7

Designed by Stephen Kraft, Washington, D.C.
Typeset in Janson by Monotype Composition
Company, Inc., Baltimore, Maryland
Printed in the United States of America by Virginia
Lithograph, Inc., Arlington, Virginia

Cover: *Sūkoku II*, Moon and pine trees (cat. no. 90)

Table of Contents

Participating Museums

Worcester Art Museum
Worcester, Massachusetts
September 19–November 1

The Toledo Museum of Art
Toledo, Ohio
November 21, 1987–January 3, 1988

Society of the Four Arts
Palm Beach, Florida
January 23–March 6

Virginia Museum of Art
Richmond, Virginia
March 26–May 8

8

Acknowledgments

It is a great honor and pleasure for the International Exhibitions Foundation to present *Surimono from the Chester Beatty Library*. Drawn from the holdings of the celebrated Chester Beatty Library in Dublin, the one hundred Japanese woodblock prints shown here are a superb collection of works by the foremost masters of the Tokugawa period (1600–1868).

Organizing an exhibition of this breadth and quality requires the cooperation and support of many people. First and foremost, we would like to thank guest director Mr. Roger Keyes, noted surimono scholar and director of the Center for the Study of Japanese Woodblock Prints in Woodacre, California, for choosing the works and preparing the accompanying catalogue. Director Wilfred Lockwood's foreword about Chester Beatty provides an informative overview of the patron and his lifelong interest in collecting. We are grateful for his valued contribution and for his assistance throughout the development of this project. Mrs. Yoshiko Ushioda, curator of Japanese art at the Chester Beatty Library, assisted in the selection of the works and the realization of the exhibition. Mr. Susumu Matsudaira transcribed and prepared rough translations of the verses in the catalogue entries. To these scholars we extend special thanks. We should also like to express our sincere appreciation to the Chester Beatty Library and its board of trustees for their generosity in loaning these splendid prints for the four-museum American tour.

His Excellency Nobuo Matsunaga, the Ambassador of Japan, has graciously agreed to serve as Honorary Patron of the exhibition during its tour. We are most grateful to the Ambassador for his interest and support. We are likewise most grateful to the directors and staff members of the four participating museums, who have provided enthusiastic cooperation at every stage.

We have been most fortunate to receive

grants in support of this exhibition from the
National Endowment for the Arts, Washington, D.C., a federal agency, and from the Dillon Fund. We are extremely grateful for the
invaluable help these institutions have provided. Once again, it is a pleasure to thank
The Andrew W. Mellon Foundation for its
continued support of our catalogue program.

This publication could not have been realized without the expertise of editor Migs
Grove, designer Stephen Kraft, and printer
Beth Kent of Virginia Litho, all of whom
deserve our sincere appreciation. We are also
grateful to Philip Wilson Publishers Ltd for
granting us permission to reprint material
from *The Art of Surimono*. Finally, we extend
our warm thanks to the staff of International
Exhibitions Foundation—Diane Stewart,
S. Stanley Dawson, Tam Curry, Mimi Holland,
Sarah Tanguy and Linda Bell—for attending
to the numerous details of this international
exhibition.

Annemarie H. Pope   Lynn Kahler Berg
Founding President   *Director*

Joseph W. Saunders
Director
International Exhibitions
Foundation

Chester Beatty: Prospecting a Collection

WILFRED LOCKWOOD

Every private collection of art bears a distinctive character, due partly to the personality, tastes and methods of the collector and to the time in which the collection was formed. Of no collection is this truer than of the great collection assembled by Sir Alfred Chester Beatty, now, the property of the Irish people. This collection, perhaps the first ever assembled of Oriental manuscripts, is the result of a lifetime of patient and diligent search for perfection, combined with an enthusiasm for exploring the unknown. These were characteristics that typified Chester Beatty in his professional life and in his collecting.

By profession, Alfred Chester Beatty was a mining engineer, perhaps the most outstanding and successful of his generation. The Beatty family was of Scots origin and settled in the Irish city of Armagh. Robert Beatty, Chester Beatty's grandfather, emigrated to St Thomas, then a Danish island in the West Indies, where he lived until 1835, when he freed his slave workers, abandoned the plantation and settled with his wife and ten children in the United States.

The family into which Chester Beatty was born in 1875 lived at what is now the site of the Rockefeller Center, later moving to Morristown, New Jersey. Beatty's father, John Cuming Beatty, was a banker and stockbroker, not a rich man, but sufficiently successful to be able to provide a good education for his three sons. Young Chester Beatty (he always disliked the name Alfred) attended Westminister School at Dobbs Ferry outside New York City and spent much of his time searching waste rock dumps and auctions for mineral specimens. In time his childhood hobby led to his chosen profession as a mining engineer. J. C. Randolph, Beatty's neighbor in Morristown and one of the first to graduate from the School of Mines at Columbia University, enthusiastically encouraged Beatty to pursue his interest in minerals, so it was perhaps natural that, on leaving school, Chester Beatty proceeded to Randolph's old university. Before beginning his mining studies at Columbia, however, Beatty spent a year at Princeton taking a special civil engineering course. Once at Columbia, which was then on its old site on 49th Street at Madison Avenue, Beatty's capacity for hard work combined with an excellent memory and a natural love of the subject to ensure that he graduated brilliantly, his total marks being among the highest in the school's history. During his time as an undergraduate, Chester Beatty visited mines in Denver and was fascinated by the complexities of the mineralogy of this area, where discoveries had been very much more scattered than in other parts of the western United States. As he looked for a suitable opening for his professional career, he became convinced that Denver would reward a skillful engineer, and so he read every available book or article which could tell him of the history of mining and at the age of twenty-three he set out for Denver. Typically, Beatty refused his father's offer of an allowance, accepting only a one-way railway ticket to Denver.

Academic qualifications in themselves were, of course, not enough to ensure a successful career in mining, and Beatty soon learned that physical stamina, courage, entrepreneurial skills and diplomacy (which he possessed in abundance) were essential for a successful career in mining. Luck, too, plays a part in mining, and Beatty had his share. He entered the mining profession at a time when the systematic extraction of the minerals of North America was just beginning. Precious metals especially drew many men to the West: silver enjoyed an early importance until 1893 when gold was adopted as the monetary standard. Of the many who tried to take advantage of these developments, few were as spectacularly successful as Chester Beatty. The obstacles in his way were formidable.

Colorado was, like much of the West, recently settled and removed from law and order, to say nothing of sanitation or other amenities. Mining is in the nature of things a hazardous occupation both financially and physically. The mines lacked the most basic equipment to protect the safety and health of the workers, and although Beatty's constitution was robust, he fell victim to the atmosphere of the mines. (Dust is a major danger to the health of miners, and the use of equipment to extract dust is regarded as essential in all modern mines—not so in Beatty's day.) The air was thick with particles of dynamited rock, and Beatty's lungs were so badly affected that he was forced into retirement at the age of thirty-five. A more urgent peril, however, came from the lawlessness, especially from the militant activities of the mining unions, endemic in the mining camps. Beatty was to survive more than one attempt on his life after he had risen to managing of the mines. His skills brought him much work establishing claims and valuing mines for sale which, in the case of fraudulent claims and attempts to deceive the valuer, exposed him to serious danger from the unscrupulous mine-owners whom he was able to unmask. He had a combination of courage, integrity and knowledge, both technical and scientific, which made him a much sought-after consultant and mine manager. Chief among those who hired Beatty were John Hayes Hammond, at that time the leading mining engineer in the United States, and the Guggenheim brothers.

It was through his association with Hammond and the Guggenheims that Chester Beatty became involved in mining copper—the metal that was to become his greatest concern. Beatty's development of the processes for commercially extracting very low-grade ore, the so-called Porphyry Coppers, is arguably his greatest contribution to the industrial history of this century. In 1902 copper mining was regarded as commercially feasible only where a yield of at least three per cent per ton of ore was guaranteed. Known deposits were scarce; consequently, the supply of copper for commercial purposes was restricted—to the extent of inhibiting the commercial development of electricity for which copper is the most efficient metal conductor. As a result, the use of electricity was largely restricted to lighting. On behalf of the Guggenheim brothers, Beatty pioneered a method of mining porphyry coppers, opening the way for the expanded use of electricity and the industrialization of modern society. Because of his technical knowledge, practical judgment and skills in diplomacy and negotiation, Beatty was soon negotiating—very successfully on behalf of the Guggenheims—with King Leopold of the Belgians for mineral rights in the newly developing Congo, establishing an association with mining in Africa that was to last throughout his career. He was constantly on the move, investigating mines and negotiating purchases on behalf of the Guggenheims all over the Western Americas: in the frozen wastes of the Yukon and North-western Canada, the deserts of Mexico, the jungles of Central America and the wilds of the Andes.

Beatty's part in the Guggenheim Exploration Company was so important that when John Hayes Hammond resigned, in 1908 as general manager and consulting engineer, Beatty was offered the post. Beatty hestitated and in the end, despite much pressure, turned down an appointment that reportedly brought with it the largest salary paid at the time. He was now, at thirty-four, in a position to disregard such matters as salary since his investments were sufficient enough to guarantee a comfortable, even luxurious, life for himself and his family. Director of most of the copper corporations in the country, he decided to establish his own business as a mining consultant.

A large old house at 6 East 73rd Street on the corner of 5th Avenue provided the backdrop for Chester Beatty's growing collections of *objets d'art*, an interest that he was now able to actively pursue for the first time since boyhood. Notably, his interests were turning toward oriental objects. Here, when not travelling on business, Beatty was able to relax with his wife (he married Grace Rickard, the sister of a business associate, in 1900) and their two children. But this happy state of affairs was not to last long. Success in his career cost Beatty dearly. Years of working in dusty mines and living in rough and primitive conditions had undermined his health, rendering him susceptible to lung infections for the remainder of his life. This came to light in 1911, a year that was a watershed in his career. As his own health began to fail and after his wife died from typhoid fever, Beatty's doctors feared a complete breakdown and recommended that he take a long rest abroad. Beatty followed their advice and set out for London with his children, his brother Gedney and the servants.

The Beatty household settled for six months in the West End of London. Here Chester Beatty began to relax for the first time since he had left college. He went to art galleries and museums and visited dealers and auction rooms in search of the antique and the beautiful. He found life in London so agreeable that he returned the following year—this time to stay, taking a lease on Baroda House in Kensington Palace Gardens, which was to remain his London home for nearly forty years, though he seems to have had little affection for it, preferring the country mansion of Calehill Park he bought in Kent in 1917. In 1913 Beatty married his second wife, Edith Dunn Stone, like himself an American and enthusiastic and knowledgeable collector of art, who preferred European art, especially French Impressionists.

In 1914, Chester Beatty and his wife travelled to Egypt, where the warm dry air of the Egyptian desert acted as a tonic to his affected lungs. He spent his winters in Cairo, where he built *Beit el-Azrak* ("The Blue House") within sight of the pyramids. It was here that a completely new world opened up to Chester Beatty the collector, for in the bazaars of Cairo he became aware of the glories of Islamic illumination and calligraphy that were to become an important part of his collection. He was attracted by more than purely visual beauty. Ancient documents on papyrus seem to have fired his imagination and soon his purchases of important texts in Greek, Coptic and Ancient Egyptian were causing a stir in the academic world. In 1931 he announced the discovery of important early Biblical fragments, including some of the very earliest witnesses to the text of the New Testament, and two years later published, at his own expense, a full scholarly edition of the texts. The promptness with which material in his collection was made available to scholars and the pains and expense to which Beatty went to ensure the proper conservation and editing of his purchases bear witness to his claim that his objective in collecting was to preserve these treasures for posterity. The great series of lavishly printed catalogues produced by leading experts over the years show that Chester Beatty was not the sort of collector who kept his collection for himself.

Beatty's health, meanwhile, fragile as it was, was sufficiently restored so that he was able to resume his business activities. That he did so and that he was to make London the center of his activities was largely due to the influence of Herbert Hoover, at this stage in his career a successful mining engineer. Hoover pointed out to Beatty the cultural and commercial advantages of living and working in the capital of the British Empire. In 1914 Beatty and a number of friends set up Selection Trust, a private company for mining finance, the capital for which was largely provided by Beatty. World war hindered the development of the company, but Beatty's conviction that peace would bring great demand for metals was presently justified and the company prospered, financing mineral exploration and exploitation throughout the world (at the time of Beatty's death in 1968 the company's shares were worth £186,000,000). During the period between the two world wars, Selection Trust financed and organized ventures in diamonds in West Africa, lead and silver in the Balkans, copper in Central America and lead and zinc in the Urals. The most lucrative field of activity was in Northern Rhodesia (now Zambia) where the copper belt was controlled by Rhodesian Selection Trust. Beatty's achievement here and elsewhere was acknowledged by his profession in 1935, when he was awarded the Gold Medal of the Institute of Mining and Metallurgy:

One of the greatest of Mr Beatty's achievements is in connection with the development and equipment of the Northern Rhodesian copper fields in which he has taken a leading part throughout. . . . It is due in very great measure to his outstanding ability and enterprise that this district has become in a comparatively short time one of the major copper fields of the world.

The diversity of his ability is well illustrated by the fact that not only has he been the outstanding figure among technical men in the development of new mineral wealth in West Africa, Serbia and Northern Rhodesia, but he has carried these companies successfully through the various stages of financing and development to productive and profitable operations. Thus to the qualities necessary to the successful pioneer in mining he added those of the constructive organizer, the conservative financier and the able administrator. It is a rare privilege for a mining engineer to be recognized leader and pioneer in any new field. It is no coincidence in Mr Beatty's case that he holds this enviable position in these separate and widely diverse fields, each of which has added very considerably to the mineral wealth of the world.

Beatty's collecting was just as systematic as his mining, building a wide network of reliable dealers and expert consultants over the years. He patronized dealers such as Tano, a Cypriot who supplied many ancient and early Christian materials and the Armenian Sarkissian who carried many Arabic manuscripts, and sought advice from the likes of Edward Edwards, formerly of the Department of Oriental Books in the British Museum. When Edwards succeeded in negotiating the acquisition of the Khedival Library (the Egyptian Royal Collection) for the British Museum in 1924, the museum was content to take the items of literary interest, while the splendidly illuminated copies of the Koran were acquired by Beatty. In this way Beatty assembled a collection which, taken as a whole, is even more valuable than the sum of its parts for it illustrates the history of literacy, and thus in some measure of civilization, from the third millenium B.C. up to the present century in virtually all parts of the world.

This then was the pattern of Chester Beatty's life until the outbreak of World War II: regular work in the Selection Trust office in London and prolonged winter holidays in Cairo or the south of France. When war broke out in 1939, Beatty, who had become a naturalized Englishman, remained in his adopted country where, as vice-chairman of the United Kingdom Commercial Corporation Ltd, his professional expertise was of great service in ensuring supplies of strategic materials.

In 1945 peace brought a General Election to Great Britain in which Winston Churchill, for whom Beatty had the keenest admiration—"the greatest of our time, with the courage of a lion"—was decisively rejected by the electorate. The Labour Government (the first to enjoy a majority in Parliament) which took power was profoundly antipathetic to Beatty, who was alarmed by the prospect that Selection Trust and the other companies in which he had invested might be nationalized. His worries were not merely about financial loss he wrote his son Chester Beatty, Junior: "As creator of Selection Trust, I do not want to sit by and see it gradually die by Socialist strangulation." It was not only the future of Selection Trust that was causing him anxiety. Life in Britain had become difficult for a man like Beatty: the dead hand of socialism, as he saw it, was everywhere; bureacracy flourished at the expense of enterprise; and adjustment to the new post-war world was not at all easy. In any case, he was now over seventy years old and was seriously considering retiring from business. Ireland, he decided, was the "best country in which to retire. The country has atmosphere. The people have so much charm—life goes on as it did elsewhere until 1939." And so, in 1950, Beatty removed his household to Dublin, though his wife was to remain in London until her death in 1952. It was, he said, "more pleasant to drink a glass of Irish beer in a garden in Dublin than to spend the rest of my life buying fountain pens to fill in forms." What he brought with him was one of the greatest collections of manuscripts and printed books ever assembled by one man, and he built a special library and gallery near to his new home to house it.

Beatty's career as a collector was, however, by no means at an end. It was to continue for another fifteen years, during which time new materials of all kinds were acquired. Perhaps the most significant new venture was into the field of Japanese manuscripts and prints, which Beatty decided were not adequately represented. As with everything else in his life, Beatty approached this project systematically, commissioning Jack Hillier, an expert in the field to seek out and acquire suitable material: "I am just eighty, and I guess I have another ten good years of active life. I have collections of books and art of most Eastern countries, but very little of Japan and I would like to fill this gap in the Library." Beatty stipulated that no print should be considered for inclusion that was not in faultless condition, the only other condition being a maximum price of £125 paid for any one item. In fact, there was relatively little interest in Japanese art, and so the price limit created little difficulty, owing to the lack of competition from other collectors. A large number of fine prints—many of which Beatty discarded because they did not meet his exacting standards—assembled by Dr M. Cooper provided the nucleus for Beatty's outstanding collection of Japanese material, including some five hundred *surimono* prints.

Beatty lived for eighteen years in Dublin, during which time the British Empire knighted Beatty for his contribution to the economic life of the British Empire and his war-time work and the Irish people showed its warm appreciation by awarding Beatty honorary Irish citizenship, the first such award ever made. Beatty spent his summers in Dublin and the rest of the year in the south of France, where he died on 18 January 1968, just two weeks before his ninety-third birthday. In accordance with his wishes, his body was brought back to Dublin, where it was buried, after a state funeral, in Glasnevin Cemetery.

By stipulation of his will Chester Beatty's collection was entrusted into the hands of a Board of Trustees for the people of Ireland. The collection constitutes a memorial to the man and bears the stamp of his personality. Primarily, though not solely, a collection of manuscripts and printed materials from all parts of the world and every stage of history,

the collection carries the mark of the hand of a perfectionist who insisted on the best available specimens in any field. Sir Chester's perfectionism is to be seen also in the fact that he subsequently decided to concentrate on oriental materials, the fine qualities of which he must have been among the first to recognize when he realized that really first-rate Western manuscripts were no longer readily available. A desire for perfection, combined with a willingness to prospect into little-known areas of art where he would have only his own taste to guide him is characteristic of Beatty as a collector. It may be worth reflecting on the innate flair and taste needed to venture into the field of oriental art seventy or eighty years ago. Chester Beatty had very little help: the carefully prepared facsimile editions, the illustrated catalogues, the general histories and specialized studies to which we can refer today were not available then. When Sir Chester began to collect, even the experts—and they were few in number—were only beginning to feel their way. Indeed, in 1934, when Chester Beatty had been seriously collecting for some 15 years, the *Encyclopaedia of Islam*, that epitome of scholarship, gave just over one page out of some five thousand to the subject of Islamic painting. In the work of searching for the best specimens and discerning the canons of taste implicit in the production of widely differing schools or civilizations and discriminating between the important and the second-rate, Chester Beatty was more than a mere collector—he was a prospector and evaluator.

In the oriental countries in which he travelled there were few national collections of art to preserve the heritage of the past. By conserving and making them available to scholars, Beatty served as an enthusiastic promoter of the study of Eastern cultures. In assembling specimens of every culture and style of the Orient, Sir Chester Beatty not only provided materials for research, but also developed by the very discrimination which he brought to the task, the lines along which research would progress. Just as he provided the materials for the development of modern industrial society, so too as a collector was he able to select just what was significant for research and in the library that bears his name provide a matchless resource for future generations of scholars and a source of pleasure and interest to the general public.

The World Renewed

ROGER S. KEYES

During the early nineteenth century visitors wandering through the crowded streets of Edo could have stopped at any of a dozen shops and street stalls to buy color woodblock prints, the city's most popular souvenirs. They were colorful, exciting, inexpensive, light and easy for a traveller to carry. Unless the traveller were a poet, however, with an introduction to one of the leading poetry circles, he would probably never see a *surimono,* one of the hundreds of color prints that were published privately every year.

Surimono were especially popular in Japan during the first third of the nineteenth century. Some were distributed as announcements of musical performances, others commemorated personal events; most of the surimono collected by Sir Chester Beatty, however, were commissioned by poets as gifts for their friends. They celebrated the return of spring and the renewal of life and human activity at the beginning of the year.

Verse surimono were an affirmation of the intimate, delicate bond between the changing human world and the stable, dependable world of nature, as well as the continuity between the past and present. They were the blossom of an ancient tree of culture that had grown in uninterrupted peace for two hundred years, the blossom of a belief that the world and mankind were not separate and that personal contentment could be achieved in the midst of the objects and events of everyday life. Since the artists and poets simply took truths for granted, their work was neither solemn nor abstract. Their conviction shines through their work like sunlight or the easy playful freshness of a breeze on a spring day.

Indeed, this freshness is an unfailing characteristic of surimono, which were also both calm and challenging, eclectic and original, sober and gay, frequently audacious, occasionally trite. Private publication has always attracted some of Japan's most intelligent, inventive and original designers, and the surimono artists who inherited the styles and technical mastery of their eighteenth-century predecessors were the experimental vanguard of a new tradition.

Even an introduction to the poetry circles of nineteenth-century Edo would not have guaranteed that the visitor would see any surimono. Like Christmas cards, most surimono, were exchanged for a very short period at the very beginning of the year, then were carefully put away, all but forgotten once the year was underway. Unlike Christmas cards, however, surimono could not be purchased readymade. A few Japanese made their own surimono (cat. no. 54), but most poets had to make special arrangements. A collaborative art form, surimono required the skills of at least seven different specialists: artists, poet, calligrapher, blockcutter, printer, text engraver, and the publisher whose chief roles were to coordinate the work, guarantee quality, and produce an edition of the print on schedule.

Verse on greeting cards is usually impersonal, unsigned and nondescript. Surimono verse, composed for the occasion by the poet, his teachers and friends, was vitally important because it was the inspiration—or at least the point of departure—for the artist's picture. It was also a constraint because the artist had to leave enough room in his design to accommodate the verse.

The verse was so important, that special calligraphers and engravers who specialized in carving written text were usually required. Once the picture block was finished, the text calligrapher inscribed the verse to fit precisely into the space the artist had allocated. The verse was then cut on a new block to align with the prescribed area on the picture block. Since image and verse were printed from different blocks, duplicate impressions of the same surimono often appear in slightly different positions. The ink color of the writing and the picture outline also varies for the same reason. This is one of many subtle refinements of surimono printing.

Verse surimono were only one part of the intricate ritual of renewal with which Japanese individuals and families began each year. Like nature renewing itself, certain familiar images and symbols appeared over and over again in surimono: the first rays of the rising sun; the first tree to flower (plum); the first bird to sing (warbler); the first buds to green (willow); and *toso*, the medicinal wine that was served to celebrate the New Year. These and other images recur year after year in the verse and pictures on surimono.

In the timeless world of art, spring is eternal; each spring is Spring. But surimono also reminded the viewer that in the human world, this spring is also different from every other, an idea that was often conveyed symbolically. Time in Japan was divided into twelve recurrent units that were named for animals of the Chinese calendrical cycle: rat, ox, tiger, rabbit, dragon, snake, horse, sheep, monkey, bird, dog, boar. Each of the twelve hours of the day was ruled by one of these animals, as was each successive day and year. A Rabbit Year was different from a Tiger Year, and surimono emphasized this. Poets mentioned the cyclical animals in their verse, and artists included them in their pictures in many playful and ingenious ways: a painting of an ox, a tiger skin rug, a legendary warrior slaying a dragon, a desk ornament in the shape of a silver rabbit, an actual dog, or more obliquely—as in sets of the themes of Thirty-six Birds, Five Tiger Generals, and The Rat's Wedding—words beginning with the letter "u" (the word for rabbit), or pictures of seashells (found on the island of Enoshima where pilgrams worshipped Benten, a goddess whose companion was a white snake.

The changing sequence of long and short

months was another way of representing the uniqueness of a particular spring and the difference between the years. Months in nineteenth-century Japan were divided into either twenty-eight or twenty-nine days, and the sequence of these long and short months, which varied from year to year, was determined by government officials. Therefore, each year had a distinct mathematical character that was often interwoven into the verse or the design of the surimono. In fact, picture calendars (*egoyomi*) were an important precursor of New Year surimono, and in the nineteenth century elements of the two were often combined.

Most families have yearly rituals. When I was a child my family had a tree every Christmas. It sat in the same corner of the same room, and we decorated it with the same lights, ornaments and tinsel. Older now, we gather at my sister's house each Christmas Eve to decorate a tree. Only a few ornaments have survived from our childhood, and although there are a few new ones each year and we always hang them differently, we each enjoy the continuity of doing this year after year. On the first few days of the New Year in Japan many still observe traditional activities: the same food is served for breakfast, the same gifts are exchanged, the same ornaments decorate the alcove, the same inscriptions are copied out as the first calligraphy of the New Year. Exchanging surimono was another tradition that could be repeated year after year, but unlike the breakfast menu or the visits to neighbors and relatives with their fixed and familiar verbal exchanges, surimono were a complete surprise. "Each day, make it new," Confucius wrote in the *Analects*. For all their references to the timeless symbols of spring, each verse on a surimono was personal, new and unique; so were the pictures. No matter how conventional the subjects, each artist found a way of making them fresh year after year.

While all New Year surimono suggested renewal, many helped create it. Some artists illustrated the poet's verse quite literally. Others used them as points of departure for spirited creative flights of their own. But however familiar the subject, however conventional the artist and however many pictures of a warbler on a plum branch a poet had seen, *this* particular warbler was always unique. And when poets reread their verses refracted back through a particularly original or striking design, they often discovered new meaning in their own words.

Those who received surimono had an experience far different from the author's. They saw the picture first and their response to the picture colored their reading of the verse. When they finally read the poem, it was not uncommon for the words to come as a complete surprise, causing them to see the picture very differently. (Cursive Japanese script needs to be deciphered slowly. Even people who can read this verse fluently, see it first as a decorative part of the design.) For instance, Kubo Shumman designed a picture of a plump, cuddly bunny rabbit for a surimono, of which the first poem reads: "How enjoyable, on New Year's Day, a steaming bowl, piping hot, of . . . rabbit soup!" Any viewer's first impression of the picture would surely be altered once they read this verse.

Perhaps an example from Hokusai's Horse set would further exemplify the intricate relationship between image and verse. The Yomo (or Four Directions) Group was the largest organization of poets in Edo and one of the largest sponsors of surimono sets in the early nineteenth century. In the spring of 1821, a Snake Year, the group published thirty-six surimono on the theme of shells. (Remember the association between shells, Enoshima, Benten and the white snake.) The following year, a Horse Year, they decided to publish a set of thirty surimono and commissioned the pictures from Katsushika Hokusai, the artist who had designed the shell prints. Once the theme was agreed upon, members of the group composed their verses and delivered them to Hokusai. A verse by Sanseitei Maumi, titled *Mayoke* (Exorcising Horses), read:

> New Year's Day:
> beside the gull-shining sea
> the sun's first rays
> make Mirror Mountain
> dazzling.

Mirror Mountain is a hill beside Lake Biwa, a large inland body of water near Kyoto often described in classical verse as the "gull-shining sea." On New Year's Day, as the sun rose in the east, the sun's rays would strike Mirror Mountain, making it reflect the light and glitter. Hokusai was no doubt struck, as we are, by the fact that the poem mentions neither horse nor exorcism. But by taking into account the poetic rules of homophonous association, he soon realized that *mayoke* really meant "exorcising demons." The verse was written with the character for horse only as a pretext to include it in the series. Once that was understood, the connection between exorcising demons and the New Year verse became obvious: the dazzling mirror was an implement used in many traditional Japanese shamanistic rituals to drive away evil spirits. With those hints, Hokusai designed his picture—a still life with a porcelain bowl, a towel rack, a lacquer pitcher and a basin (cat. no. 49). The lacquer basin is filled with water; the bowl contains a flowering adonis (*fukujus*, a plant that blooms at New Year), a few sprigs of spear flower and a miniature pine tree.

Imagine your response as another member of the Yomo Group, after receiving this print from the poet Maumi as part of the New Year exchange. "Exorcising Horses." It makes no sense at all! If you look at the picture more closely, however, you notice that each of the four objects in the picture is decorated with a landscape and that the inscription on the bowl—"Mii, Ishiyama and Hira"—refers to three of the eight canonical views of Lake Biwa. Soon you discover the long bridge at Seta, the octagonal floating temple at Katata, the castle at Awazu, and the "returning sails" of Yabase. That makes seven subjects, but there is still no sign of Karasaki, the eighth view. Now you turn your attention to the verse. Once you read "gull-shining sea," you recognize Lake Biwa and congratulate yourself upon deciphering that much of the puzzle. The water in the basin represents the lake, with at least seven of the "Eight Views" surrounding it. "Mirror Mountain." Well, the silver surface in the black basin certainly looks like a circular metal mirror in its lacquered case, so there is the mirror. Printed in silver, it reflects the light and looks dazzling. Suddenly you remember the title: Exorcising—mirrors exorcise demons. *Mayoke*, "Exorcising demons"! Of course!! But you could not have made the connection unless the poem told you—or perhaps I should say allowed you to recognize—that the surface of the water in the basin might also be a mirror. Eventually, your mind returns to the eight famous places around Lake Biwa, the artist's generous addition to the design. You've found seven of them; where could the eighth be? Karasaki. Oh yes, there it is—the Karasaki Pine!

Not all New Year surimono are this complex, but each created a region of time and heightened awareness in which a person could see an image or read a verse, even a verse one had written oneself, in a new way. Images were not required to be this complex, but whenever they were, the viewer/reader would most often become part of the process of discovery without any special effort. This is an example of how a culture's values can be embodied in its arts.

How intelligent, sophisticated, deliberate and self-aware the surimono designers and their patrons were. But what meaning and value do these pictures have for people like ourselves today who cannot read cursive Japanese and do not know that the "gull-shining sea" is Lake Biwa, that the word for *horse* sounds like the word for *demon* or that mirrors were used for exorcisms? I raise this question because most people who love surimono enjoy them irrespective of their overtones and literary content. How much are they really missing?

When most of us, including myself, approach a form of art with which we are unfamiliar, we bring many unconscious habits and associations to the experience—just like the original viewers of Shumman's Rabbit or Hokusai's Horse prints. This is natural, but limiting.

Surimono attract and absorb our attention because their surfaces are extremely sensuous and rich. They are printed on a beautiful, thick, nearly unsized, long-fibered and absorbent paper that gives the expensive pigments an unusual luminosity and depth. When our attention is absorbed, two related things can happen. We might experience what the Tibetans call *drala*, the vivid, almost magical quality of presence that objects assume when our attention becomes more absorbed in perceptions than in thought. We might also enter into an identifying state. In this state we experience for ourselves some of the inner qualities of the people who made these prints: serenity, exuberance, mastery, satisfaction.

The experiences I have described are mediated more by imagination and feeling than intellect. But the Japanese in the nineteenth century had no word for intellect in our sense. Their word for *mind* was *kokoro;* it was located in the chest and also meant *heart.*

While Western cultures investigated the reaches of thought, the Japanese explored the realms of human feeling, those broad areas of human experience where taste, imagination, sensibility, intuition, emotion and awareness converge. They recorded their discoveries in art forms like surimono.

Successful art does not challenge its viewers, so much as lead them momentarily into adopting an unfamiliar point of view. But personal habits are tenacious and swiftly return us to the familiar ground of our past associations. The surimono makers were aware of this tyranny and created a form that led the viewer gently but irresistibly out of the pathways of habit into the open meadows of a shared and common view. Surimono is an art that celebrates a shared vision of the everyday world. The prints were created by artists living in an old culture that was stable enough to give its citizens peace for more than two centuries. Surimono are deliberate and spontaneous, serious and playful. They were conceived with dignity, respect, intelligence and humor. They celebrate wonder, delight and shared knowledge, remind us that the sacred is present in our ordinary lives, and help renew in us the human gift of creating a common world.

The fully illustrated catalogue is divided into three sections: Ukiyo-e artists, Shijō artists and Handscroll and Books and albums. The first and largest section includes single-sheet prints produced in Edo (now Tokyo) between the 1760s and the 1840s; the second, single-sheet prints produced by artists of the Shijō school between the 1850s and 1860s. These sections are arranged alphabetically by artist with the artist's works listed in chronological order. The third section includes privately printed books and albums of all styles. Since many contain works by more than one artist, they have been arranged in chronological order. Dimensions are given in centimeters, height preceding width. The information or verses on the surimono have been translated and reprinted where it seemed important and practical. Verses have not been translated of the miniature anthologies because the pictures are only indirectly related to the verse or of most prints with haiku because their images are either simple illustrations or independent of the verse.

Ukiyo-e artists

Kōkintei Banzan active *c.* mid 1820s

Banzan (or Hanzan) was a poet who designed a few square surimono in the 1820s, including a set of *Three Trees* for the Sugawara Circle and some illustrations of his own verse.

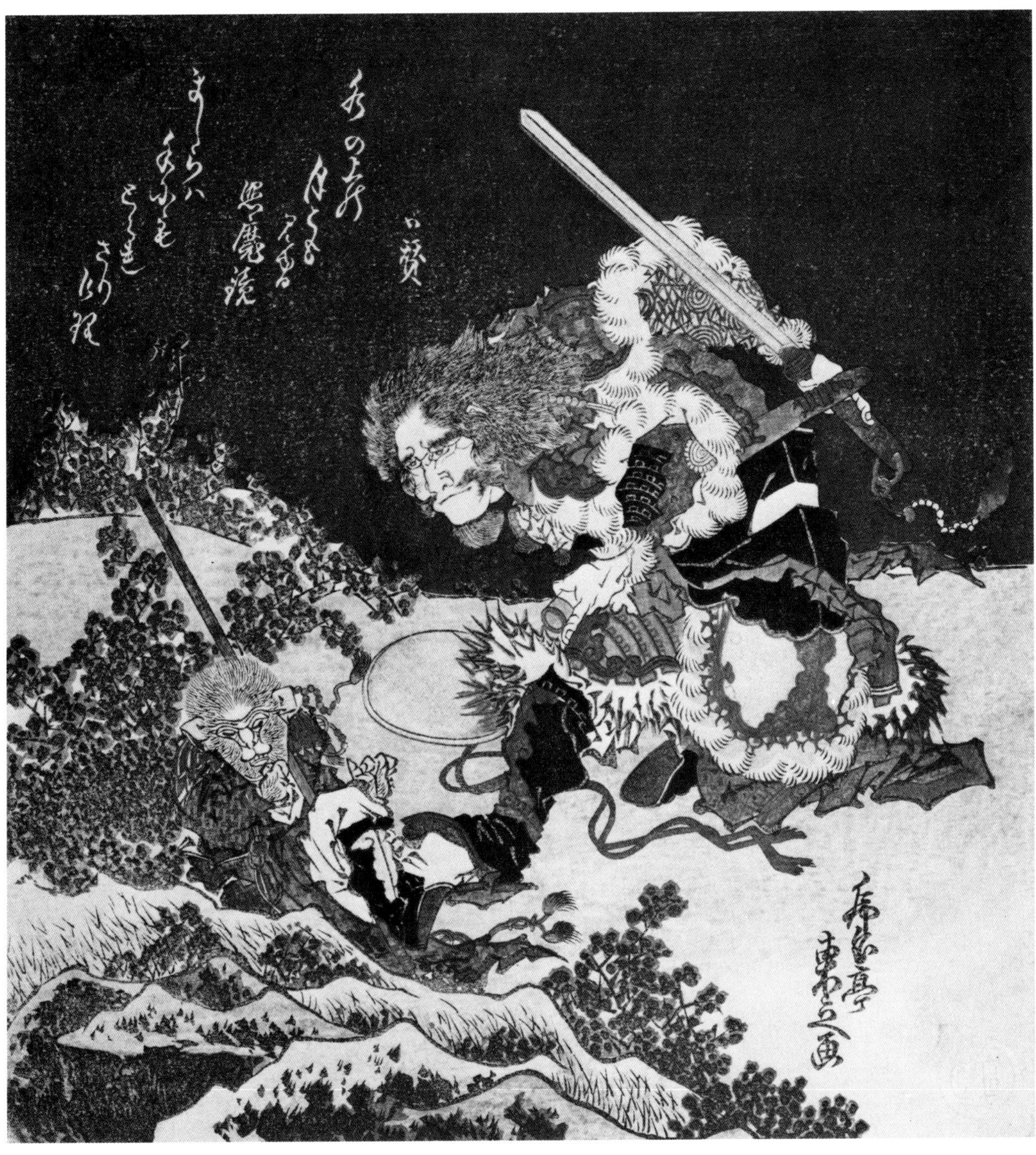

1

Chinese warrior and monkey
possibly 1824
19.3 × 17.2 cm
signed Kōkintei Kanshi (?)
Beatty 2157

The Chinese warrior is holding a tasseled silver mirror, which the poem identifies as a *shōmakyō*, or mirror that makes evil spirits visible. The mirror reveals to him that his opponent is actually a monkey; the picture may illustrate an episode in the novel *Saiyūki*, "Chronicle of a Journey to the West," in which Yuan Zhong, a seventh-century Chinese priest, travels to India in search of Buddhist scriptures with Songokū, a monkey possessing supernatural powers who could assume human form. The presence of a monkey suggests that the picture may have been designed in a Monkey Year, either 1824 or 1836. The style of the drawing and the fact that the artist's other prints were published in the 1820s make the choice of 1824 more likely. If so, the background color is probably not Prussian blue, since that color is not said to have been used in Edo before 1828. The poem was written by the artist and the word *kōsan* that follows it probably means "oral composition."

Mizu no ue no tsuki tomo miyuru shōmakyō majiraba te nimo torarezarikeri

"The moon on the water was also seen in the magic mirror, but the hand could not grasp it"

Keisai Eisen

1790–1848, active from *c.* 1809

The son of the calligrapher Ikeda Shigeharu, Eisen was born in Edo, studied with a Kanō painter, Hakkeisai, and then with Kikugawa Eizan. He specialized in pictures of women, book illustrations and erotica, but designed a number of surimono between the late 1810s and late 1820s. He used the *gō* Ippitsuan before his signature on his earliest surimono; afterwards he signed them Keisai Eisen, or simply Keisai, changing the way he wrote the character *sai* in 1825 from a square to a cursive form.

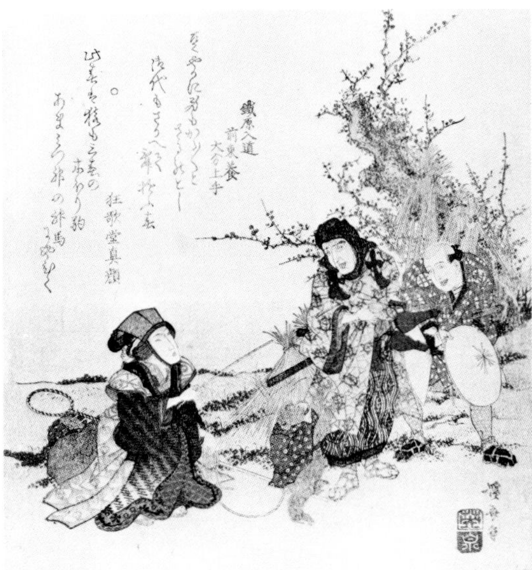

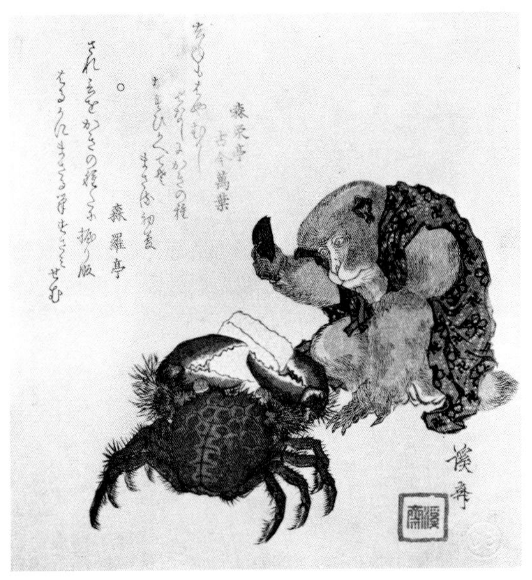

2

The samurai poet Tetsuhara Nyūdō and a
companion watch a performing monkey
1824
20.8 × 18.7 cm
signed Kēisai hitsu
seal Eisen
Beatty 1992

The monkey begs for the rice ball held by the
elderly poet, whose robe is decorated with his
personal emblem, a turtle. His companion's
surname, Murai, is written on the two circular medallions on his robe, while the woman's
over-robe and sash are patterned with the fan-
shaped emblem of the Yomo poetry group of
which Magao was the leader. The first poem
puns on the word *saru*, which means both
"monkey" and "depart"; the second compares
the monkey with the toy wooden ponies that
were made in the town of Miharu in the
Tamura district of Fukushima Prefecture.
There is a pun on Miharu and *haru*, which
means "spring."

*Mameyaka ni mi mo karugaru to saru no toshi
miyo mo sakaete maiasobu haru*

"We set out in good health and high spirits;
spring plays and dances; the emperor's reign
prospers in the Monkey Year"
 Tetsuhara Nyūdō saki no Tōyō Daibu Jōzu

*Kono haru wa saru mo miharu no kibori koma
amamitsu kami no shimme ni ya hiku*

"Isn't this Spring's monkey a wooden pony
from Miharu, led like the sacred horse of the
gods who fill the sky?" *Kyōkadō Magao*

3

Monkey offering a crab a dried persimmon
seed
1824
20.8 × 18.6 cm
signed Keisai
seal Keisai
Beatty 2059

At the beginning of the Japanese children's
story called "The Battle of the Monkeys and
the Crabs," a monkey gave a dried persimmon
seed to a crab in trade for a rice ball. Both
were pleased with the exchange. The monkey
immediately satisfied himself by eating the
rice ball, while the far-sighted crab planted
the seed, which eventually grew into a fine
persimmon tree. Both poems pun on the
words *saru* (monkey) and *masaru*, which means
"to surpass" or "to excel." The second verse
contains several other ingenious puns as well.
The monkey's robe is decorated with a reverse
swastika, which is the emblem of the poet
Shinratei and his circle.

*Kozo mo haya mukashibanashi ni kaki no tane
musubi kaete zo masaru hatsu yume*

"How quickly last year became an old tale: a
rice ball for a persimmon seed; in the first
dream of the Monkey Year, each gets the
better of the deal" *Shin'eitei Kokin Manyō*

*Zaregoto o kaki no tane dani nigirimeshi harukani
masaru fude susamisemu*

"I seize my brush and write in jest: 'Rice ball,
persimmon seed, monkey, crab; each and all
by far the best' " *Shinratei*

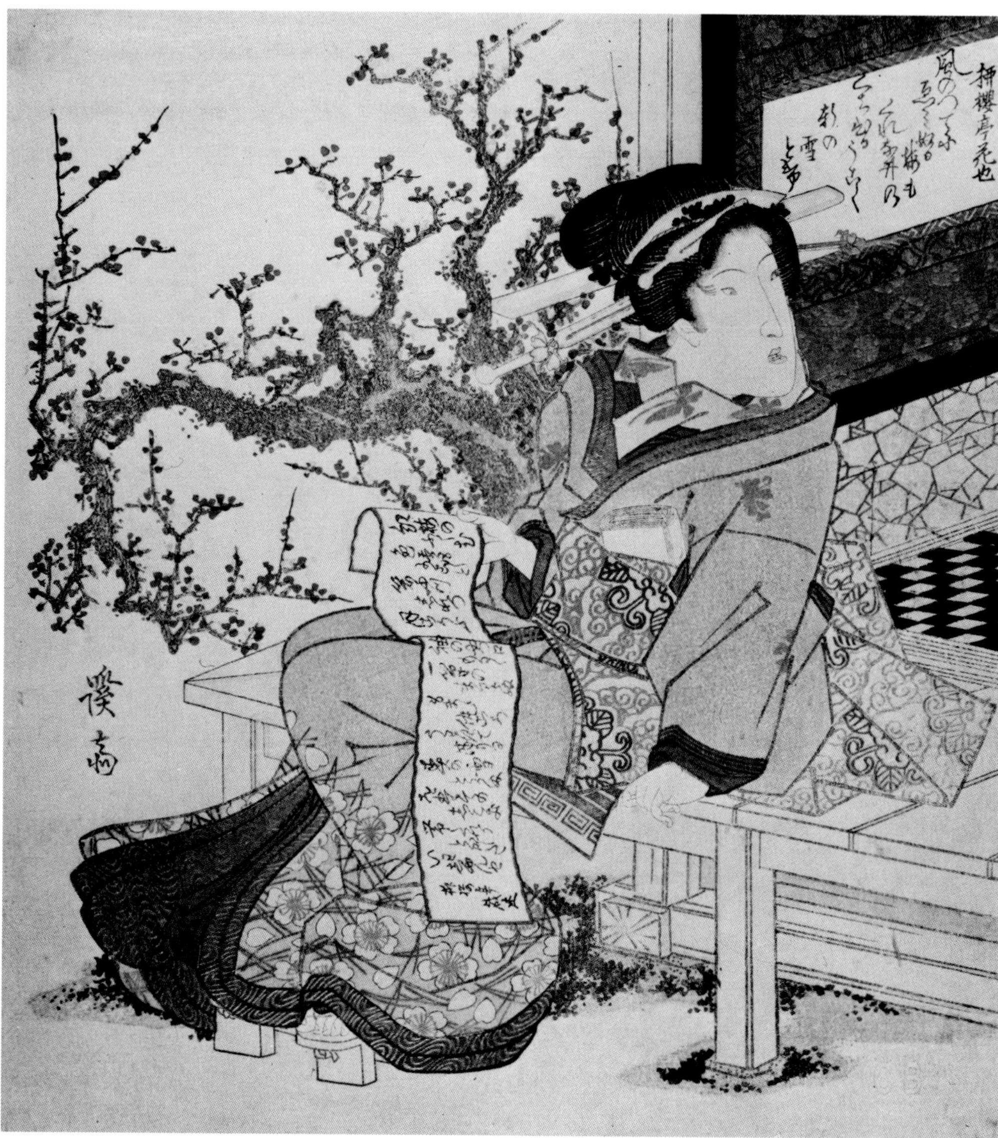

4

Geisha seated on a porch beside a plum tree
mid 1820s
21.1 × 18.5 cm
signed Keisai
Meade; Beatty 2306

The geisha is holding a letter, which contains eight couplets composed by the poet Hananari. Hananari also wrote the poem on the hanging scroll to the right, which compares the geisha's smile to the red flowers of a plum tree. This may be a portrait of a geisha who was particularly close to the poet, since Hananari's emblem of a flying butterfly appears on her robe, collar and hairpins.

Kaze no tsute ni eminuru ume mo kurenai no kuchibiru ugoku noki no yukidoke

"Through the mediation of the wind, the snow melts on the eaves; the crimson of both lips and plum break into a smile"

Ryūōtei Hananari

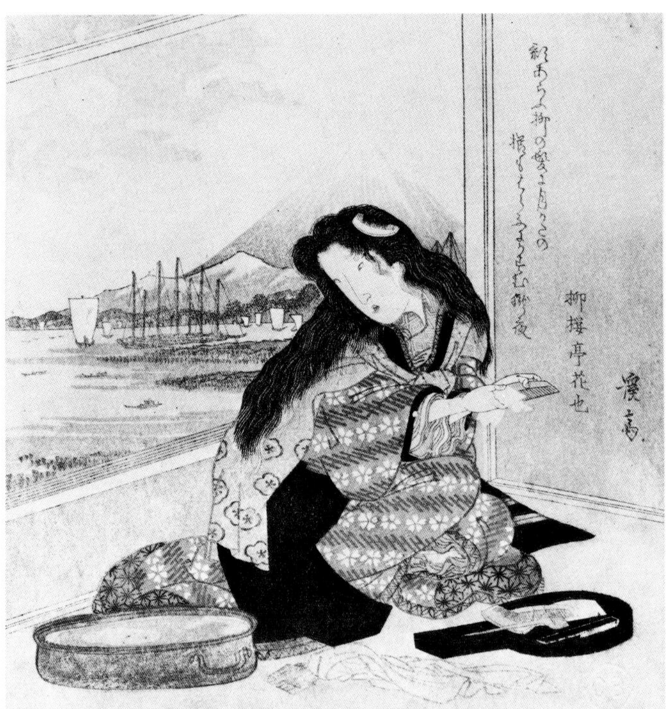

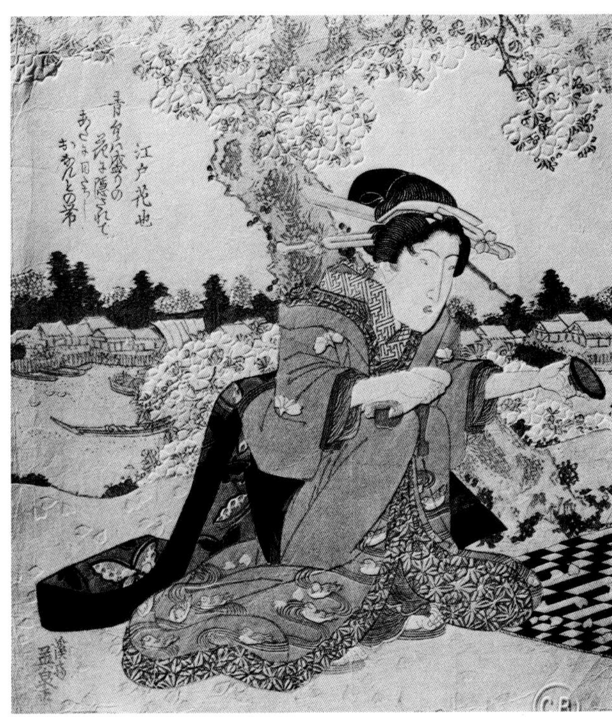

5

Woman drying a comb and watching the reflection of the moon in a basin
mid 1820s
20.1 × 18.2 cm
signed Keisai
Beatty 346

There is a lovely contrast in this print between the figure and the soft, painterly landscape outside the window; and a graceful similarity between the woman's pose and the shape of the mountain rising in the distance. The artist has shown equal skill in finding suitable visual equivalents for each of the poet's images. Another impression in the Fitzwilliam Museum, Cambridge, bears the seal Eisen after the artist's signature.

Kage arau yanagi no kami ni tsukigata no kushi mo harau ni kasumu oboroyo

"The tresses of the willow wash away the shadows, the misty night wipes the moon-shaped comb"
                                        Ryūōtei Hananari

6

Geisha kneeling beneath a cherry tree
mid or late 1820s
21.0 × 18.1 cm
signed Keisai Eisen ga
Rose; Beatty 1993

The geisha sits beneath a cherry tree in full flower and holds an empty wine cup in her hand. The artist has drawn gulls, a bird associated with the Sumida River, on the woman's blue robe. The poem speaks of a sky-blue sash; perhaps the position of the river behind the woman's waist was meant to suggest a sash. The poem also includes a pun on *onando* (sky-blue) and *nando* (storehouse), suggesting that the geisha is like a precious object that has just been brought out of storage. The print is the left-hand panel of a diptych which is complete in the Victoria and Albert Museum. The right panel shows another geisha inscribing a poem slip and includes another poem by Hananari, signed Ryūōtei.

Aozora wa sakari no hana ni kakusarete ada ni medachishi onando no obi

"The blue sky is hidden by the cherry blossoms: how lovely is the sky-blue sash"
                                        Edo no Hananari

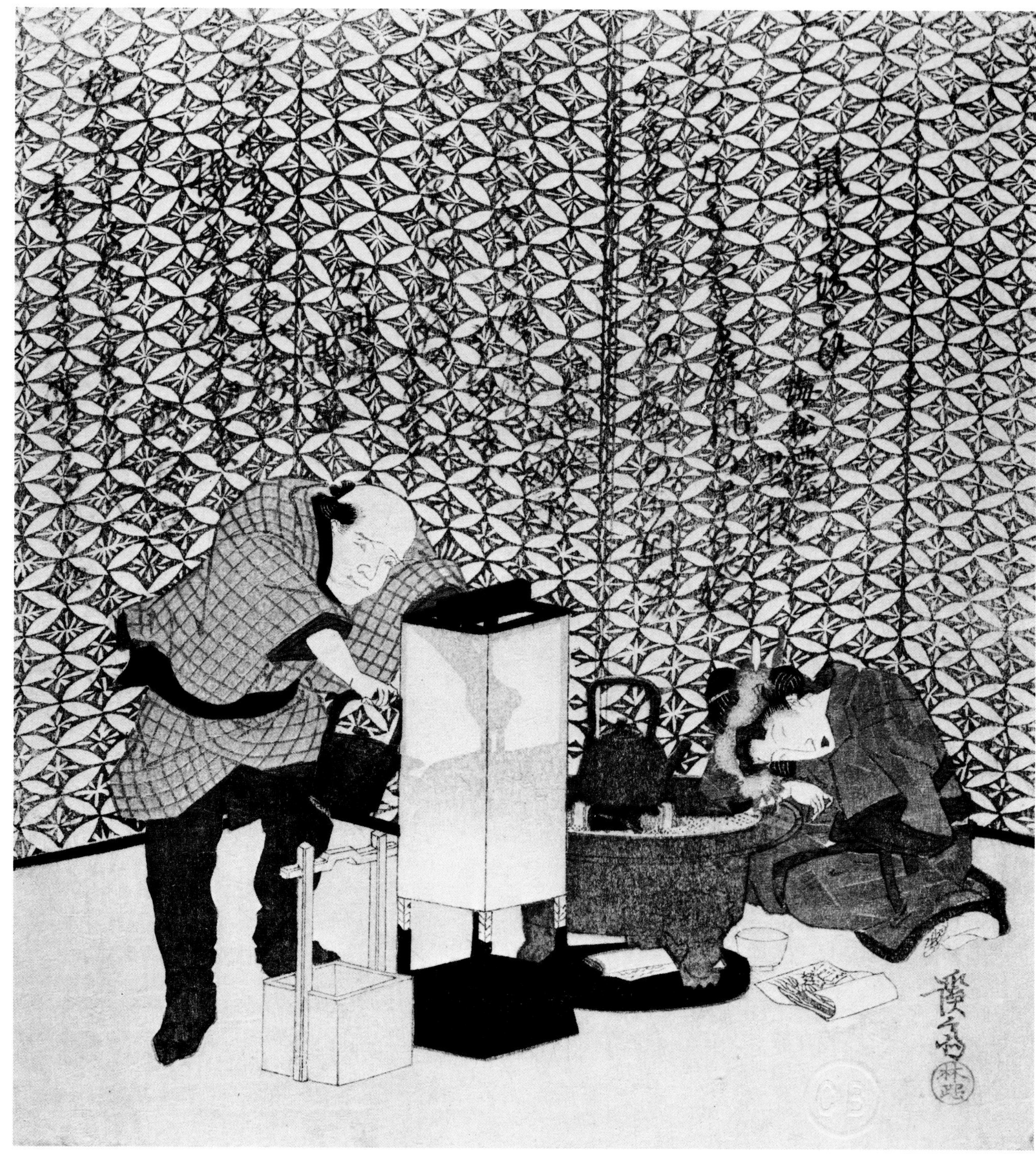

7
Happy rats
1828
20.3 × 18.3 cm
signed Keisai
Hayashi; Rose; Beatty 2058

This is a picture of New Year's Eve in the Yoshiwara district. A courtesan has retired to bed behind the tall screen in the back of the print, leaving her young understudy asleep by the brazier; a woodblock print of a treasure ship, to aid her dreams, rests beside her on the floor. The servant on the left is replenishing the lamp with oil.

There are two states of this print. In the first, the pattern on the backing of the screen is continuous, as here. In the second, the picture was included in the set *Nezumi zukushi jūnihō*, "Twelve Treasures with Rats," and an oblong cartouche was cut in the color blocks at the upper right to accommodate the series title. An impression of this state is illustrated in Hillier (1976) no. 806. The light blue-gray pattern of the screen makes the gold poems indistinct on the early impressions; in the second state the screen is printed with a darker color and the poems are illegible.

In the first poem, *nezuminaki* (rat squeaks) is a word for the whispering voice of a courtesan calling out an invitation to a prospective client. The other poems mention the treasure ship and the courtesan on the other side of the screen, but the gold metallic pigment used to print them has rubbed away in several areas and most are too indistinct to transcribe. The names of the poets are Umimatsunoya Kuroeda, Hamanoya Masago, Mangentei Takamori and Shūchōdō.

Nezuminaki shikiru byōbu no ☐☐☐ *mon akete hanasanu kuruwa no hatsuyume*

"The pattern of the dividing screen is like a whispered invitation in the licensed quarters; not to part at dawn is the first dream of the New Year"   *Umimatsunoya Kuroeda*

Yashima Gakutei active 1815–52

Gakutei was the illegitimate son of a samurai, named Hirata, in the service of the military government. After his birth, his mother married into the Yashima clan. He is said to have begun his studies with the painter Tsutsumi Shūei and to have continued with the surimono designer Hokkei, but there is no visible evidence of a relationship with either artist in his published work. He was an accomplished kyōka poet, studying first with Mado no Muratake and later with Rokujuen. His first dated work was a book of popular fiction *Modorikago mata no aigata*, "The Returning Palanquin: Meeting Again," which he wrote and illustrated. This appeared in 1815, around the time his first commercial prints were published. Once he began to design surimono and illustrations for poetry anthologies, however, he produced very little commercial work. His first surimono, commissioned by Muratake and carrying Gakutei's own verse, appeared in 1816; they were signed Harunobu. From 1817 he began signing his prints Gakutei, and until 1819 used a characteristically broad signature with a distinctive hook at the bottom of the last character. Around 1819 he began to design large sets of surimono, first for the Honchō Group and then for the Katsushika Circle of poets. Around 1821 he began to fill the backgrounds of these prints with bold geometric patterns printed in pale colors; by 1824 he had created a style unlike that of any other print designer, in which he completely filled the picture surface with color and printed patterns over one another with moiré-like effects. After 1824 Gakutei began to draw larger figures with broader patterns and simpler shapes; the boldest of these prints seem to have been designed and published around 1827 and 1828. About that time he moved to Ōsaka, where he designed a series of landscape prints, *Naniwa meisho tempōzan shōkei ichiran*, "A Set of Views of Mt Tempō, A Famous Site in Ōsaka," which were

published in 1834. He continued to contribute
illustrations to poetry anthologies until 1845
and in 1852 contributed an illustration to
Chaban imayō fūryū, "Modern, Elegant
Teahouse Comedies," a book with illustrations
by Kunishige, an Ōsaka artist. This seems to
have been Gakutei's last work. A number of
books appeared between 1856 and 1860,
written by a Gakutei; this was Gakutei II, a
pupil, who is said to have taken the artist's
name after his death. His personal name was
Okabe Sukezaemon and he lived at Hirokōji
in Edo, until he moved to Yokohama in 1874
or 1875. He was a writer and apparently did
no illustrations. A self-portrait of the first
Gakutei was included in a poetry anthology
published in the late 1810s or early 1820s.
He is kneeling calmly before another poet,
but his face is turned away from the viewer.

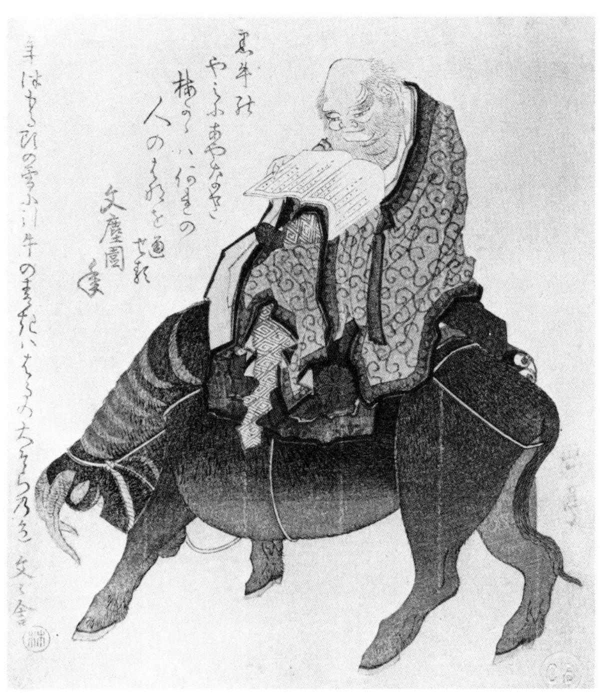

8
Lao Zi riding an ox
1817
21.2 × 18.7 cm
signed Gakutei
Rose; Hayashi; Beatty 2011

Lao Zi, the legendary Taoist sage, is often
depicted in paintings riding a black ox. The
traditional association led Gakutei, or perhaps
the poet Bumbunsha, to choose him as the
subject for this print, published at the beginning of an Ox Year, although Lao Zi is very
rarely seen in Japanese woodblock prints. The
poems speak of black or blue-black oxen and
years piled like snow upon one's head. The
poets may have been reflecting on their own
age, since there is no direct reference to Lao
Zi.

*Kuroushi no yami ni ayanaki umegaka wa izure no
hito no hana o tōseru*

"The Night of the Bull is pitch black and the
fragrance of the plum passes someone's nose"
                                    Bunjin'en Somuki

*Toshi tsumoru kashira no yuki ni hiki ushi no aoki
wa haru no ōzora no iro*

"The years pile like snow upon one's head,
though the ox one leads is as young and blue
as the wide spring sky"   *Bumbunsha*

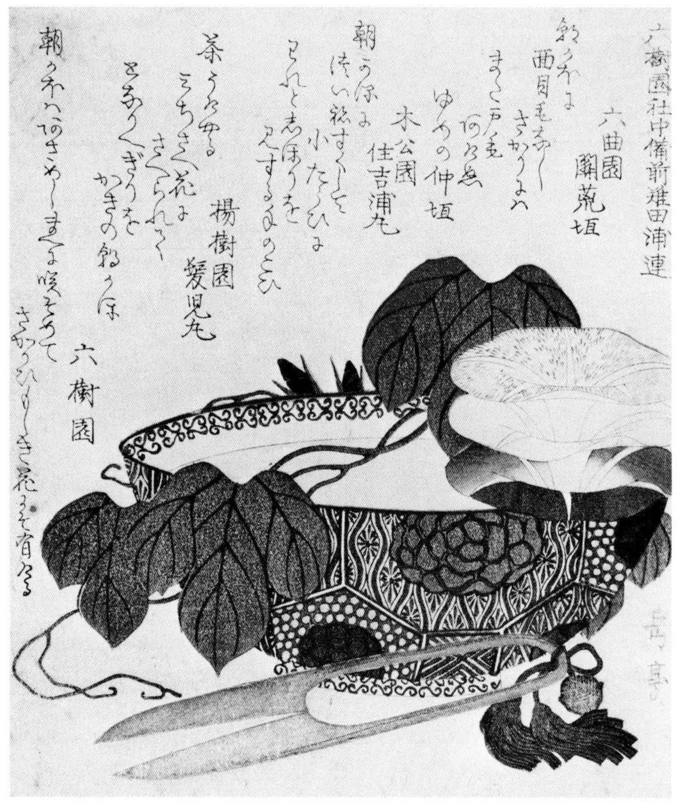

9

Morning glories, scissors and porcelain bowl
c. 1818
20.1 × 16.8 cm
signed Gakutei
Rose; Beatty 2060

Morning glories were cultivated and hybrid-
ized in Japan, and books were published illustrating their many varieties, long before Men-
del began his experiments with sweet peas in
Europe. The poets from Kijitaura must have
been morning glory fanciers, since Gakutei
illustrates three distinct varieties, one within
the other, at the edge of the polychrome porcelain bowl. In the first verse, the poet is
ashamed because he is still asleep when the
morning glory blossoms. In the second, the
poet has also overslept, but finds consolation
in the environment. There is a pun on *shibori*,
which means "tie-dyed," but also "double-
colored" when applied to morning glories.
The first three poems recall a famous haiku
by the poetess Kaga no Chiyo (1703–1775):
Asagao ni tsurube torarete morai mizu (My well
bucket is held by morning glories; I go and
ask for water). The third kyōka poet is returning a favor, but is caught by the sight of the
beautiful flowers and forgets his obligation;
there is a pun on *kaki*, which means both

"fence" and "break." The first three poets are
members of the Kijitaura Circle in Bizen
Province.

*Asagao ni memboku mo nashi sakari ni wa mada to
mo akenu yume no nakagaki*

"The morning glory fills me with shame: in
full bloom, while the gate in the fence of my
dreams still has not opened"
                    Rokkyokuen Seki Aragaki

*Asagao ni tsui nesugushite kotarai ni ware to shibori
o misuru tenogoi*

"I overslept and missed the morning glories;
but the towel in the basin has the same
pattern"   *Bokukōen Sumiyoshi Uramaru*

*Chauke yaru michi sae hana ni saerarete tonari e
giri o kaki no asagao*

"On the way to give some tea cakes to the
neighbors, some flowers caught my eye; the
morning glories on the fence make me break
my obligation"   *Yōjuen Kamikomaru*

*Asagao wa asameshi mae ni sakisomete sakari
himojiki hana ni zo arikeru*

"Morning glories start to bloom before breakfast; they must be very hungry flowers"
                                Rokujuen

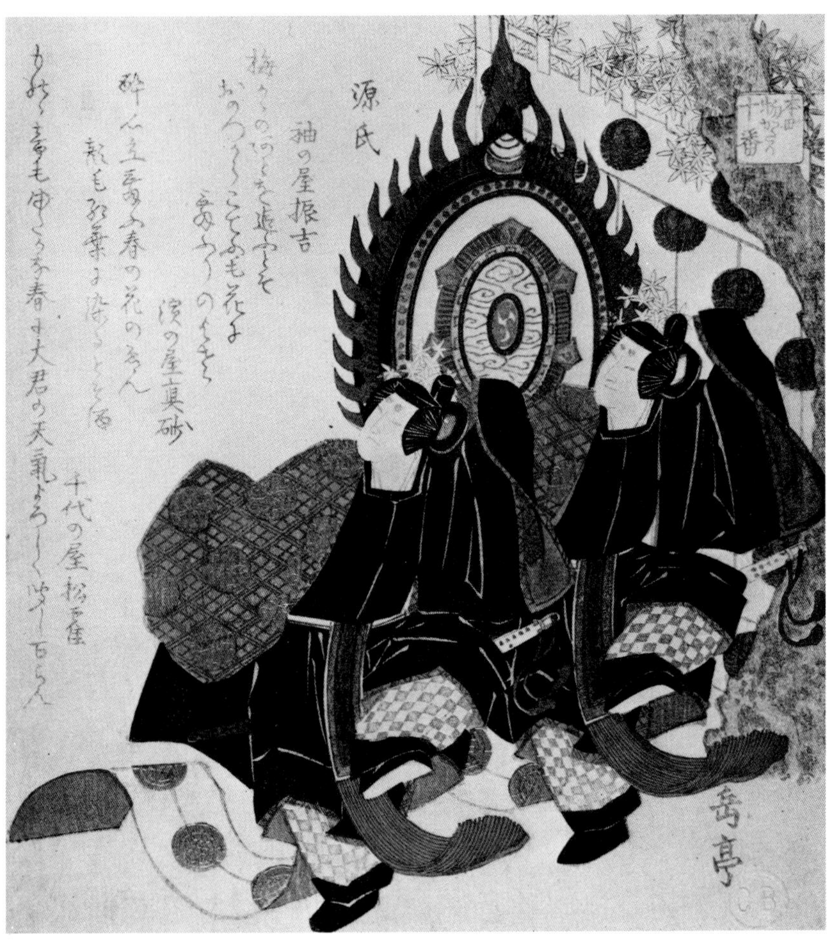

10

Prince Genji and Tō no Chūjō performing the
Dance of the Blue Waves
series Ten Romances for the Honchō Circle
c. 1819
20.3 × 18.2 cm
signed Gakutei
Beatty 1048

In chapter seven of the *Tale of Genji*, the emperor visits the Red Sparrow Court in autumn; an outdoor entertainment is held for
him, which gives the chapter its name, *Momiji
no ga* (The Festival of Red Leaves). "When at
last under the red leafage of tall autumn trees
forty men stood circlewise with their flutes,
and to the music that they made a strong
wind from the hills sweeping the pine-woods
added its fierce harmonies, while from amid a
wreckage of whirling and scattered leaves the
Dance of the Blue Waves suddenly broke out
in all its glittering splendour—a rapture seized
the onlookers that was akin to fear" (*Tale of
Genji*, Waley trans. (1935), ch.7). Gakutei's
picture conveys the splendor of the dance
without the awesome accompaniment of the
storm and falling leaves. The poems speak of
dancing butterflies (butterflies often fly in
pairs) and of the Flower Feast, a banquet held
beneath a cherry tree, which is the title of the
eighth chapter. The last poem adopts the formal style of the *Tale of Genji*.

*Umegaka no ato o ou to zo onozukara kochō mo
hana ni maiburi no yosa*

"As they chase the departed fragrance of the
plum blossoms, the butterflies naturally perform a lovely dance"   *Sodenoya Furiyoshi*

*Yoigokoro tachimau haru no hana no en kao mo
momiji ni somuru tosozake*

"Feeling drunk he stands and dances at the
Feast of Flowers in Spring, his face dyed with
wine, like maple leaves"   *Hamanoya Masago*

*Mono no ne mo yutaka na haru ni ōgimi no tenki
yoroshiku kikoshimesuran*

"Spring is beautiful, the music is full, the
emperor listens with pleasure on this beautiful
day"
                    Chiyonoya Matsuzuru

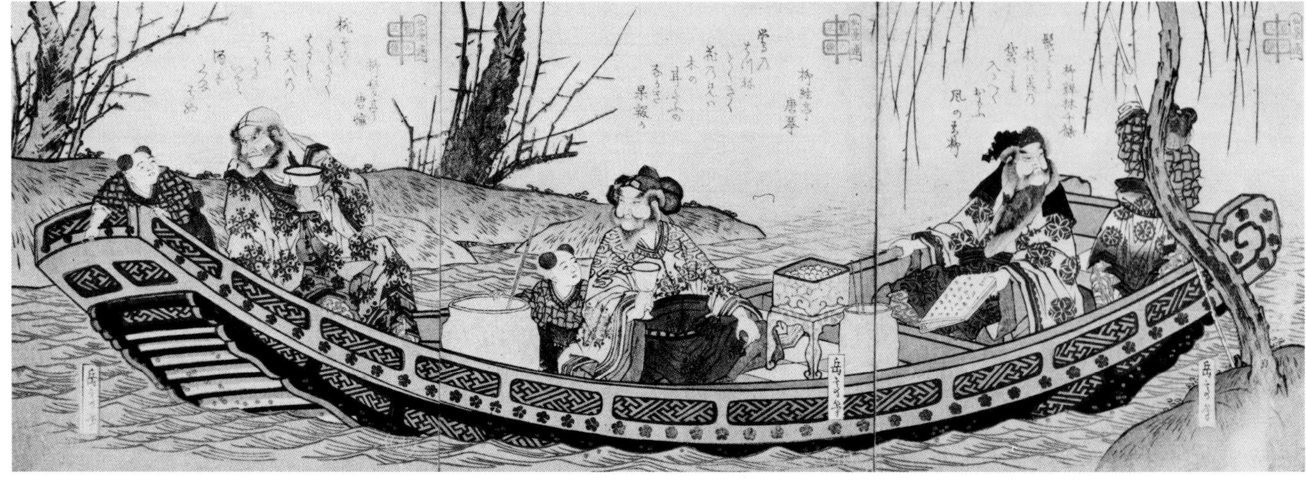

11

Guan Yu, Liu Bei and Zhang Fei
series Three Heroes of the State of Shu for the
Sendai Circle
c. 1820
triptych, 21.9 × 56.8 cm
signed Gakutei hitsu
Beatty 2137

The three heroes of the Romance of the
Three Kingdoms are most frequently shown
taking their oath of brotherhood in a peach
orchard (see cat. nos. 16a–c). In this picture
they are enjoying a spring excursion in a flat-
bottomed barge on a river lined with plum
trees and willow. Black-bearded Guan Yu is
seated in the stern of the boat holding a book;
long-eared Liu Bei is seated beside a jar of
wine and tray of food amidships; and Zhang
Fei is seated in the prow holding a wine goblet. Because each of them is accompanied by a
small child, they seem by contrast even more
stern, solemn and dignified. The poets belong
to the Sendai Circle, whose emblem encloses
the series title on each of the prints. Sendai is
a large city in northern Honshū at some distance from Edo. The military government required the lord of the region to keep a large
establishment in Edo and the Sendai poets, in
all likelihood, were attached to his entourage
and stationed there. The poems link attributes
of the Chinese heroes to conventional images
and epithets for Spring. *Mimitabu* (earlobes)
are also the mushrooms called "wood ears."
Long earlobes are a symbol of good fortune.

*Hige to miru eda wa kasumi no fukuro ni mo
irubeku omou kaze no aoyagi*

"The branches of the green willow in the
wind look like a beard which ought to be put
in a bag of mist"   *Ryūsōrin Senjō*

*Uguisu no hatsune toku kiku hana no ani wa ki no
mimitabu no nagaki kahō ka*

"The plum tree hears the first song of the
warbler: its long 'wood ears' promise luck"
                                   Ryūgentei Karagoto

*Momozono no momo saku haru wa jōhachi no
hokoraka ni iza sake mo kumabaya*

"Ten feet tall, I pour my wine with pride, in
springtime when peach flowers are blooming
in the orchard"   *Ryūhatsutei Karawa*

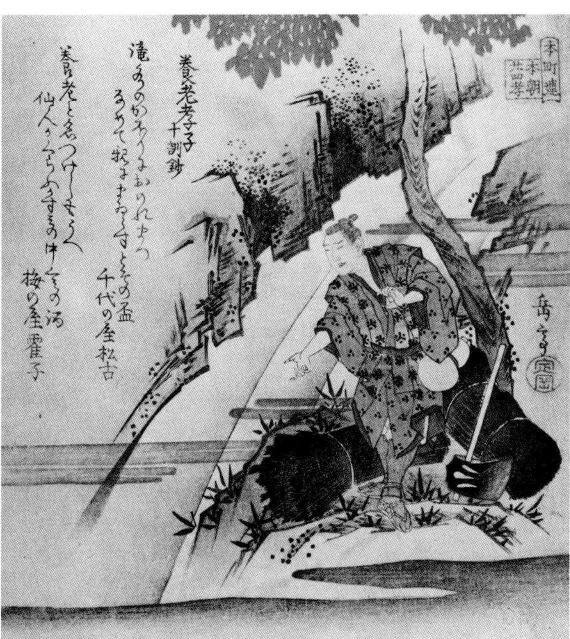

12

The filial son at Yōrō Waterfall

series Twenty-four Japanese Paragons of Filial Piety
for the Honchō Circle

c. 1820

21.0 × 18.6 cm

signed Gakutei

seal Sadaoka

Beatty 2082

Filial devotion was one of the pillars of Confucian morality and a canonical group of twenty-four examples, established in China at a relatively early date, was often referred to in art and literature. The stories of the Paragons were repeated in Japan and found their way into Japanese woodblock prints at the beginning of the eighteenth century. Many Chinese subjects were transformed into Japanese equivalents at the beginning of the nineteenth century.

Honchō was the name of a district in Edo. It was also a literary word for Japan and on the strength of the pun, the group commissioned Gakutei to design a set of Japanese Paragons of Filial Devotion. Since the subject was new and some of the examples were obscure, the name of the exemplar was followed by the literary work in which his story was told.

The story of Kosagi, a poor woodcutter in the province of Mino (modern Gifu Prefecture), was told in the *Jikkinshō,* "Ten Lessons," an anthology of about 280 didactic tales completed in 1253. The woodcutter's aged father had one pleasure in life: the meager ration of wine his son brought him each day. One day Kosagi had no money to buy wine and was distressed that he would therefore deprive his father of his pleasure. As a substitute, he scooped some water from a nearby waterfall. The gods were so touched by his devotion that they turned the water to wine and, because of this legend, the waterfall was called Yōrō, or "Nourishment for Old Age."

Sweet springs were said to flow in times of peace. In a Nō play by Zeami, the Emperor

Yūryaku (456–479) sent an envoy to inspect the sweet waters of Yōrō Waterfall. The envoy met the aged father and his son and heard the origin of the sacred spring. The Empress Genshō visited the waterfall herself soon after her ascension to the throne and changed the name of the year period to Yōrō in 717. The poems link the fragrant water of the cascade with *toso,* the medicinal wine served at the New Year, and the water drawn from the middle of the waterfall with pure wine drawn from the middle of the cask.

Takimizu no kaori ni onore mazu namete oya ni mairasu toso no sakazuki

"Amid the fragrance of the waterfall, the son drinks first, then offers the wine cup to his parents"
　　　　　　　　　　　Chiyonoya Matsufuru

Yōrō to nazukeshi mo ue sennin ga kurau kasumi no nakakumi no sake

"It is named 'Nourishment for Old Age'; the wine is scooped from the mists that are eaten by the immortals"
　　　　　　　　　　　Umenoya Tsuruko

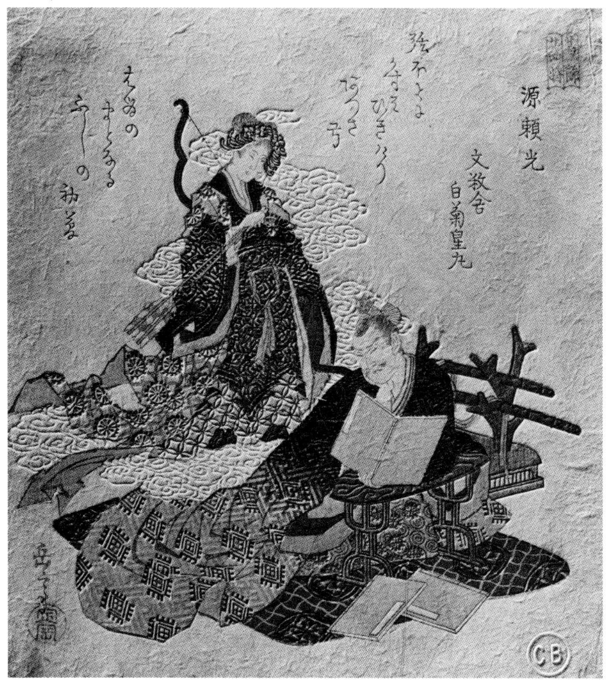

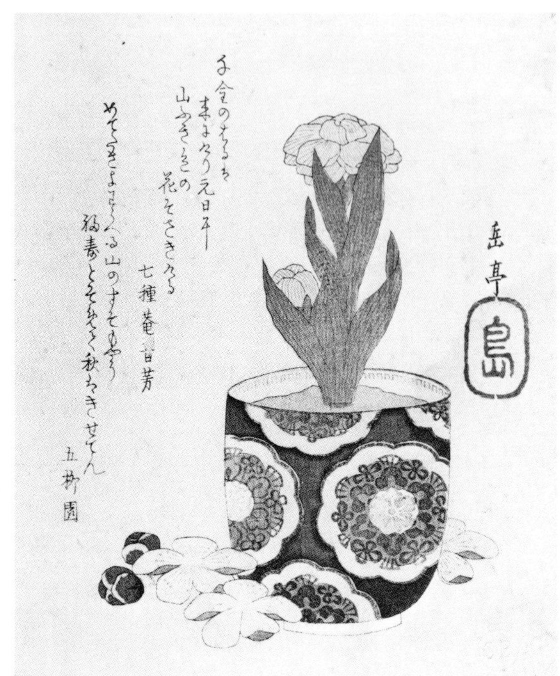

13

The conception of Minamoto no Yorimitsu
(Raikō)
series Twenty-four Generals for the Katsushika
Circle
c. 1821
21.1 × 18.8 cm
signed Gakutei
seal Sadaoka
Beatty 2120

Minamoto no Yorimitsu (948–1021) was the
son of the famous archer Tada no Mitsunaka.
Mitsunaka was fond of studying the Chinese
classics and one night Jie Hua, the daughter
of the great Chinese archer Yang Yaojing,
appeared to him in a reverie. She told
Mitsunaka that he was the most worthy
archer in Japan and presented him with her
father's bow. In the course of their exchange
Jie Hua seems to have become pregnant; at
any rate, she is pregnant in Gakutei's print
and there must be a tradition that she was the
mother of Yorimitsu (or Raikō, the Chinese-
style pronunciation of his name by which he
is better known).

*Gen hodo ni kasumi hikikeri azusayumi haru no
mato naru fuji no hatsuyume*

"In the first dream, Mt Fuji is the spring
target; the catalpa bow drew the mist with its
bowstring"   *Bunkyūsha Shiragiku no Hoshimaru*

14

Plum blossoms and adonis in porcelain bowl
c. 1822
21.4 × 17.1 cm
signed Gakutei
seal Yashima
Beatty 2061

Fukujusō, or adonis, grew wild in the vicinity
of Edo and blossomed naturally during the
third or fourth month of the lunar year. It
was cultivated, however, for sale and enjoy-
ment at the New Year and was so common
then that it was often called *ganjitsusō*,
"Flower of New Year's Day." The poisonous
root of the plant was used as a cardiac stimu-
lant and this may have been one reason why
it was called *fukujusō* (the plant of happiness
and longevity). The second poem combines
autumn and spring imagery; the print may
have been published late in the year.

*Senkin no haru wa kinikeri ganjitsu ni yamabuki
iro no hana zo sakikeru*

"Precious Spring has come and flowers with
golden color have bloomed on New Year's
Day"   *Nanakusaan Otoyoshi*

*Medetasa yo waraeru yama no suso moyō fukuju to
zo mede aki wa kiseten*

"How wonderful! Autumn has clothed the
foothills of the smiling mountains in a robe
with patterns of long life and happiness"
                                      Goryūen

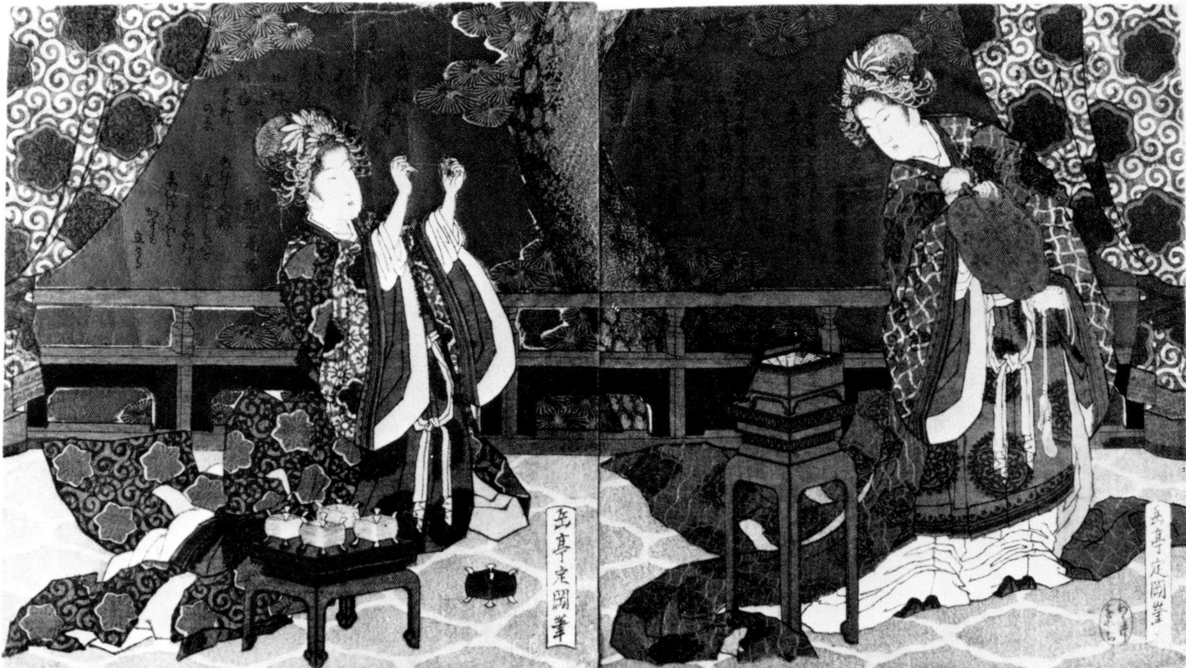

15

Two Chinese women examining thread and a
spider's web in a box
series Diptych for the Drum Group
c. 1824
21.4 × 37.3 cm
signed Gakutei Sadaoka hitsu
Wakai; Rose; Beatty 2138

One of the two Chinese women in this picture
is looking at a spider's web in a box, the other
is threading a needle; the exact identification
of the women is uncertain, but when this
diptych was first published it carried poems
about the Tanabata Festival in the seventh
month of the year. One of the women, therefore, may be the legendary Chinese princess Ji
Nü, the weaving lady, who is honored during
that festival. Ji Nü was a daughter of Tian
Di, the Lord of Heaven, and spent her time
making clothes for his other children. One
day she fell in love with a herdsman and
married him. When she neglected her work,
however, her father separated the two and
they were only allowed to meet one day of
the year. Their meeting was celebrated in the
Tanabata Festival.

In the first state of the print, the background is a blue sky with white clouds; the
woman on the left holds a needle in her left
hand and the piece of colored thread in her
right hand is connected to the spool beside
her on the floor; there are verses by four

Ōsaka poets. Genuine impressions of this state
are in the Metropolitan Museum of Art; a
good copy of the right-hand panel, published
by Tsumura Isakichi in the early 1890s, is
often encountered. In the second state, the
poems by the four Ōsaka writers were replaced with verses by five Edo poets. An
impression of the right-hand panel of this
state is in the Fogg Museum of Art. In the
third state, the blue sky was replaced with a
gold background and a hand-stamped title was
added in the upper-left corner of the right
panel, identifying the Drum Group of poets.
The only examples of this state seem to be
those here illustrated.

Judging from the poems about the Tanabata
Festival, the print was originally published for
distribution in the city of Ōsaka in the seventh month of one year. The poems by the
Edo poets all mention spring and the New
Year, so perhaps the prints were reissued in
the spring of the following year.

*Sasagani no su o harukaze ni sasowarete itokuri
idasu niwa no aoyagi*

"The spider's web is blown in the wind and
the green willow in the garden spins thread"
Kashūtei Tanehide

*Saohime no kesa watariken yamayama e kasumi no
hashi no kakaru akebono*

"Dawn suspends from hill to hill the bridge of

mist the Goddess of Spring will cross this
morning"   *Kōrensha Tomoyoshi*

*Sasagani no ito e matsuba no hari soete kasumi no
kinu no shitate ageseri*

"To the spider's thread, one adds a pine
needle and tailors a garment of mist"
                              Yamato Watamori

*Tsuki mo hi mo yururi to matsuru odamaki no
kumode ni karamu aoyagi no ito*

"The sun and moon both calmly sew; the
threads of a green willow are coiled around
the spidery arms of a spool"
                              Shunjorō Mitsune

*Akete kesa haru no keshiki o misu ya hari ito
hikeru hodo kasumi tachikeru*

"Mist rises as I pull the thread to raise the
bamboo blind to display the spring landscape
this early morning"   *Katanoue Koreneri*

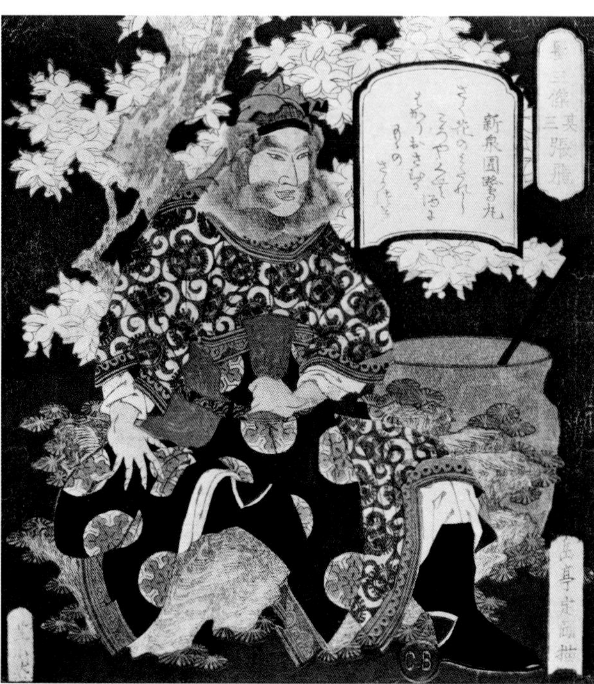

16a

Number three: Zhang Fei
series Three Heroes of the State of Shu
c. 1824
21.0 × 18.6 cm
signed Gakutei Sadaoka byō; engraved and printed
by Shiba Konori
Beatty 500c

Zhang Fei is shown holding a western-style
goblet, seated next to a wine vat with its ladle
projecting to one side. The poem alludes to
the meeting in the peach orchard.

*Sakuhana no midareshi koro ya kumu sake ni
hakari osamuru momo no sakazuki*

"The peach cups dip wine and settle their
plans when the blossoms are in full flower"
                              Shinsen'en Sagimaru

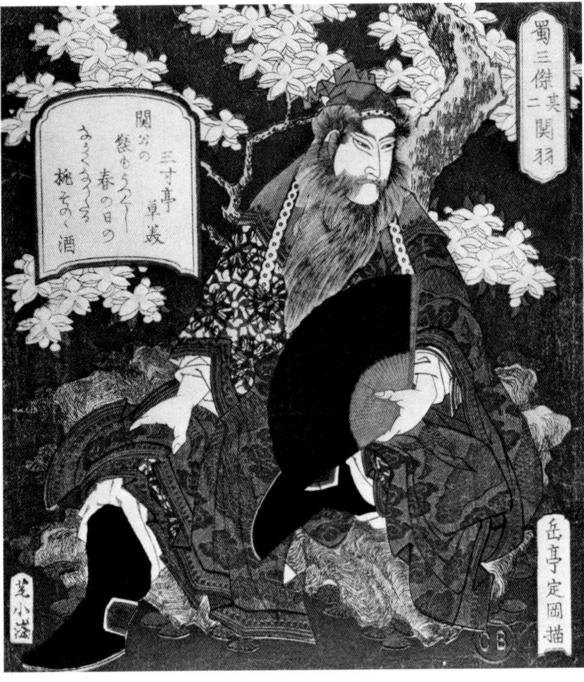

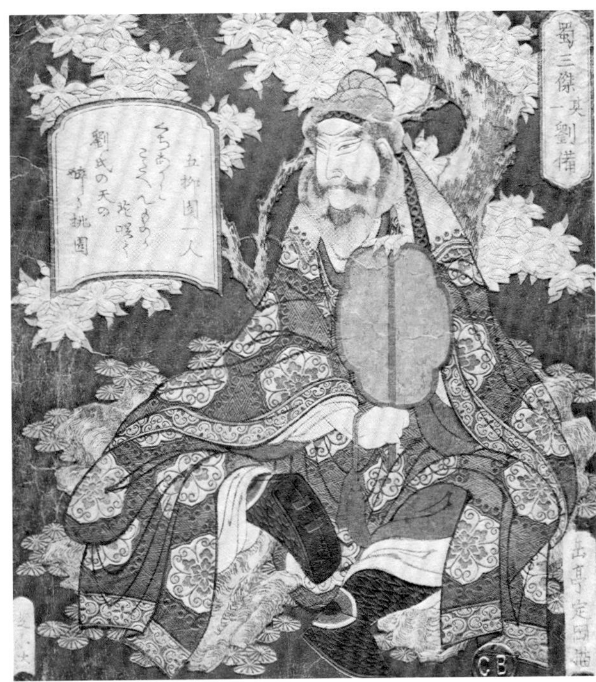

16b

Number two: Guan Yu
series Three Heroes of the State of Shu
c. 1824
21.0 × 18.5 cm
signed Gakutei Sadaoka byō; engraved and printed
by Shiba Konori
Beatty 500b

This is the second panel of the triptych. Guan
Yu was proud of his glossy, luxurious, black
beard, which is the subject of the poem.

*Kankō no hige mo utsukushi haru no hi no nagaku
naritaru momozono no sake*

"The wine in the peach orchard lasts as long
as Guan's lovely beard and the beautiful
spring day" *Sanzuntei Kusami*

16c

Number one: Liu Bei
series Three Heroes of the State of Shu
c. 1824
21.1 × 18.7 cm
signed Gakutei Sadaoka byō; engraved and printed
by Shiba Konori
Beatty 500a

Guan Yu, Zhang Fei and Liu Bei, three heroes of the Chinese novel *Romance of the Three
Kingdoms*, met together in Liu Bei's peach orchard one spring and discussed their futures
as they drank wine beneath the blossoms. The
poem seems to say that no one would deny
that when the flowers are in bloom, one could
become drunk in Liu's heavenly orchard.

*Kuchi akashi kotaen mono ga hana sakite ryūshi no
ten no yoeru momozono* *Ichindo Goryūen*

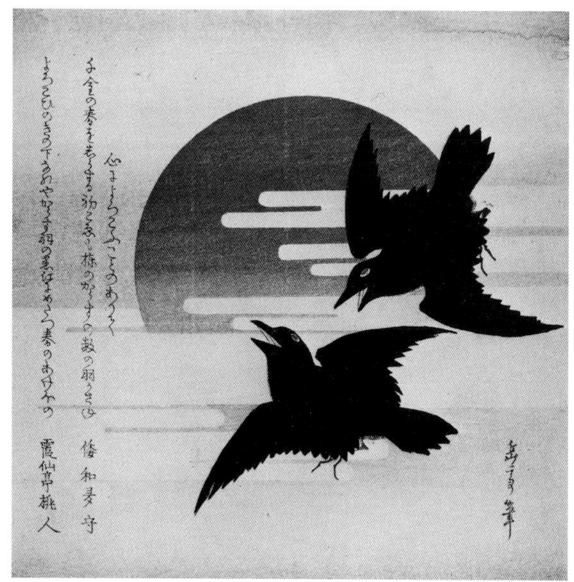

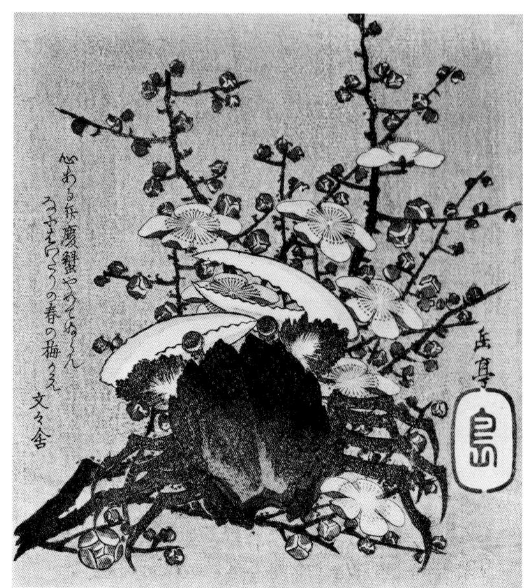

17
Crows and rising sun
c. 1825
19.1 × 18.1 cm
signed Gakutei hitsu
unidentified collector's seal on verso;
Beatty 2436

The poems are titled *Kokoro ni yorokobu koto no
arite*, "With Gladness in the Heart." The second alludes to lacquer made in the town of
Kuroe, "Black Inlet," in Wakayama Prefecture
and puns on the Chinese-style pronunciation
of the character for gladness and the word for
tree, both of which are pronounced *ki*. The
print may have been published in 1825, a
Bird Year.

*Senkin no haru o shirasuru hatsukoe mo mune no
karasu no kazu no hagasane*

"The wings of the crows on the rooftop over-
lap, their first cries announce the priceless
Spring" *Yamato Watamori*

*Yorokobi no ki no shita nare ya karasuba no kuroe
ni medatsu haru no akebono*

"Spring dawn: are the crows, so famous in
Kuroe lacquer, beneath the character for gladness or beneath a tree?" *Kasentei Momondo*

18
Benkei Crab and plum blossom
c. 1826
20.9 × 18.3 cm
signed Gakutei
seal Yashima
Beatty 954

The crab was the personal emblem of
Bumbunsha Kanikomaru ("Little Crab"), the
leader of the Katsushika Group of poets. It
was the subject of many prints containing
Bumbunsha's poems and it seems likely that
he commissioned these directly from Gakutei,
Hokusai, Kunisada, Taito II and other artists.
The Benkei Crab is about three centimeters
wide; the poem probably alludes to an episode
in the life of General Yoshitsune. Yoshitsune
had been put to flight by his brother, Yoritomo,
at the end of 1185 and embarked with his
retainers in a fleet of ships from Daimotsu, a
harbor near the present-day city of Amagasaki,
not far from Ōsaka. A storm arose and many
ships were lost. The storm was caused by the
angry ghosts of enemy warriors slain by
Yoshitsune's forces in a previous battle. When
the ghosts were appeased by the prayers of
the warrior priest Benkei, Yoshitsune's ship
was able to escape. Naniwa, as Ōsaka was
once called, was famous for its plum
blossoms.

*Kokoro aru benkeigani ya medenuran naniwa wa-
tari no haru no umegae*

"Wouldn't a Benkei Crab with a heart offer
praise to a branch of spring plum at the
Naniwa crossing?" *Bumbunsha*

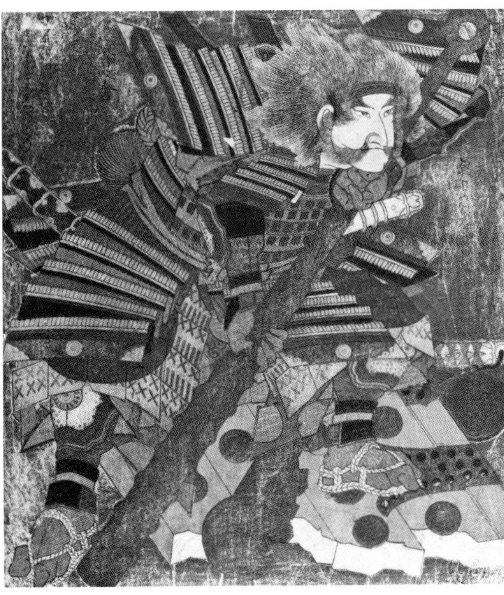

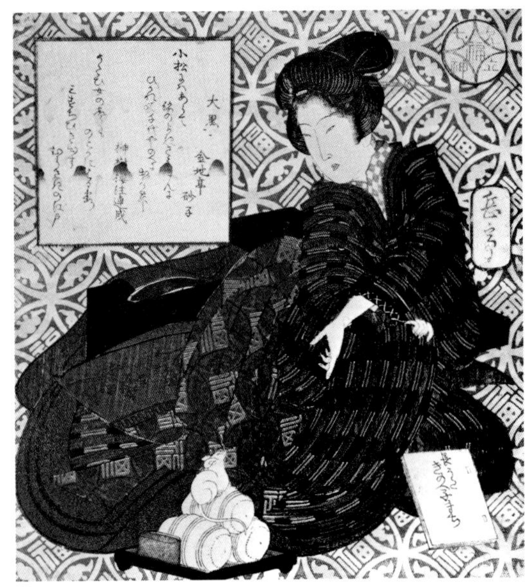

19

Asaina Saburō Yoshihide breaking the door of
Sanetomo's palace

series Three Broken Doors
c. 1827
21.6 × 18.4 cm
signed Gakutei
Beatty 897

According to legend, Asaina (or Asahina) was
the son of General Wada no Yoshimori (1147–
1213) and the female warrior Tomoe Gozen.
He is best remembered for the part he played
in the revenge of the Soga brothers in 1193,
which has been commemorated in many kabuki plays and woodblock prints. Later, in
1213, one of Yoshimori's sons and one of his
nephews joined an insurrection. When the
shōgun Minamoto no Sanetomo refused to
pardon the nephew, Yoshimori attacked his
place to seize the official he felt was responsible. During the seige, Asaina broke down the
palace door and this is the subject of Gakutei's
print. The poems by Bunkyūsha Kanimi and
another undeciphered poet which are printed
on the gold background are indistinct in
places.

20

Daikoku as a woman with a rat
series Allusions to the Seven Lucky Gods
c. 1827–28
21.1 × 18.8 cm
signed Gakutei
Beatty 898

This is one of seven pictures of women with
attributes of the Seven Lucky Gods; they
were commissioned by the Shippō Circle of
poets, whose emblem of four adjacent arcs in
a circle is used for the title cartouche and for
the background of the print. Many of the
poets whose names appear on the square
poem sheets beside each figure have names
which begin with *fuku*, (happiness); this character is at the center of the cartouche and of
the circles in the background, each of which
also contains four bats, an emblem of longevity. This motif is again repeated on the woman's sash. The woman is reaching out towards
a white rat seated on top of three miniature
imitations of straw-wrapped rice bales. The
rat is the messenger of the God Daikoku, the
subject of the print, usually represented atop
a pair of rice bales. A festival for Daikoku was
held on one of the first Rat Days of the year.
Devotees would keep vigil, eat black beans
and forked radishes, and pray for happiness
and prosperity until the Hour of the Rat
(11:00 p.m. to 1:00 a.m.), when the festival
would properly begin. The vigil was called
kinoene machi, "Waiting for the Rat"; this is
also the title on the libretto by the woman's
knee. The intense colors of the print suggest a

date in the late 1820s, at the end of Gakutei's career as a surimono designer; perhaps the set was published in 1828, a Rat Year. Several prints in this set were carefully copied in the early 1890s, but none of the copies bears the handstamped signature that appears on genuine impressions. There is a pun in the first poem on *ne*, which means both "rat" and "sound." The word *dekemai* might also be read *tekemai*, a variant of *tekomai*, a dance performed by geisha during festivals.

Komatsu ni wa arade ne no yoki samisen ni hikarete chiyo ya nobe ni dekemai

"Not picking pine shoots on the Day of the Rat, but accompanied by a good sounding samisen, time dances in the fields"

Konjitei Sunago

Utaime no koe mo nodoka ni harugasumi misuji hikidasu murasaki no edo

"The singer's mild voice carries like a spring mist as the purple city of Edo plays the samisen"

Sakakirō Shimenari

Utagawa Hiroshige

Hiroshige was born in Edo, the son of a supervisor of a brigade of firemen. He studied the rudiments of painting with a neighbor, Okajima Rinsai, and in 1811, at the age of fourteen, began to study with the ukiyo-e artist Toyohiro. His first print was published in 1814, but it was not until 1818 that he began producing prints in any number. Around 1821 he designed his first square surimono; during the next decade he may have designed two dozen or more, a small number compared to his thousands of commercial prints. From the mid 1840s, Hiroshige also designed a number of picture calendars, most of them drawn in a sketchy style derived from the Shijō school of painting. After his death in 1858, this tradition was continued by Hiroshige II and their styles are often difficult to distinguish. Hiroshige is best known for his landscape prints, but he also designed many illustrations for anthologies of kyōka verse, often in the simple abbreviated style displayed in the Chester Beatty surimono.

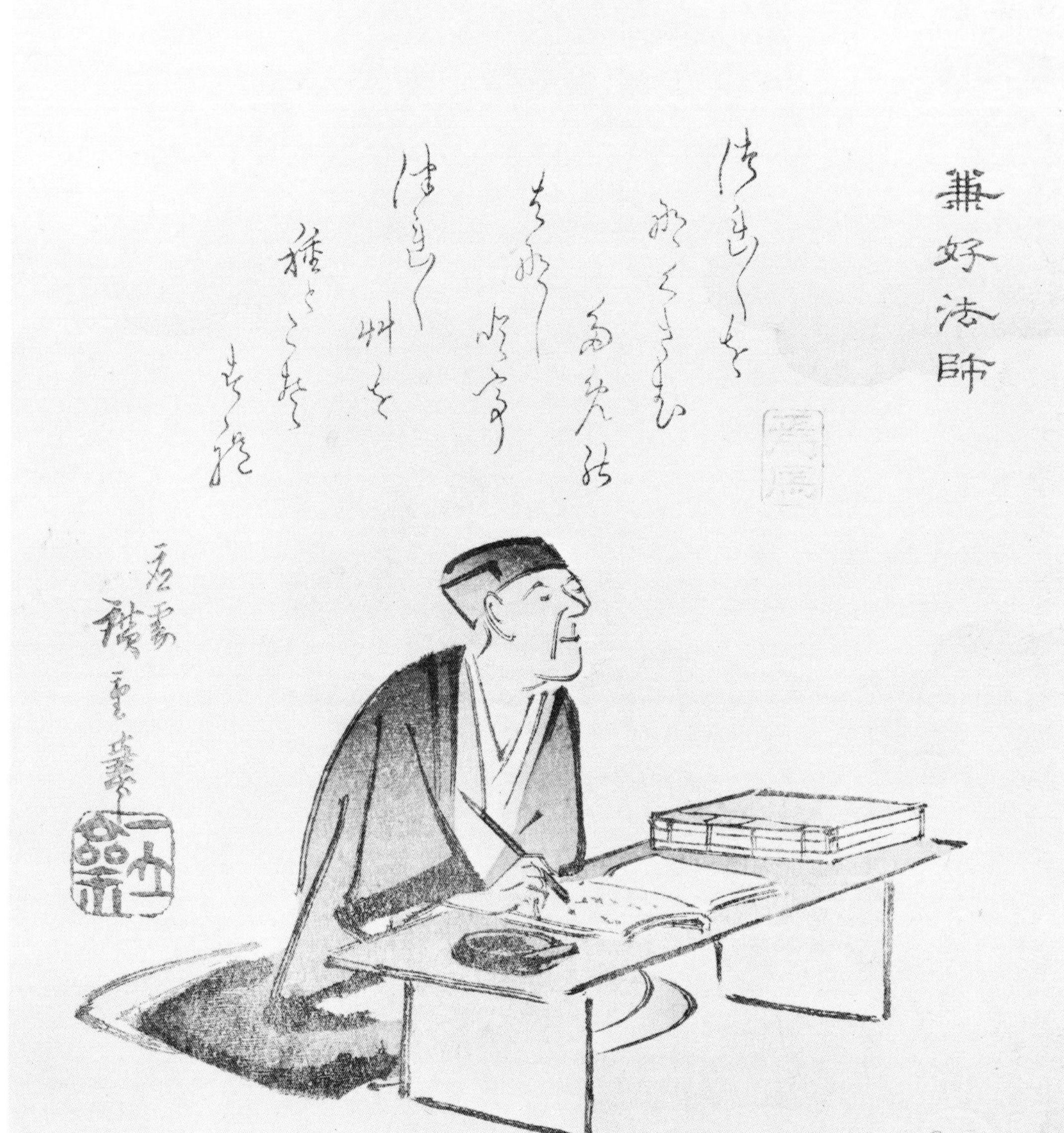

21

<table>
<tr><td>

The priest Yoshida Kenkō
c. mid 1840s
20.0 × 16.9 cm
signed Ōju Hiroshige hitsu
seal Ichiryūsai
Beatty 2243

</td></tr>
</table>

Yoshida Kenkō (1283–1350) was a court official who took religious orders in 1324 to devote himself more exclusively to literature and poetry. A miscellaneous collection of his prose writings, *Tsurezuregusa*, written between 1324 and 1331, is his most famous work. During the 1840s, Hiroshige illustrated several verse anthologies with simple imaginary portraits of poets drawn in this gentle, relaxed and painterly style. The poem is based on the opening passage in *Tsurezuregusa*, whose title literally means "The Grass of Idleness." The red seal of the publisher Tsutaya Kichizō in the Nakabashi district of Edo is stamped on the back of the print.

*Tsurezure o nagusamu tame no hanashi tote
tsurezuregusa o tane to koso suru*

"To beguile away the empty hours I tell stories; these become the seeds of the Grass of Idleness"

Emba II

Totoya Hokkei

Hokkei was an early pupil of Hokusai and his first work appeared in 1799, immediately after Hokusai had relinquished the name Sōri. He originally earned his living as a fish seller, but as he became successful as a designer of privately commissioned album sheets and surimono, he retired from this profession and devoted himself entirely to art. Although he designed some surimono in the 1800s and 1810s, he did not discover his genius for design until the end of the 1810s. This may have come about through a collaboration with Shumman; at any rate, Hokkei seems to have taken Shumman's place as the designer of the most exquisite and refined surimono after that artist's death in 1820.

On his early surimono, the right and left sides of *hoku*, the first character in his name, are nearly equal in size. In the middle of the 1820s, as his prints begin to become more dramatic, the left side of the signature becomes increasingly larger. After 1830 the figures in Hokkei's prints become smaller, while the drawing and engraving become tighter; the signature also becomes smaller, but the proportions of the left and right sides of the first character remain the same.

Beside surimono and illustrations for poetry albums, Hokkei designed a few illustrations for popular fiction and some commercially published prints, including a splendid set of thirteen landscapes in a horizontal half-block format entitled *Shokoku meisho*, "Famous Places in the Provinces," which were published around the early 1830s, probably about the same time as Hokusai's set of famous bridges and waterfalls. Besides Hokusai, Hokkei was also said to have studied painting with Kanō Yōsen'in (1753–1808).

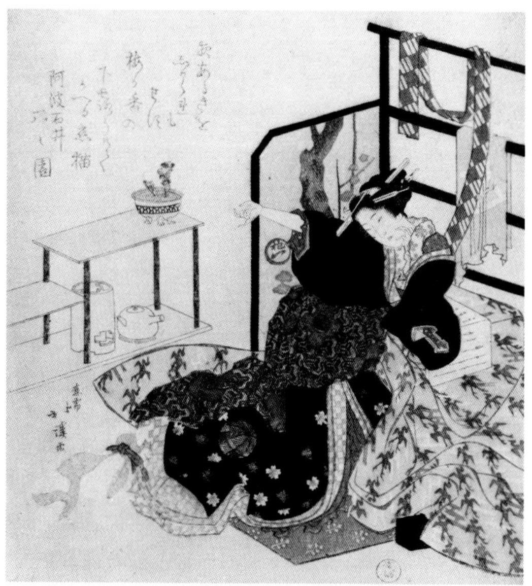

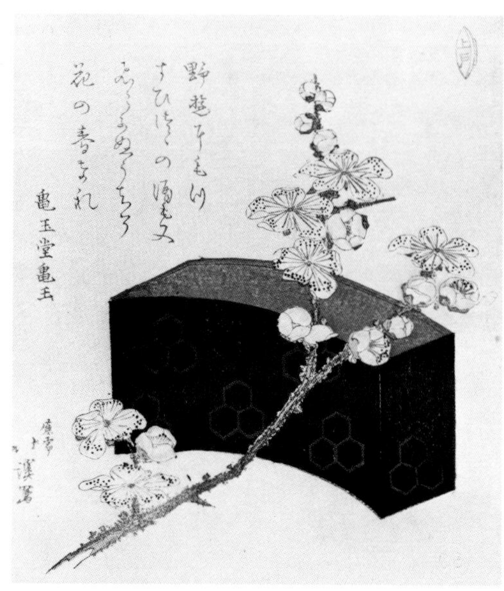

22

Geisha playing with cat
c. 1820
20.6 × 18.5 cm
signed Ōju Hokkei ga; engraved and printed by
Shumman
Beatty 2433

The young woman kneels beside a *kotatsu*, a
small warming pit covered with a wooden
frame and fabrics. She was reading but now
dangles a decorative ball of thread on a string
in front of the cat; the cat is printed without
an outline and the string is embossed. Behind
the *kotatsu* is a clothes rack with a painting of
a plum tree by Sakai Hōitsu, the artist who
revived the Rimpa style of painting in the
early nineteenth century. The blue towel on
the rack bears the emblem of the Gogawa
poetry group, as does the porcelain bowl with
the flowering adonis plant at the left. The
picture bears the seal of Shumman, a surimono designer who also produced work for
himself and other artists. Shumman died in
1820, and this must be one of the last prints
that he helped produce. *Koineko*, or "love cat,"
means a cat in heat, and the sensuous erotic
suggestions in the verse are reflected in the
intense colors and swirling movement around
the woman in Hokkei's design.

*Yoaruki o shikarare mo sezu ume ga ka no shimotsuyu
ukete kaeru koineko*

"The cat in heat was not scolded for night
prowling; she returned damp with the fragrance of plum from the under-dew"
   Rokurokuen of the town of Ishii in Awa Province

23

Plum branch and portable wine flask
c. 1820
20.9 × 18.0 cm
signed Ōju Hokkei sha
Beatty 2047

The black lacquer canteen with its red top
and silver stopper is decorated with the tor-
toise shell emblem of the poet Kigyoku "Turtle Jewel." The wine cup in the upper right-
hand corner of the print may be a personal
emblem of the poet or his group; it bears the
characters *jōgo* (drinker). The colors in this
print are particularly delicate: there is a light
pink background and a pink blush with surface polishing on some of the embossed plum
buds; the branch itself is light brown at the
end, but green where it leans against the wine
flask.

*Noasobi ni motsu suizutsu no sake mo mata hirakanu
uchi zo hana no haru nare*

"The flask of wine we carried on our outing
in the fields: Spring came with its flowers
before we opened it again" *Kigyokudō Kigyoku*

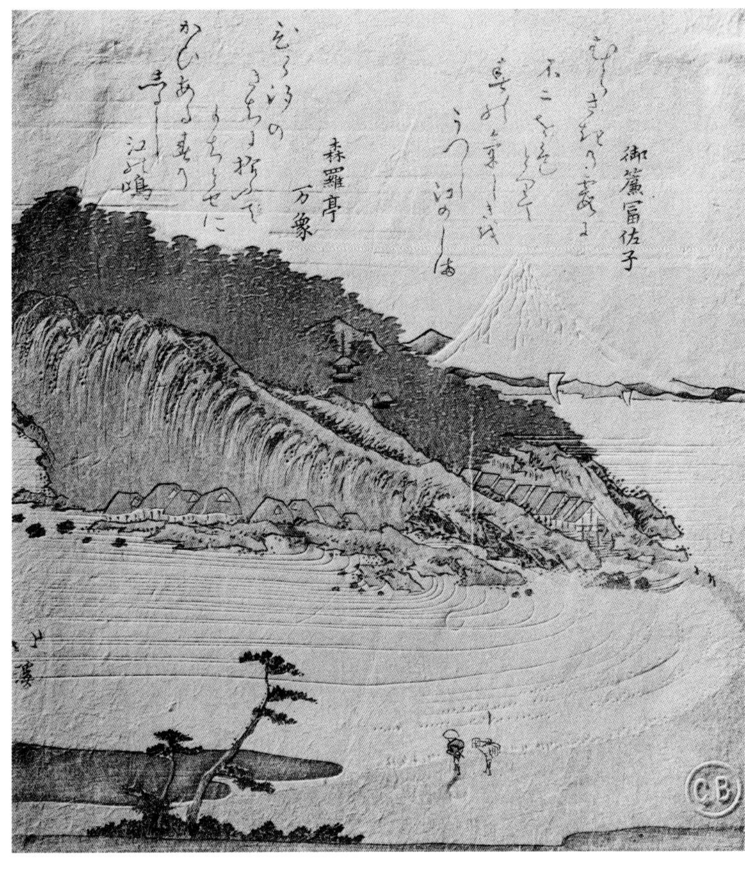

24

Mt Fuji and the island of Enoshima from
Shichiri Beach
1821
21.1 × 18.2 cm
signed Hokkei
Beatty 2154

Originally, Enoshima was said to have been
the lair of a malevolent dragon. When an
earthquake raised the island and exposed the
entrance to the dragon's cave, the Goddess
Benten descended from heaven and married
the dragon, putting an end to its terrible
deeds. Over time, the legend was modified,
and the dragon who had been Benten's hus-
band became a companion in the form of a
white snake.

Enoshima Island is near Kamakura and was
approached along a sweeping stretch of sea-
shore called *shichirigahama*, the Seven-*ri* or
Seventeen-mile Beach. During the Tokugawa
period, Enoshima was joined to the mainland
by a narrow spit of sand and rock that was
exposed at low tide. Because it was not far
from Edo, it was a frequent destination of
pilgrims from the capital and, from the 1780s,
often appears as a subject in woodblock
prints. Because of the association between
Enoshima, Benten and the snake, surimono
often used the island and its famous shells as
symbols for the Snake Year. Indeed, most
surimono with pictures of Enoshima, or references to the island in their poems, were published in 1809, 1821 or 1833.

In the first poem there are overlapping puns
on *utsushi* (reflect), *utsushi-e* (pictures), and
Enoshima. In the second poem there is a pun
on *kai* (shell) and *kai aru* (fruitful); there is
another pun on *sachi*, which means both "good
fortune" and "product of the sea."

*Murasaki no kasumi ni fuji o irodorite haru no
keshiki o utsushi enoshima*

"Mt Fuji is colored with purple mists and the
picture of Enoshima reflects the spring landscape"   *Misu no Fusako*

*Hiku shio no sachi ni hirōte mochitose ni kai aru
haru no shirushi enoshima*

"With its shells, gathered from the bounty of
the ebbing tide, Enoshima is the emblem of a
bountiful Spring"   *Shinratei Manzō*

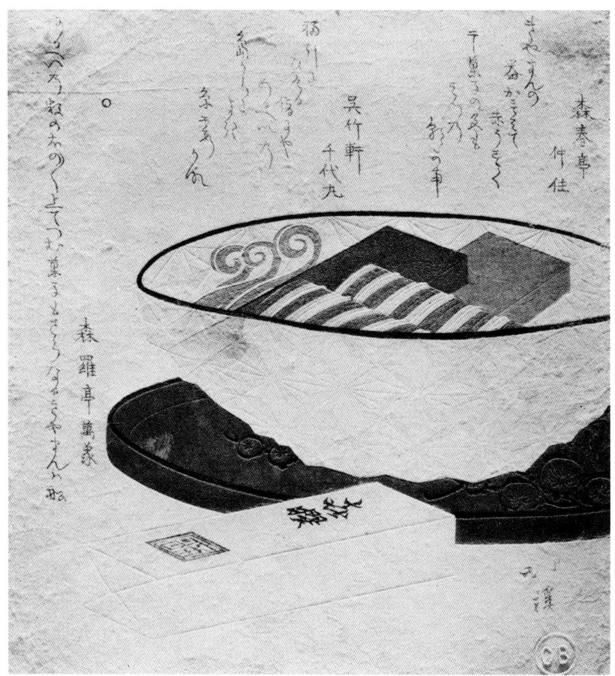

25

Sweets in a cut-glass bowl
1821
21.6 × 19.0 cm
signed Hokkei
Beatty 2045

A bowl of translucent glass rests on a lacquered tray with a decoration of plum blossoms in the Rimpa style. The two long brown objects in the bowl are pieces of *yōkan*, a cake made principally of red beans and sugar. The paper-wrapped parcel embossed in the foreground contains *kisemmaki*, a type of *yōkan* colored with gardenia juice and named after the medieval poet-priest Kisen Hōshi. The pink and green objects in the bowl are *aruhei*, a modeled sugar sweetmeat introduced by the Portuguese, who called the material *alfeloa*. The green ones are meant to represent young fern shoots. Cut glass was also introduced by the Portuguese, who apparently called it *diamante* because the glittering facets so resembled diamonds; the pronunciation changed to *giyaman* in Japanese and the word was eventually applied to glass in general. One would ordinarily find the name or insignia of the confectioner on the square vermilion seal of the cake wrapper, but in Hokkei's print the seal contains the cyclical signs, *kanoto mi*, for 1821, a Snake Year.

In the first poem there is a pun on *higashi*, which means both "sweets" and "east." There is another pun on *mitsu* (honey) or a sweet syrup and *mitsu no asa*, "The Three Mornings," a poetic expression for New Year's Day, since it was at once the first morning of the day, the month and the year. In the second poem there is an association between mist and the word *hiku* (to draw), and a pun on *aru* (there is) and *aruhei* (the sugary sweet). *Fukubiki* (pulling for luck) was a lottery-like drawing for small prizes; participants would pull strings attached to small concealed objects. In the last poem, there is a pun on *honobono* (dimly) and *ho* (sail). There is another pun on *sara* (dish) and *saranaru* (naturally).

Giyaman no utsuwa kasumite akausuku higashi no iro mo mitsu no asa kana

"The glass bowl is misty, the light pink color of sweets in the east makes a sweet New Year dawn"
Shinshuntei Nakazumi

Fukubiki ni hikeru ato ni wa aruhei no shimagara mo yoki itogasumi kana

"After we pulled strings in the lottery, there were sugar sweets with lovely stripes like threads of mist"
Gochikuken Chiyomaru

Aruhei no kazu no honobono agete tsumu kashi mo sara naru giyaman wa fune

"Raising dim sails of sugar sweets, loading the dish with cakes; naturally, the glassy bowl is a ship"
Shinratei Manzō

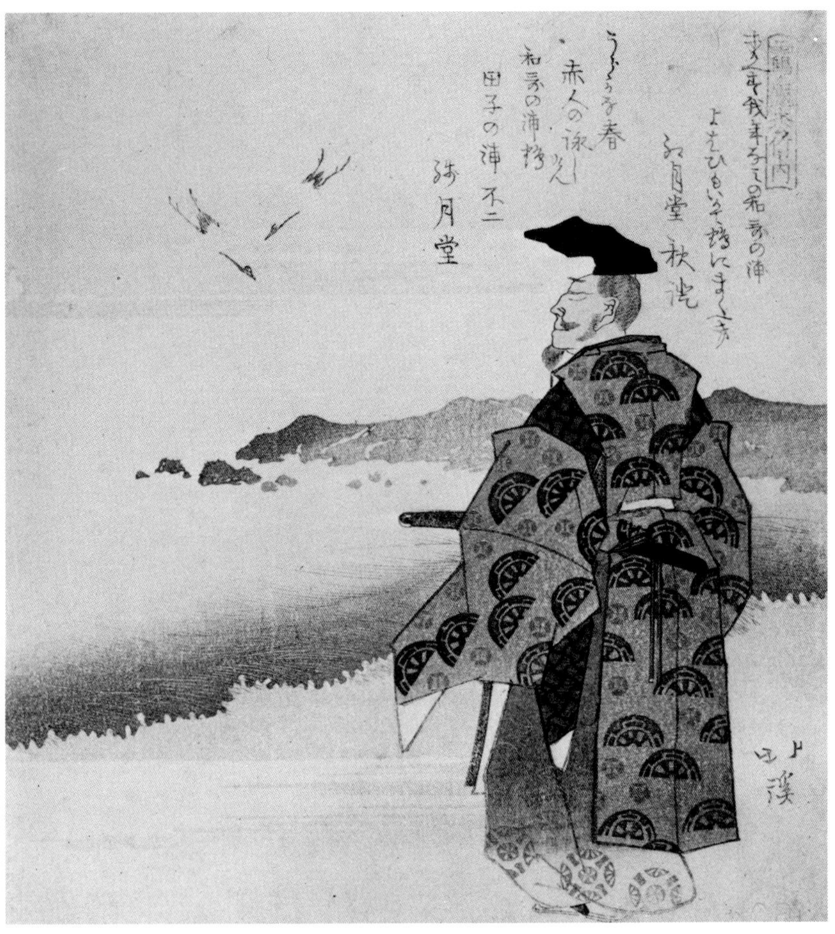

26

The poet Yamabe no Akahito watching cranes
at Wakanoura
series Cranes, Turtles, Pine and Bamboo
1821 or 1822
21.1 × 18.7 cm
signed Hokkei
Beatty 956

Yamabe no Akahito was a court poet of the
eighth century; later generations honored him
with the title of Sage (or Saint) of Poetry and
included him among the thirty-six *kasen*, or
"Immortals of Verse." Many of his poems
were included in *Man'yōshū*, "The Collection
of Ten Thousand Leaves," the first anthology
of Japanese verse. One of the most famous of
these was a long poem prompted by the journey of the Emperor Shōmu to the province of
Kii in the winter of 724. This poem ended
with the words: "As the tide flows into Waka
Bay, whose lagoons are lost in flood, the
cranes go crying towards the reedy shore."
The poet Akahito was therefore often linked
with the cranes at Wakanoura, or Waka Bay,
and Hokkei presents us here with an imaginary portrait of the poet, standing in his court
robes and watching a pair of cranes in the
sky. There were four prints in Hokkei's set;
one of them seems to mention a Horse Year,
but two mention *kai awase*, a shell game often
associated with a Snake Year. Cranes were a
symbol of long life and the poet Akizumi reflects that his life could never be as long as
theirs. In the second poem, Zangetsudō refers
to another famous verse in which Akahito ex-
pressed his awe at suddenly seeing the peak of
Mt Fuji from the beach at Tago.

*Uchikaesu waga toshinami no wakanoura yowai mo
ikade tsuru ni makubeki*

"Years of age repeat like pounding waves at
Waka Bay; will I be defeated by the cranes?"
Kōgetsudō Akizumi

*Uraraka na haru akahito no eijiken wakanoura
tsuru tagonoura fuji*

"On beautiful spring days must Akahito have
composed his poems about the cranes at Waka
Bay, Mt Fuji from the beach at Tago"
Zangetsudō

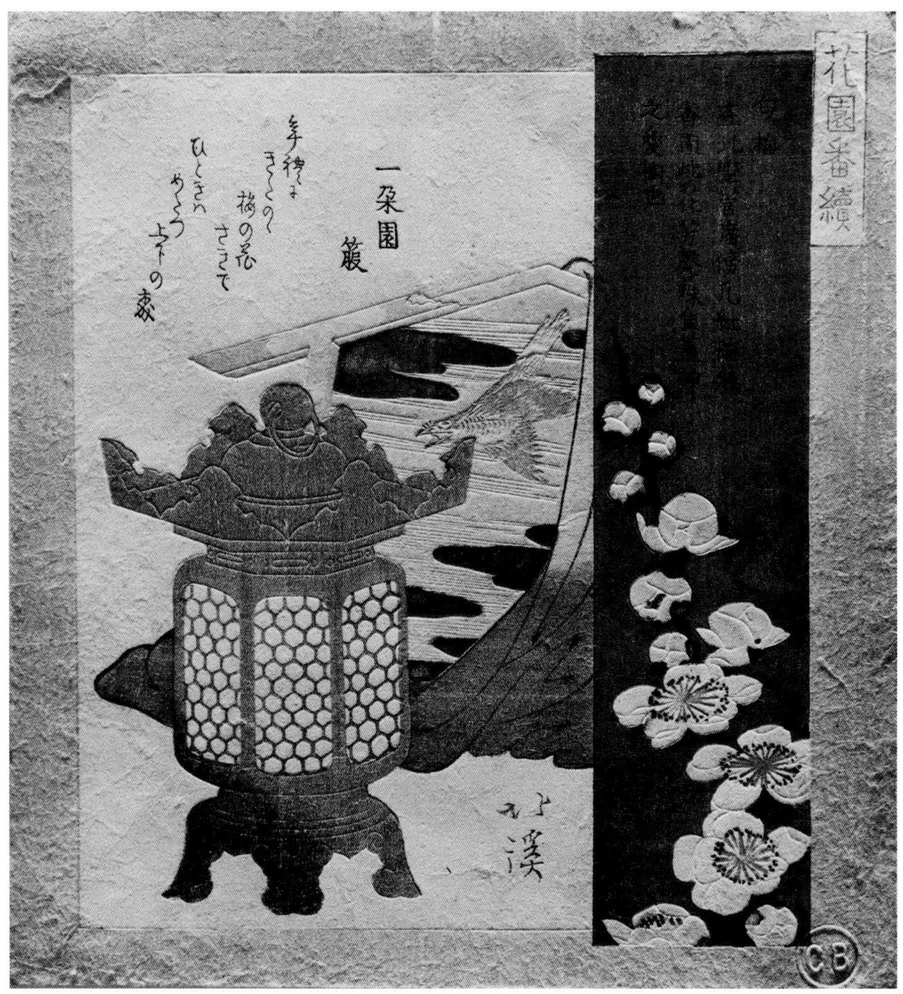

27

Temple lantern, temple plaque and fragrant
plum
series Series for the Hanazono Group
c. 1822
21.3 × 18.8 cm
signed Hokkei
unidentified Japanese collector's seal on verso;
Beatty 2044

Hokkei's print is from a series of complemen-
tary double images with colored borders; this
artifice is used to make the pictures look as
though they are pasted on album pages. The
larger picture to the left of each pair is always
a still life; the narrow panel on the right always contains a branch of plum blossom,
whose species is often identified beside the
accompanying verse or inscription.

The objects in the print are a bronze temple
lantern and a votive painting of a *hototogisu*, a
bird similar to a cuckoo. The Japanese poem
above the objects contains a pun on *kamishimo*,
the name of a formal men's costume, which
literally means "upper and lower." There is
another pun on *hanasaki*, which means both
"near" and "flowers blossoming." It also mentions Kitano, an area on the northern edge of
the city of Kyōto where a tomb was built in
959 for the great statesman, calligrapher and
poet, Sugawara Michizane (845–903); his fa-
vorite flower was the plum. Over the centuries, Sugaware was transformed from an historical figure into a deity and came to serve as
a patron saint of scholars and calligraphers.
Under the patronage of Toyotomi Hideyoshi
in the late sixteenth or early seventeenth century, a shrine was built at Kitano in honor of
Sugawara.

*Nenrei ni kitano no ume no hanasakite hitokiwa
medatsu kamishimo no mori*

"During the New Year visits, the men in formal robes stand out as distinctly as the upper
and lower forests near the flowering plum
trees at Kitano"
                              Ichidaen Ebira

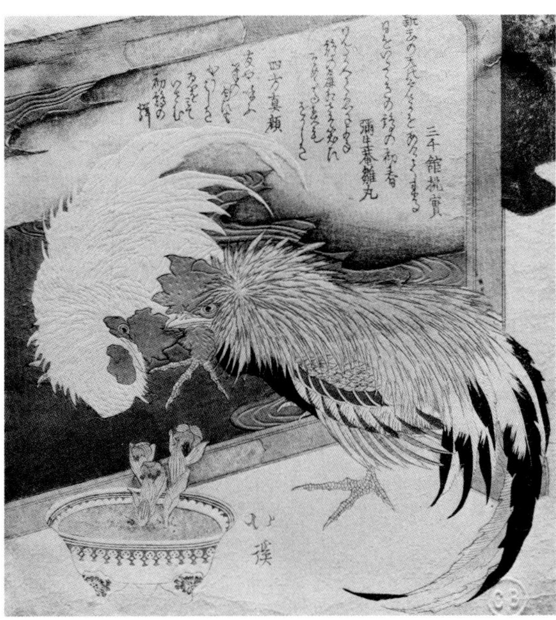

28

Rooster threatening a painted cock
1825
21.9 × 18.9 cm
signed Hokkei
Beatty 2019

By the 1790s, the ukiyo-e artists who depicted
shiny surfaces and reflected images in their
woodblock prints had developed an ironical
awareness of the difference between image
and reality, representation and object. Rather
than philosophize, however, early nineteenth-
century artists like Hokkei, and poets like
Magao and his followers, used their insights
to create visual metaphors like the one in this
print.

The design, engraving and printing of a
surimono took considerable time and work. A
picture which was distributed during the first
few days of the year would have been begun
before the end of the previous year; thus this
print was to be distributed at the beginning of
1825, but will have been designed and engraved in 1824. The poets who commissioned
Hokkei's print of the rooster wanted the date
and cyclical signs for 1825 engraved conspicuously in the upper-right corner of the print:
this was not a common practice; perhaps the
cyclical signs were included because they
were identical to those on the first calendar
prints designed by Harunobu in 1765, sixty
years earlier. However, the date on the print
mistakenly reads Bunsei 7 (1824), rather than
Bunsei 8 (1825), the date of the Bird Year. It

was not difficult to replace a number on a
woodblock, but the mistake was apparently
not caught until the edition had already been
printed. A separate block was therefore cut in
the shape of a cloud, and the entire date was
covered with gold pigment and effaced. One
early impression, perhaps a proof, without the
gold cloud is reproduced in the Hayashi sale
catalogue. On all other impressions that are
presently known the date is effaced. In the
first poem there is a pun on *akeru* (to open)
and *ageru* (to raise). In the third poem there is
a pun on *hatsutori* (the first cock-crow), and
torihiki (transaction).

*Aratama no ama no tosaka o akete kuru hi o
itadaki no tori no hatsuharu*

"Early Spring in the Year of the Cock, who
wore the sun for its comb and raised it when
the rough-cut door of Heaven opened"
Senzenkan Momozane

*Mitagaeta e ni yoru tori no sosōsa wa warai
sometaru haru mo okashiki*

"The disappointment of the cock who attacks
the painting by mistake: the first laugh of a
humorous Spring"   *Yayoian Hinamaru*

*Tomo ya yobu fude no nioi mo kōbashiki e o mite
isamu hatsutori no hiki*

" 'Friend or foe?', he cries, bravely facing the
painting scented with the fragrance of the
brush: the first transaction, at cock-crow, of
the Bird Year"   *Yomo Magao*

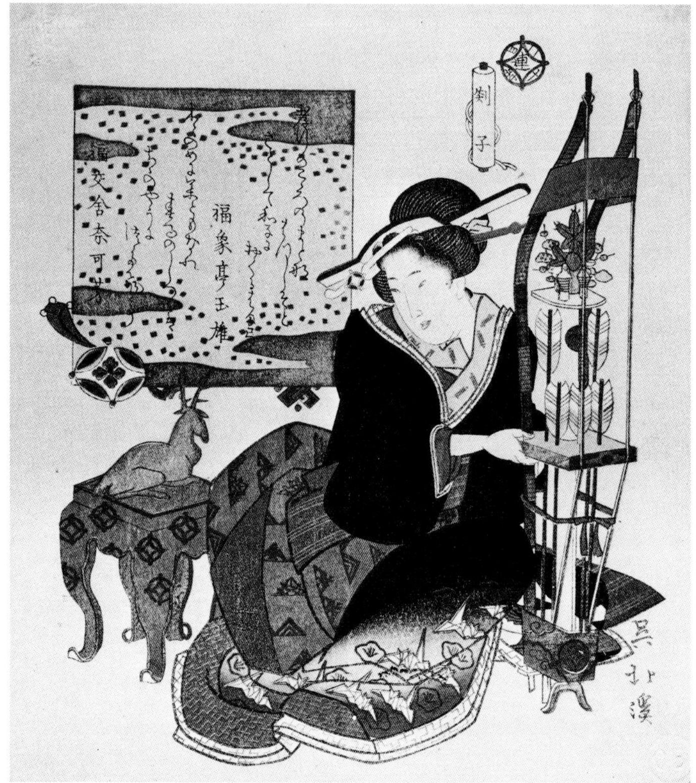

29

series Woman holding a ceremonial toy bow/*Cui Shi*
Twenty-four Paragons of Filial Piety for the
Seven Treasures Circle
c. 1825
21.7 × 18.9 cm
signed Go Hokkei
Beatty 2056

Each print in this series depicts a young
woman holding an object, or performing an
act, that recalls one of the Twenty-four
Chinese Paragons of Filial Piety, a group familiar to any Japanese of the Edo period who
had the rudiments of a Confucian education.
The prints were designed for the Shippō, or
"Seven Treasures," circle of poets; their emblem appears on the top of each print, beside
a small handscroll marked with the name of
the paragon represented. The verses are written on a square resembling a poem sheet; it is
decorated with gold flecks and emblems of the
Seven Treasures, traditional symbols of luck
and fortune derived from Buddhist art. The
secondary names of all poets in the Seven
Treasures Group start with the word *fuku*
(luck). The group's circular emblem frequently appears as a decorative element in the
series, as, for example, on the lacquer table
and on the base of the bow in this print.

Cui Shi (or Saishi in Japanese) had an aged
mother who was toothless and unable to chew
her food. His wife, therefore, nursed the old
woman for several years and, when the wife
died, Cui Shi's mother summoned her friends
and relations to describe her daughter-in-law's
kindness. Although his wife nursed his
mother, Cui Shi himself was enrolled among
the Paragons; presumably for making sure
that she did. The woman in Hokkei's print is
holding a *hamayumi*, a decorative arrangement
of bows and arrows that was often given to
children at the New Year as a talisman against
evil spirits. The bow has nothing to do with
the story of Cui Shi, but does aptly illustrate
the first poem. The deer is a symbol of longevity; it may also have been included in the
print because of its association with hunting.

*Kōkō no kokoro no mato na hazushi zo to satoshite
wako ni okuru hamayumi*

"Do not fail to hit the target of a filial heart,
she admonishes her son, giving him the toy
bow"
          Fukushōtei Tamao

*Kigi no me ni konomi tomo nare harusame to
shizuku wa chichi no yō ni tsutaite*

"Become fruit, oh drops of spring rain, as you
trickle like milk on the buds of every tree"
          Fukkōsha Nakayoshi

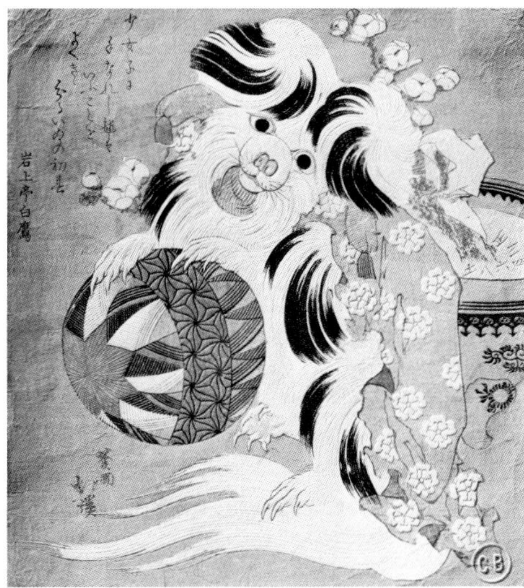

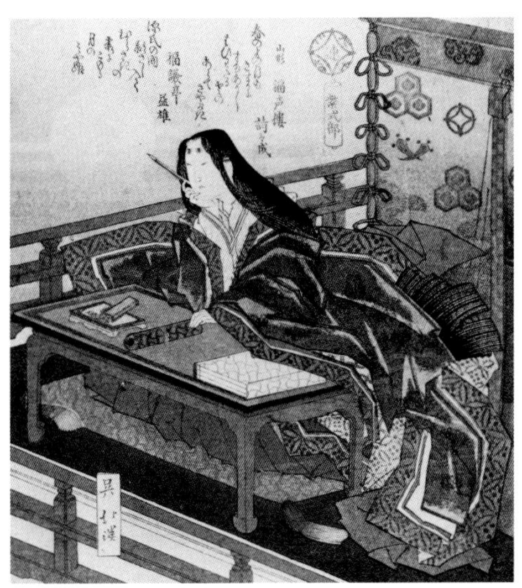

30

Pekinese dog with decorative ball
1826
20.6 × 18.5 cm
signed Aoigaoka Hokkei
Beatty 2018

The beguiling little dog is seated beside a
footed porcelain planter containing a miniature plum tree. The dog is dressed in a silk
cape, which fastens around the neck with a
crepe cord, and leans against a ball decorated
with patterns of colored thread and secured
by a band of cloth. Pekinese dogs were not
native to Japan but were introduced from
China. They seem to start appearing in color
woodblock prints around 1790, although a
careful search might show that they are depicted earlier. This print is a picture calendar;
the numerals for the long months of 1826, a
Dog Year, are clearly written on the soil inside the planter: 1, 3, 4, 6, 8 and 11.

*Otomego ni tenareshi mari wa iu koto o yoku
kikiwakuru inu no hatsuharu*

"The ball is used to the little girls; it listens
carefully and understands what they say, like
a dog in early Spring"   *Ganjōtei Shirataka*

31

Murasaki Shikibu seated at a writing desk
series Three Great Women for the Seven Treasures
Circle
c. 1826
21.2 × 18.5 cm
signed Go Hokkei
Rose; Beatty 2021

Lady Murasaki (*c.* 978–*c.* 1014) was a lady-in-
waiting at the Heian court. After many years
of service, she retired to a temple at Ishiyama,
overlooking Lake Biwa, and wrote the *Tale of
Genji*, the earliest and finest Japanese prose
romance. The room in which she was said to
have composed the book was called *Genji no
ma*, the Genji Room; it overlooked the lake
and commanded a magnificent view of the
autumn moon. Perhaps because of this,
Ishiyama Temple was later associated with
the autumn moon in the Eight Views of Lake
Biwa, a common subject for paintings and
woodblock prints in the Edo period. The first
poem contrasts the clear moon at Ishiyama
with the clouded moon at two places to which
Prince Genji was exiled. The second puns on
Murasaki's name, which means "purple."

*Haru no yo no tsuki mo sasugani suma akashi
haiwataru kumo no arade sayakeki*

"The moon is clear on this spring night; without the clouds that creep over it at Suma and
Akashi"   *Fukuseirō Shishinari of Yamagata*

*Genji no ma kage sashiirete murasaki no kasumi ni
komoru tsuki no miyahime*

"The Princess of the Moon, robed with purple mist, sends moonbeams into the Genji Room"
   Fukukentei Masuo

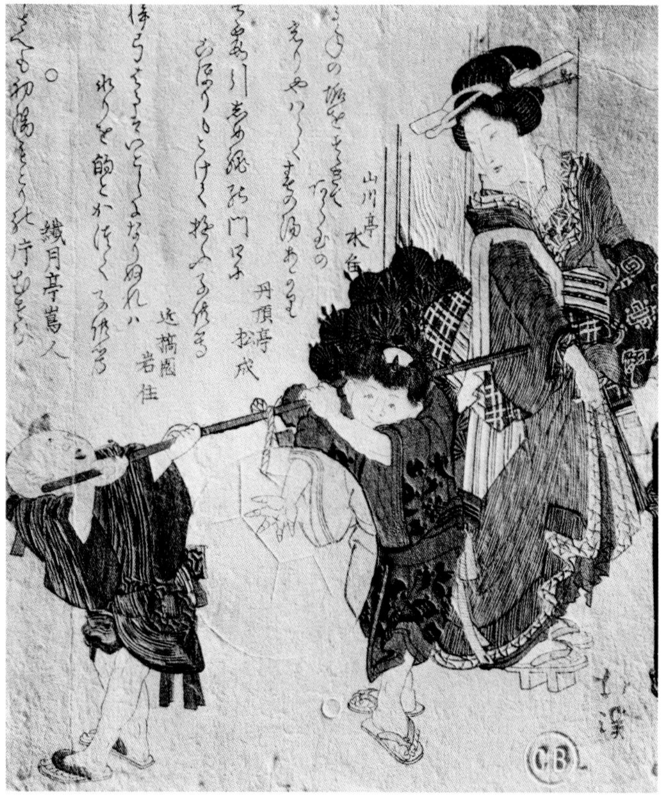

32

Woman watching children with a sheet of ice
at the entrance to a bathhouse
1827
20.3 × 16.8 cm
signed Hokkei
Beatty 2151

Standing at the entrance to a bathhouse, a
woman watches two children carry a sheet of
ice suspended from a bamboo pole. The ice
has been removed from a cistern on the right,
placed in the street for use in case of fire. The
ice is printed in light blue, with embossed
lines for cracks, and the red robe of the child
on the right is printed in light pink where it is
covered by the transparent ice. This impression is trimmed at left and right; it lacks the
name of the bathhouse, *ume no yu* (Plum
Bath), the wooden plaque on the side of the
cistern and the last line of the final poem. On
an untrimmed impression in the Fogg Art
Museum, the plaque reads *minamichō inohori*,
"South Street, Boar Canal," a neighborhood
in the Fukagawa district of Edo. The second
and third characters in the inscription may
also be read as *hinoto i*, the cyclical signs for
1827, a Boar Year. In the third poem there
are puns on *haru*, which means "spring" and

"to draw a bow," and on *i*, which means
"shoot" and "boar." In the last poem there is a
pun on *tokeru*, which means "melt" and "untie."

*Furutoshi no aka o susugite aratama no hikari
yawaragu haru no yuagari*

"A spring bath softens the rough-cut sun-
beams and washes off the soil of the old year"
Sansentei Suikaku (or Suigyo)

*Harugasumi hiki shimenawa no kadoguchi ni kōri
mo tokete asobu kodomora*

"Spring mist is drawn like a sacred rope
across the entrance gate; ice melts and children play" Tanchōtei Matsunari

*Azusayumi haru wa idoshi ni narinureba kōri o
mato to katsugu kodomora*

"Spring, like a shot from a catalpa bow, turns
into the Year of the Boar; the children carry
the ice like a target" Kinkōen Iwazumi

*Obi sae mo hatsuyu modori no katamusubi [sorosoro
tokuru haru no kōri wa]*

"Even the sash, loosely fastened for the trip
home from the bath, gradually comes untied,
like slowly melting ice in Spring"
Sengetsutei Shimando

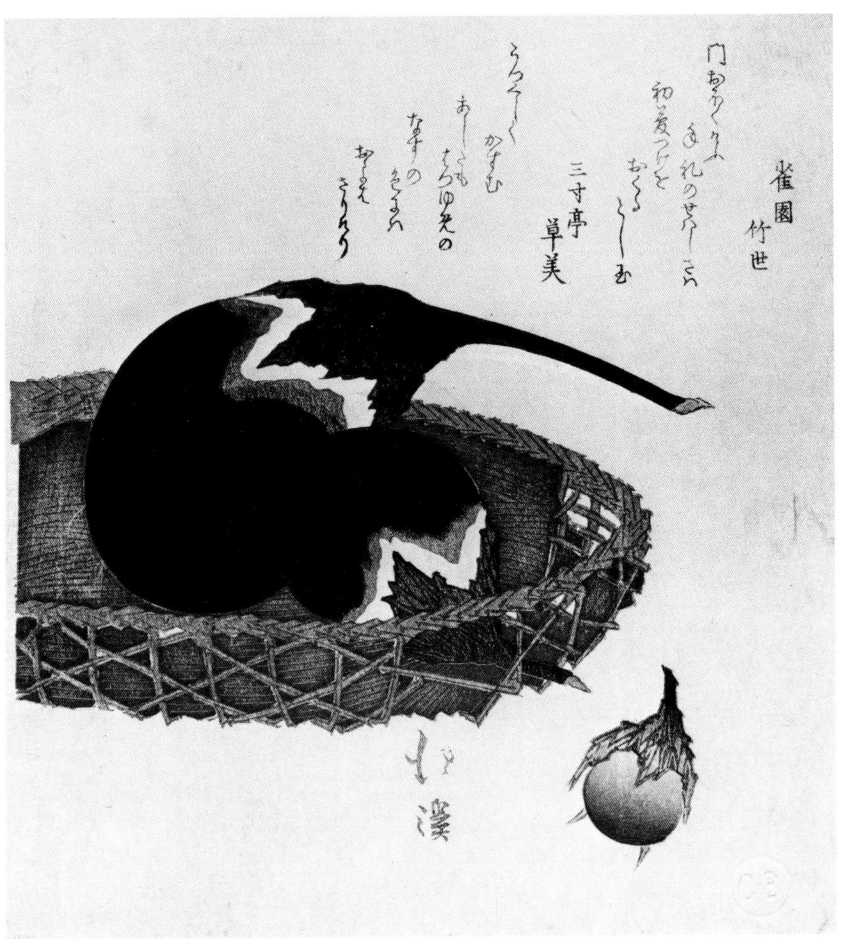

33

Basket of eggplants
from an untitled series of Three Lucky Dreams
c. 1828
20.3 × 18.2 cm
signed Hokkei
Beatty 2052

The Lucky Dreams were three unrelated images—Mt Fuji, a hawk and eggplants; if they appeared in one's dreams on the first or second night of the New Year, they would bring luck in the coming months. To encourage good dreams, people often slept with a woodblock print of the *takarabune*, the treasure ship of the Seven Gods of Good Fortune, under their pillow (see cat. no. 7). Many artists designed prints with all three images included in the design, but Hokkei seems to have been the only artist who designed a still life, as it were, of each subject. The two other prints in the set show the peak of Mt Fuji and the hawk on its perch; both are reproduced in Ward (1976), pls. 17–18. The poems by Seiyōkan Umeyo and his pupils give no indi-

cation of the date of the set; the simple style and colors seem early, but the large stroke to the left of the character for *hoku* in the signature shows that the design is relatively late. The first poem mentions *hatsuyume zuke*, "First-Dream Pickles," which were made from eggplant, and compares the round fruit to a jewel. This picture was copied several times at the end of the nineteenth century: one version has a red pepper beneath the basket, others have the signature located at the side.

Kado ōku kyō nenrei no sewashisa wa hatsuyumezuke o okuru toshidama

"At many busy gates today people pay their respects and give jewel-like First-Dream Pickles as New Year presents"   *Suzumeen Takeyo*

Utsukushiku kasumu ashita mo hatsuyume no nasu no iro niwa oyobazarikeri

"Even the beautiful misty New Year dawn does not surpass the color of the eggplant in the first dream of the year" *Sanzuntei Kusami*

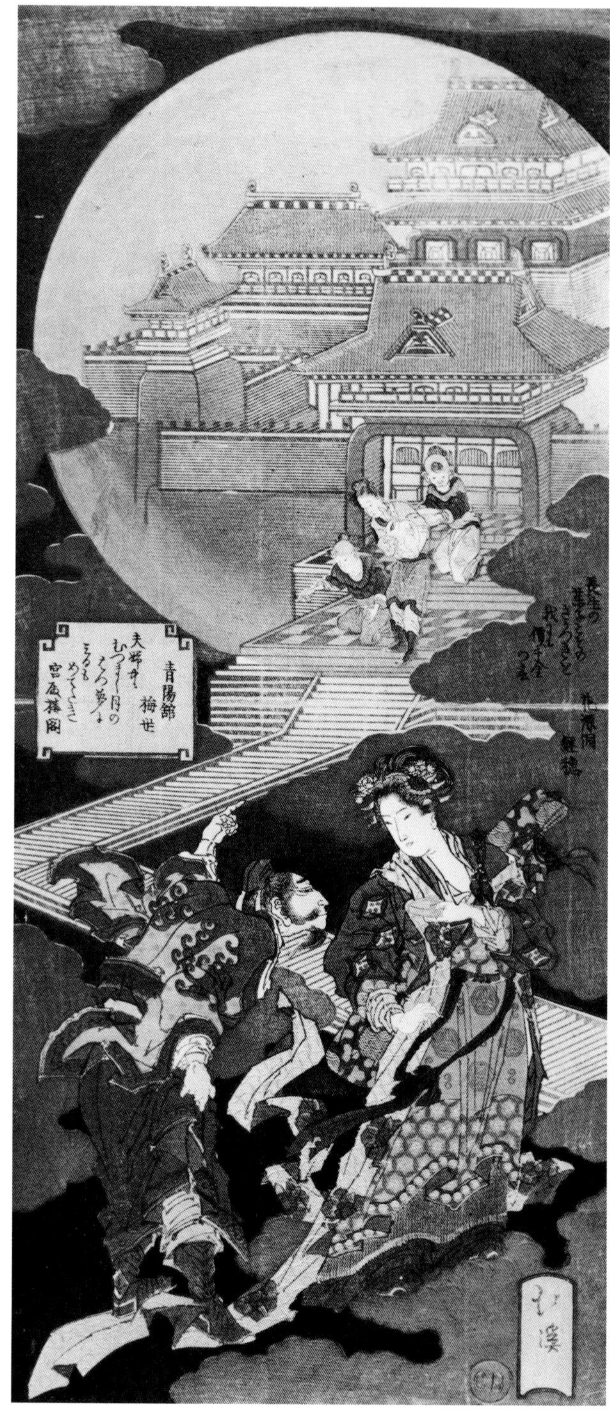

34
Chinese couple outside the Palace of the
Moon
1831
vertical diptych, 42.2 × 18.2 cm
signed Hokkei
Beatty 2136

The woman with a silver dish or cup in one
hand and a zither suspended in a brocade case
over her shoulder is standing on a cloud outside the Moon Palace. The Chinese man ges-
turing towards the palace is supported by the
train of her robe. In the background, a young
woman at the gate of the palace holds the
Moon Rabbit, an indication that the print was
published in 1831, a Rabbit Year. Because the
poems speak of a loving couple and the elixir
of immortality, the subject of the print is
probably the meeting of Yang Guifei (Yōkihi
in Japanese) and Luo Gongyuan, a Taoist magician in the service of Xuan Zong, the last
emperor of the Tang Dynasty. Xuan Zong
met Yang Guifei towards the end of his life
and became so infatuated with her that he
neglected matters of state. This neglect led to
a serious rebellion, during which Yang was
killed. The emperor was heartbroken and sent
the Taoist magician to search for her in the
afterworld. In the Nō play *Yōkihi*, the magician found Yang in the palace at Hōrai, the
Land of the Immortals, and she gave him a
hair ornament as a memento to present to the
emperor. In Hokkei's print, the scene has
been transposed to the Palace of the Moon,
probably because of the association of the
moon with the rabbit; also, perhaps, because
the magician once took the emperor on an
astral voyage to the Palace of the Moon in a
search for the elixir of immortality. The emperor and his consort often played music together and that may be why the woman in
Hokkei's print carries a zither on her back.

In the first poem, *mutsumaji*, which means
"harmonious" or "friendly," was also a poetic
word for the first month of the year. In the
second, *chōsei*, which means "immortality,"
was the name of the palace in which Xuan
Zong lived with Yang Guifei.

Meoto naka mutsumajizuki no hatsuyume ni miru
mo medetaki kyūden rōkaku

"A loving couple is fortunate to see the towers
of the Moon Palace in their first dream of the
first month of the year"   *Seiyōkan Umeyo*

Chōsei no kusuri ni toso no sakazuki o ware nimo
atai senkin no haru

"And give me, too, a cup of New Year wine
with the elixir of immortality; it is worth a
thousand gold coins in the Spring"
Kagendō Tsugiho

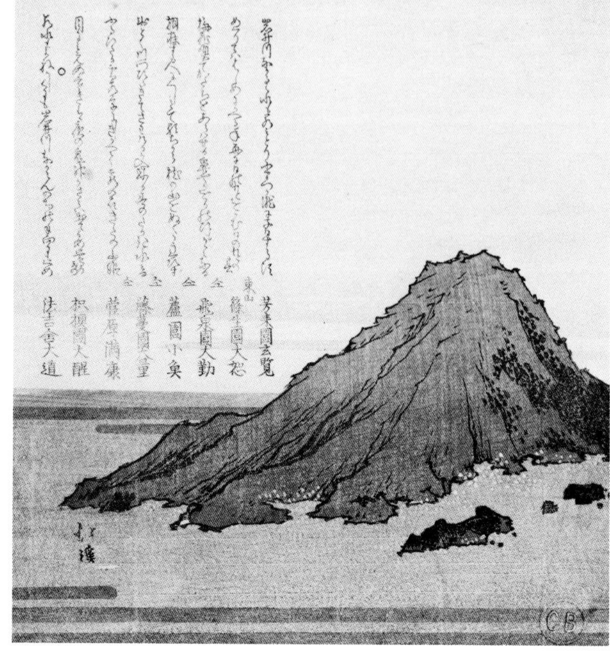

35

New-Year sunrise at Mt Kinka with a view of
the Iwai River in Iwate Province
early or mid 1830s
triptych, 19.9 × 54.2 cm
signed Hokkei
Beatty 494

Kinkazan, "Golden Flower Mountain," is a
small picturesque volcanic island, four or five
kilometers in diameter, off the coast of the
Ojika Peninsula in Iwate Province, in northern Japan. It was originally called Michinoku
Mountain, but after gold was discovered there
in 749 it was renamed Koganehanasakuyama,
"The Mountain where Golden Flowers
Bloom." That name was eventually contracted
to Kinkazan. The first and second poems both
mention the island; two of the last poems
mention the Iwai River, which flows from the
slopes of Mt Kurikoma on the border of
Miyagi, Iwate and Akita Prefectures and joins
the Kitakami River near Ichinoseki, at a considerable distance inland from Kinkazan.

There are in fact no rivers on the Ojika Peninsula, so the hillside with the embossed
stream on the right must be an imaginary
view of the mountainous headwaters of the
Iwai River. Hokkei probably included this
scene in his triptych to accommodate the
fancy of the provincial poets who commissioned the prints. Their names suggest that
many of them were Buddhist priests.

Many commercial woodblock prints published in Edo in the nineteenth century were
designed as triptychs, but this format was
rarely used for the privately published surimono. Hokkei designed two interesting sets of
landscape prints in the early or mid 1830s.
The finer and more striking was *Shokoku
meisho*, "Famous Places in the Provinces," in
horizontal half-block format; the other was a
series of Chinese-style landscapes printed pre-
dominantly in blue, like this view of Mt
Kinka. Because of their number, the verses by
the following poets have not been transcribed
or translated here:

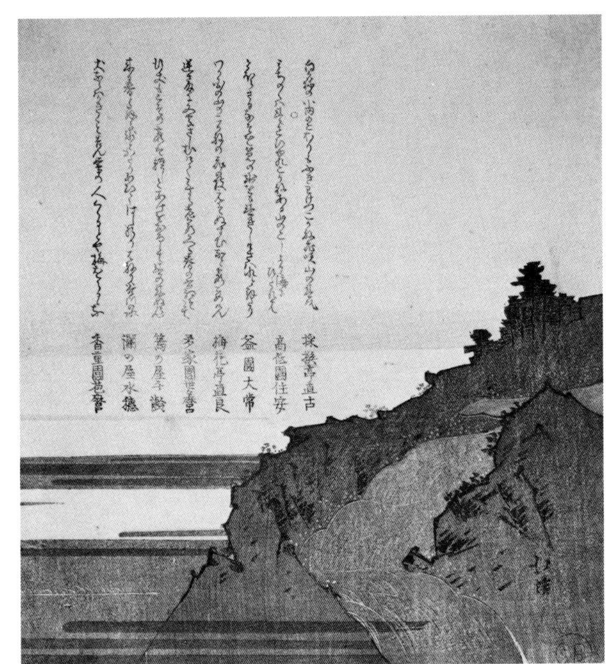 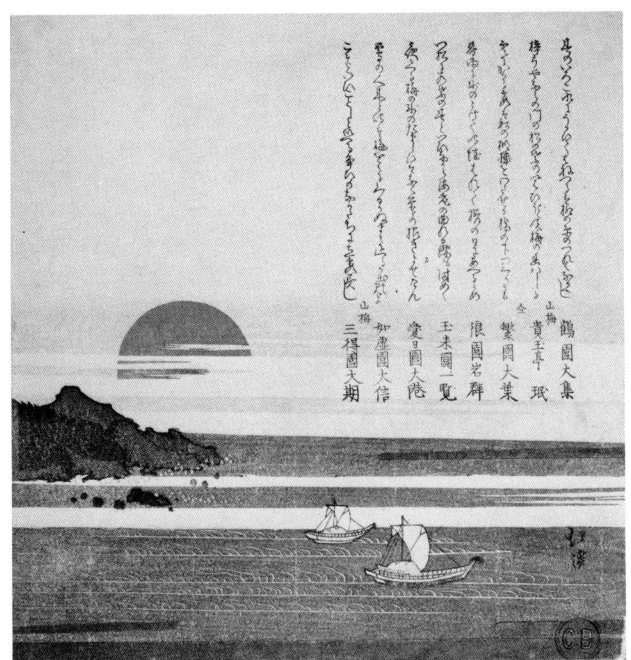

<table>
<tr><td>

Left panel

Hōraien Genran
Zōshōen Daijō of Higashiyama (or Tōzan)
Hisen'en Daikin of Higashiyama
Roen Shōgyo of Higashiyama
Tōman'en Dairyō of Higashiyama
Sugawara Mankō of Higashiyama
Kikuen Daisei
Hōkitsusha Daidō

</td><td>

Center Panel

Kakuen Daishū
Kigyokutei Min of Yamaume
Han'en Daiyō of Yamaume
Rōen Iwamure
Gyokuraien Ichiran
Aijitsuen Daikō
Jokyoen Daishin
Santokuen Daiki of Yamaume

</td><td>

Right panel

Saikantei Naofuru
Kōteien Sumiyasu
Ekien Daijō
Baikatei Naoyoshi
Takaen Yoyomaro
Atsunoya Chitose
Naminoya Mizuho
Kōjūen Tsutomaro

</td></tr>
</table>

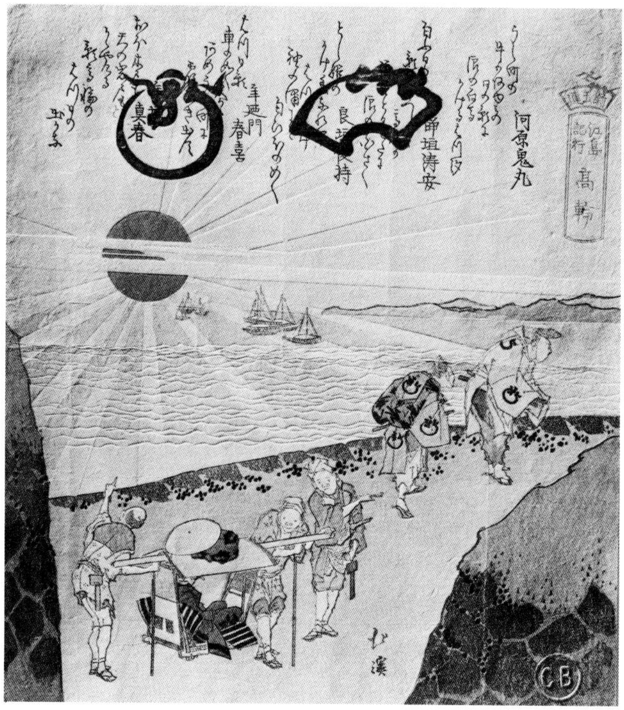

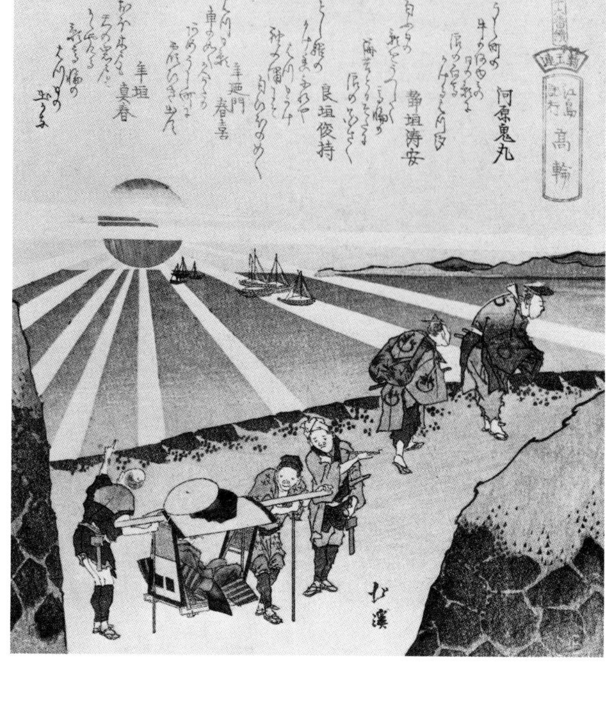

36a

Takanawa
series Record of a Journey to Enoshima for the
Shingyoku Circle
1833
20.6 × 17.8 cm
signed Hokkei
Beatty 2039

Three poets from the Shingyoku Circle begin
their journey to Enoshima at Takanawa as the
New Year sun rises over Edo Bay. Two men
with the group's emblem on their robes walk
towards the right, as the third poet, a woman,
watches the sunrise from her palanquin. This
is the first state of the print, with the gold
emblems of the group in the sky and the mark
of the Katsushika Group at the upper right
above the title; it contains an engraver's error
in the fifth line from the left, which has been
corrected by hand in red ink from *mo* to *to*.
The water in this impression is light blue and
a light-brown block is used for several of the
costumes. The poems mention Takanawa, the
point of departure from Edo for travelers jour-
neying west and south. The first poem mentions Ushimachi, Ox Street, a district of
Takanawa which faced the bay; Sodegaura
("Sleeve Bay") and Ōkido are also places near
Takanawa. The last poem compares the first
sunrise at Takanawa with the appearance of
the Sun Goddess, Amaterasu, from the cave
in Heaven where she had concealed herself.

*Ushimachi no ushi no ayumi no hi no kage ni nami
no shirouma kakeru hatsushio*

"The first tide spurs the white horses of the
waves, as the oxen at Ushimachi approach
with slow steps like the rays of the sun"
Kawara Onimaru

*Niou hi no kage o utsushite takanawa no nori toru
zo dani nami no hana saku*

"When they gather seaweed at Takanawa, the
waves are blossoming flowers, reflecting the
fragrant waves of the sun"   *Shizugaki Namiyasu*

*Toshihime no kakegō nareya hatsu hikage sode no
ura ni zo nioi honomeku*

"Is it the perfumed sachet of the Princess of
the New Year? The first rays of the sun
faintly scent one's sleeve at Sode Bay"
Yoshigaki Toshimochi

*Hatsuhikage kuruma no gotoku hisakata no
ameushimachi no kasumi hikidasu*

"The first rays of the sun are like a cart drawing the mist of the tawny sky at Ushimachi"
Toshinoto Haruki

*Ōkido mo ama no iwado mo kagayakeru kage
takanawa no hatsuhinode kana*

"Both Okido and the Cave of Heaven shine in
the rays of the first sunrise at Takanawa"
Toshigaki Maharu

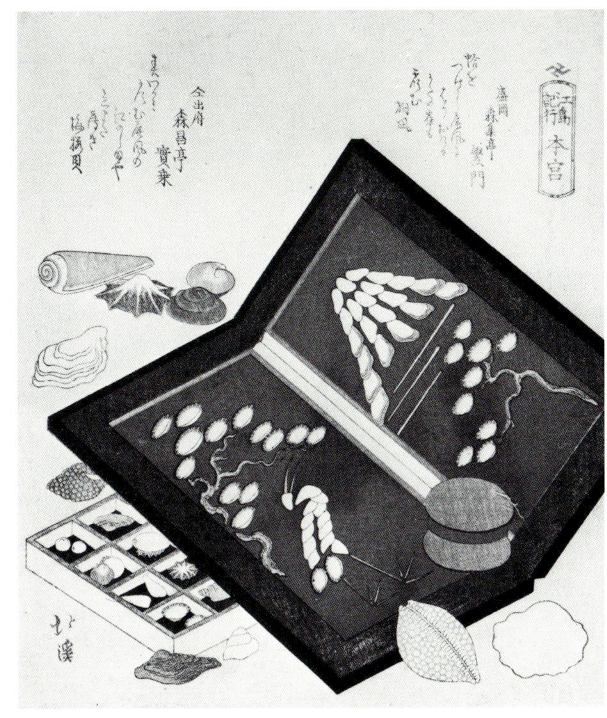

36b

Takanawa
series Record of a Journey to Enoshima, Sixteen
Pictures for the Shingyoku Circle
1833
21.0 × 18.0 cm
signed Hokkei
Beatty 957

This is the second state of the print, with the
engraver's error in the fifth line from the left
changed from *mo* to *to*; it lacks the gold emblems above and replaces the emblem of the
Katsushika Group above the title with the
hand-stamped subtitle, "Sixteen Pictures." In
this state, the water is dark blue and the same
color is used on several of the costumes.
Enoshima was sacred to the Goddess Benten,
whose messenger was a white snake, and the
set was published in 1833, a Snake Year.

Matthi Forrer has located fourteen of the
sixteen subjects from this set in Western collections. The general rarity of surimono in
Japan may be judged by Isaburō Oka's com-
ment on an impression of this print, reproduced full size in color in *Ukiyoe taikei* (vol. 8,
pl. 71): "The stamped seal on the picture calls
for sixteen subjects, but this is the only picture from the set I have ever seen."

37

Motomiya
series Record of a Journey to Enoshima
1833
21.4 × 18.4 cm
signed Hokkei
Beatty 799

Enoshima was famous for its shells and shell-
work screens, which are the subject of this
still life. Motomiya was the main shrine on
the western tip of the island; two other
shrines were located near the top of the hill.

*Hamaguri o tsukeshi byōbu ni hariokeru uta no
suzume mo kasumu asanagi*

"The sparrow in the poem fastened on the
clam-shell screen is covered with mist in the
morning calm"   *Shinshūtei Shigekado of Morioka*

*Haruwakami kasumu byōbu no enoshima ya iro
mada usuki ume sakuragai*

"Spring is young, so the color of the screen of
mist on Enoshima is pale like plum and
cherry shells"
*Shinshōtei Sanenori (or Minori) of Morioka,
presently in Edo*

Teisai Hokuba 1771–1844, active 1798–1842

Hokuba was an inactive retainer of the shōgun; later in his life he took lay religious orders. He was active in the 1800s and 1810s as an illustrator of popular fiction, but also designed a few surimono during this period and continued to design illustrations for privately printed poetry anthologies thereafter. If *Kokusho sōmokuroku* is correct in identifying Hokuba as one of the designers of *Kyōka kachō shū*, "Poems about Birds and Flowers," a poetry anthology compiled by Sensōan and published in 1798, then he was one of Hokusai's earliest pupils, and adopted the name Hokuba while Hokusai was still using the name Sōri. His next dated work is another poetry anthology, *Kyōka maku no uchi*, "Poems from Inside the Curtain," published in 1802.

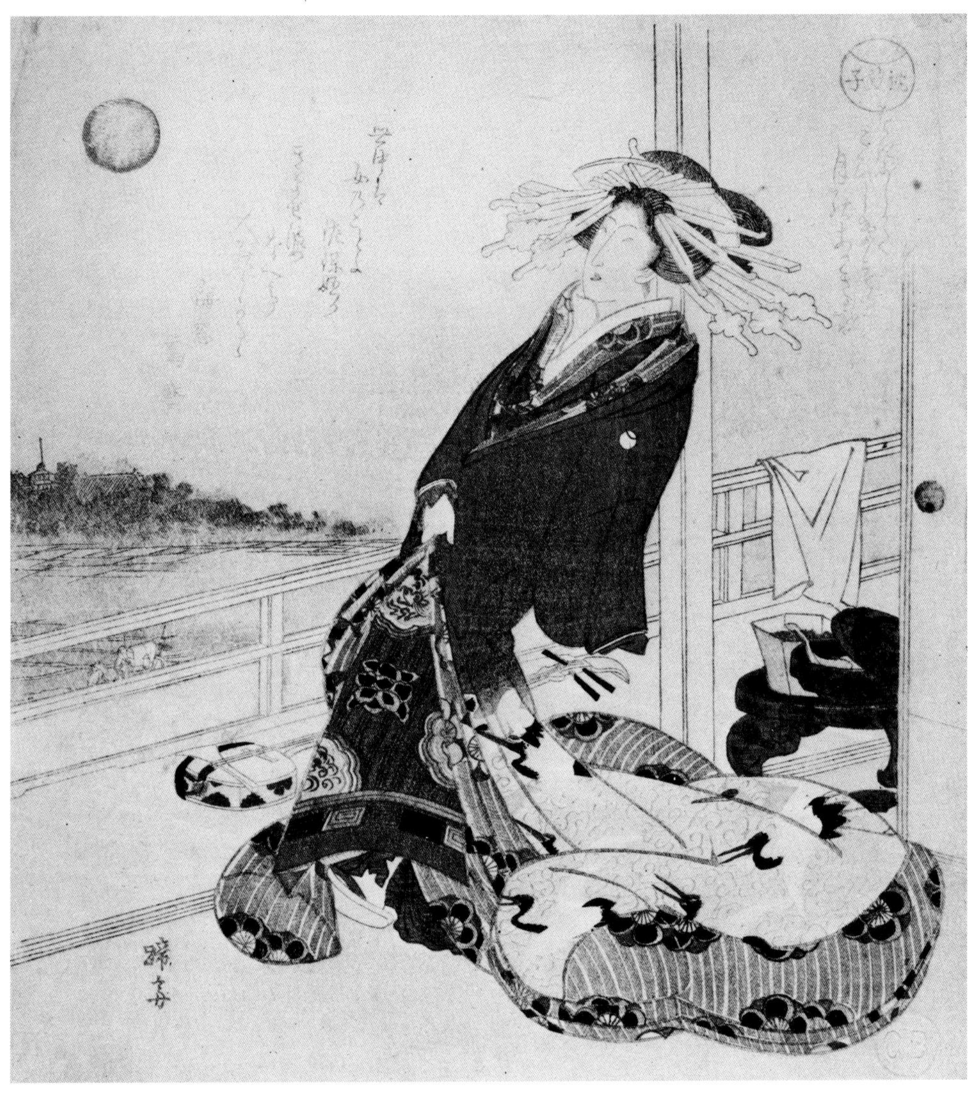

38

Courtesan looking at the moon from a room in
the Yoshiwara
series The Pillow Book
c. late 1810s
21.6 × 18.8 cm
signed Teisai
Beatty 1242

The courtesan is leaning against a post and
looking at the silver moon. A samisen lies
beside her on the floor; a low lacquer table
with food stands behind a sliding door. A
palanquin in the middle distance carries a
client away from the Yoshiwara and on the
horizon the pagoda and main hall of Kinryūzan
Temple rise quietly above the trees. There is
a lovely and intentional contrast between the
brilliant colors of the interior in the foreground and the soft, hazy twilight of the landscape in the distance. The woman's robe is
marked with the circular emblem of the
poetry group that commissioned this series of
illustrations for passages from the *Pillow Book*,
a prose miscellany completed by the court
lady Sei Shōnagon around the year 1000. A
set with a similar title cartouche was designed
by Shumman in the mid or late 1810s; Hokuba's
prints may have been designed as part of that
set, or as a sequel to it. The picture illustrates
a passage from chapter thirty of the *Pillow
Book*: "Things that arouse a fond memory of
the past: a night with a clear moon."

*Yo no naka wa onna no koto ni saohime ga
kimaseba nabete hito no ukaruru*

"What it is like to be a woman in the world:
when the Goddess of Spring appears all the
men become cheerful"   *Baisō Uguisumaro*

Shōtei Hokuju

1759–mid 1820s, active *c.* late 1790s–1824

Hokuju produced a few paintings and surimono, but he specialized in landscape prints with perspective and other signs of Western influence. The first of these seem to have appeared in the late 1790s, since an entry in *Bukō nempyō*, "A Chronology of Edo," for the Kyōwa period (1801–1803), mentions Hokuju as "skilled at perspective pictures." His date of birth may be inferred from a painting of Katō Kiyomasa on which he wrote that he was in his sixty-second year; the picture seems to have been painted in 1824.

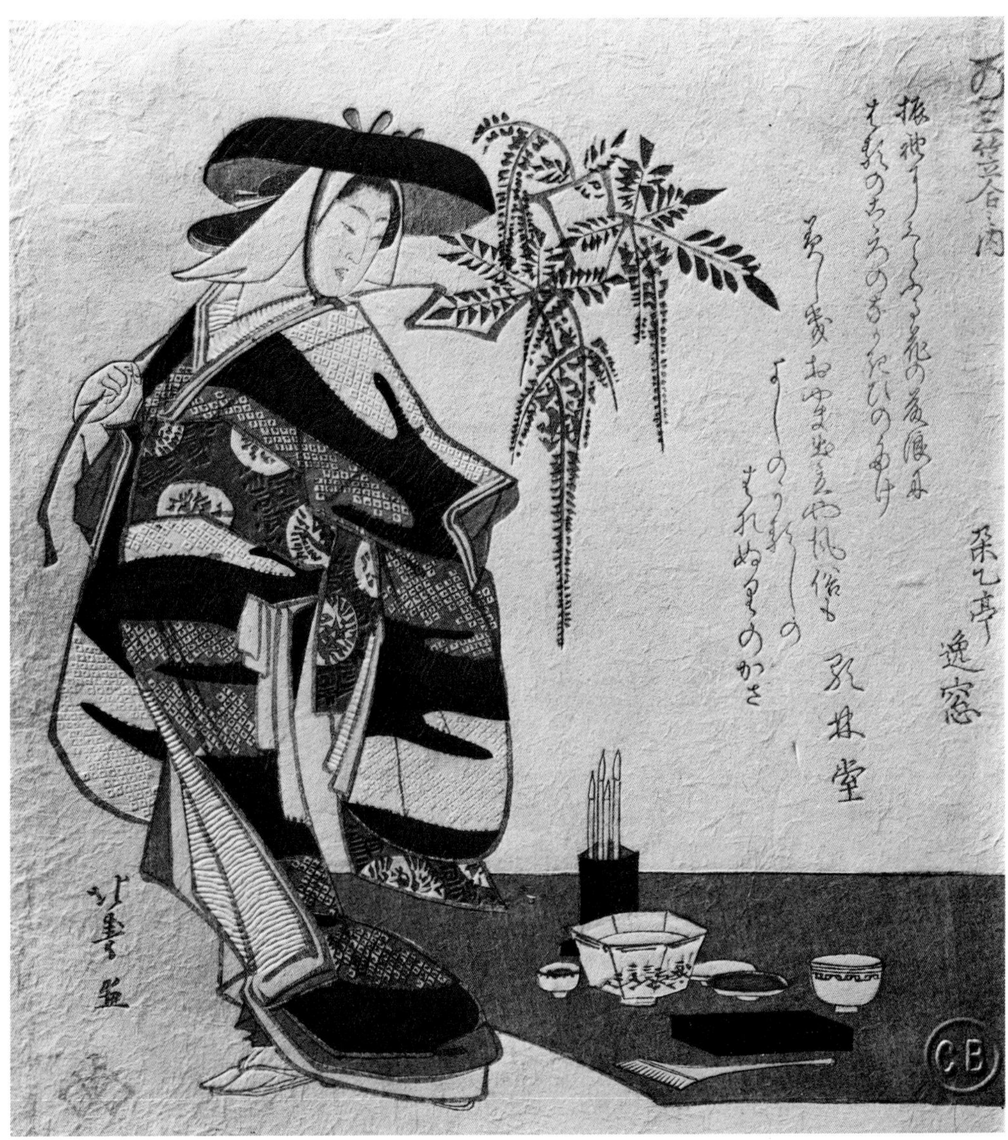

39

Painting equipment and a wistaria maiden
series Three Hats
c. 1820
20.8 × 18.8 cm
signed Hokuju ga; engraved by Egawa Tomekichi
Beatty 2248

The "wistaria maiden" was a common subject of the folk paintings made in the town of Ōtsu on the Tōkaidō Road. The woman in Hokuju's print is a Pygmalion; she was created by the artist whose materials are arranged on the red mat at the right. His painting has come to life and the woman he created is walking away, casting a mere backward glance. The hand-stamped emblem in the lower-left corner belongs to the engraver Tomekichi and appears on several surimono by Kunisada, Hokusai and others published around this date.

In the second poem there is a pun on *yoshi* (good) and Yoshino, the name of a mountainous region in Nara Prefecture which seems to have been famous for its lacquer.

Furisode ni kuraburu hana no fujinami ni haru no kokoro no nagaki hi no take

"The trailing calyxes of wistaria are like flowing sleeves; the heart of Spring is a long day"
Daotsutei Soremado

Utsukushiki oyama detachi ya fūzoku mo yoshino urushi no harenuri no kasa

"A beautiful woman appears with a lovely costume and a parasol of Yoshino lacquer"
Karindō

Katsushika Hokusai 1760–1849, active from 1779

Hokusai began his career as a print designer in 1779 as a pupil of Katsukawa Shunshō, using the name Shunrō; his first calendar pictures were designed under that name in 1789. In 1792 Shunrō retired from commercial print design and was inactive until the spring of 1795, when he contributed an illustration to a poetry anthology. For the following year he designed a number of surimono and privately published album sheets, which he signed Hokusai Sōri and Hyakurin Sōri, names he continued to use on surimono and album sheets until 1798. From 1799 to 1809 the artist designed many surimono in the long and small formats. All of them were signed Hokusai; those additionally signed Gakyōjin were designed between 1801 and 1805; those signed Katsushika Hokusai, from *c.* 1807 to 1810. In 1810 Hokusai adopted the name Taito and during the next decade designed relatively few surimono, most of these in the square format. In 1820 the artist celebrated the completion of his first cycle of sixty years by changing his name to Iitsu, roughly meaning "One Again." He designed a large number of square surimono in 1820 and in the two following years designed his masterpieces in the format, the Shell and Horse sets (see cat. nos 47–49). In 1824, Hokusai designed five square surimono of actors in scenes from kabuki plays performed at the New Year. Thereafter he practically withdrew from the design of privately published prints, although a few square surimono appeared in the early 1830s, including a view of Mt Fuji (cat. no. 51) and a picture of a resting fisherman, which may be a self-portrait. The large picture of surveyors that was published in 1848 was also privately commissioned; it was Hokusai's last woodblock print.

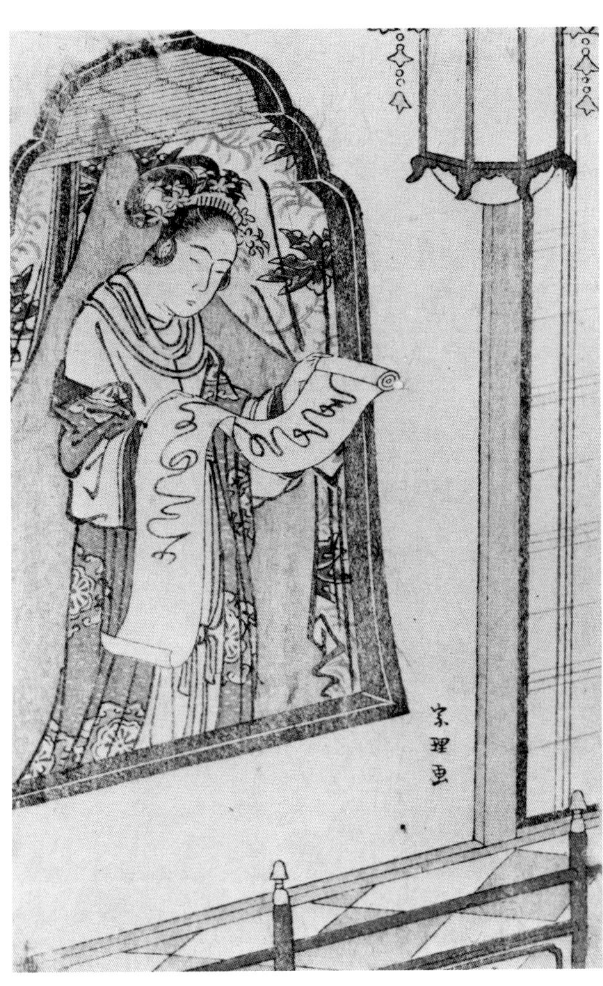

40

Chinese princess standing at a window
1796
13.2 × 8.0 cm
signed Sōri ga; engraved and printed by Toen
Beatty 2201

This is a picture calendar; the numbers for
the long months of 1796 —2, 4, 7, 9, 11 and
12—are written in cursive script on the letter
in the woman's hand. The color and design
are particularly fine for an early calendar
print; but there seems to be no obvious allusion to any particular legend or tale.

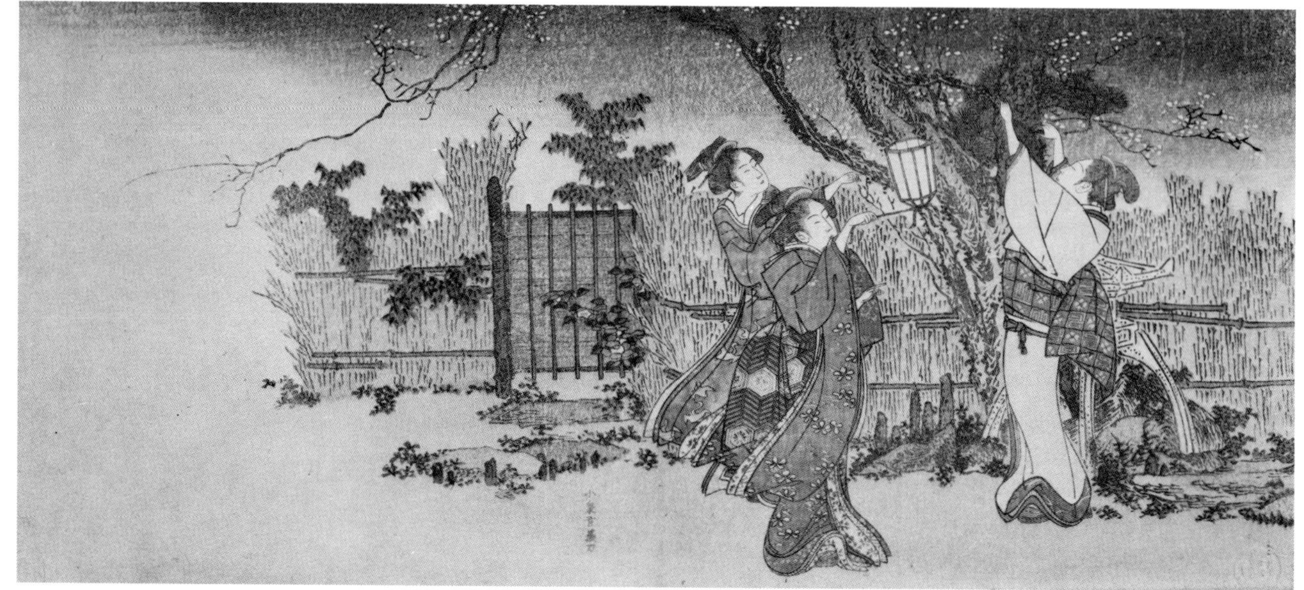

41
Three women beside a plum tree
c. 1796
19.1 × 36.2 cm
unsigned; engraved by Koizumi Ariyoshi tō
Beatty 813b

In 1792, Hokusai stopped designing commercial woodblock prints and disappeared from public view. In 1796 he reappeared with a different name, Sōri, as a designer of privately commissioned surimono and illustrations for albums of kyōka verse. This picture of a woman breaking a flowering branch from a plum tree has a vertical centerfold and came from one of these albums. Although it is unsigned, the drawing of the figures and the painterly textures of the tree, the stones, the fence and the vegetation are all characteristic of Hokusai's work around 1796. The characters printed in red at the center left of the print are the name of the engraver. A similar picture by Hokusai of three women by a well, signed Kanchi Sōri and sealed Hyakurin, is illustrated in *Hokusai et son temps*, M. and J. Guillaud, ed., fig. 6.

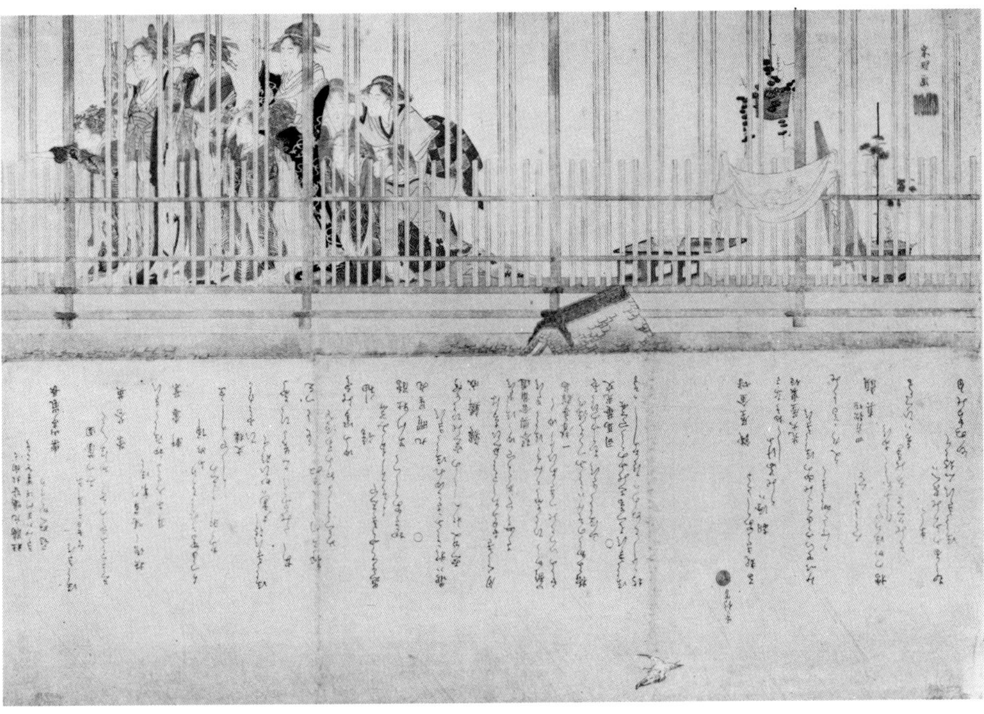

42

Hokusai and Kyōden
Courtesans and attendants watching a cuckoo
late 1790s
39.6 × 55.9 cm
signed Sōri ga, Kyōden Sha
seal undeciphered
Beatty 2236

Hitomoto, Hitotsue and Tagasode, three high-ranking courtesans of the Daimonjiya, a brothel in the Yoshiwara, stand beside the protective wooden latticework on the second story of their establishment and look out at a cuckoo which flies past them. The women are accompanied by four teenaged *shinzō*, who were their understudies, and two child companions, called *kamuro*. The cuckoo was not drawn by Hokusai, but by the well-known popular writer Santō Kyōden, who began his career as a woodblock-print designer in the 1780s under the name Kitao Masanobu. The print was originally issued folded in six parts with only the right third of the picture showing. When this flap was opened, the cuckoo appeared outside the window close to the courtesans in the left third of the picture. The picture is illustrated unfolded here, so the cuckoo appears upside down at the bottom of the sheet. There is a poignant contrast between the bird in free flight and the women behind the latticework, which seems like the bars of a cage.

The poems all speak of autumn. As three of them are by the courtesans whose portraits appear in the print, the picture may have been commissioned by the owner of the Daimonjiya or a patron of the establishment to commemorate the autumn gathering when the poems were composed. The poems are prefaced with a quotation from a Chinese poem: "A cuckoo cries and all face north." Hokusai seems to have understood the phrase to mean that everyone turned to face the direction of the bird, but a quotation in Morohashi seems to imply that the cuckoos themselves always faced north when they sang or cried. An impression of the upper half of the print was reproduced in the Vignier and Inada catalogue (vol. 5, no. 147, pl. XLVIII), but no other complete impression with Kyōden's cuckoo and the text is presently known. Kyōden collaborated with Hokusai in some poetry anthologies and on at least one other long surimono during the late 1790s: a picture of women gathering young herbs and peasant women with bundles of twigs (*Ukiyoe taikei*, vol. 8, pl. 119).

The poets include Rakuzantei Ranchō, Sakae Hanahide, Noki Umeba, Bunrō Hitomoto, Mototsue, Tagasode, Kuyō Hoshimaru, Suzuki Urokonari, Kinkōsha Kadomichi, Isseitei Muradori, Shibaan Kōkō, Zeniya Kinrachi, Saki no Ōya Urazumi and Yomo Utagaki Magao.

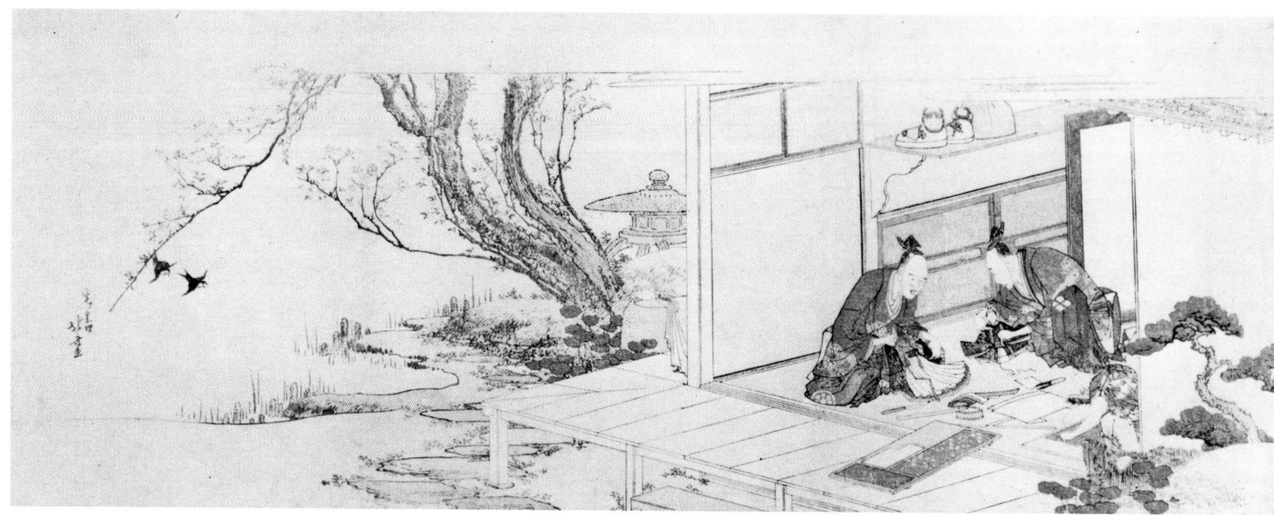

43

Doll makers
1799 or 1800
21.4 × 54.5 cm
signed Saki no Sōri Hokusai ga
Beatty 2239

The workmen in ceremonial dress are assembling a pair of dolls; knives, scissors and other equipment lie beside them on the floor. The young apprentice at the right is backing sheets of thin cloth with paper to make them easier to cut, form and sew. After backing them, he mounts them to dry on a wooden board. The Doll Festival was held on the third day of the third month, when the cherry trees are in blossom; Hokusai's print was probably published to announce an event scheduled in that season. As in many of Hokusai's early suri-mono, there is a fine balance between the scene of human activity and the tranquil land-scape: the printing and the unfaded colors of this impression are particularly beautiful. The two vertical creases show where the picture was originally folded. No other impressions of the print are known.

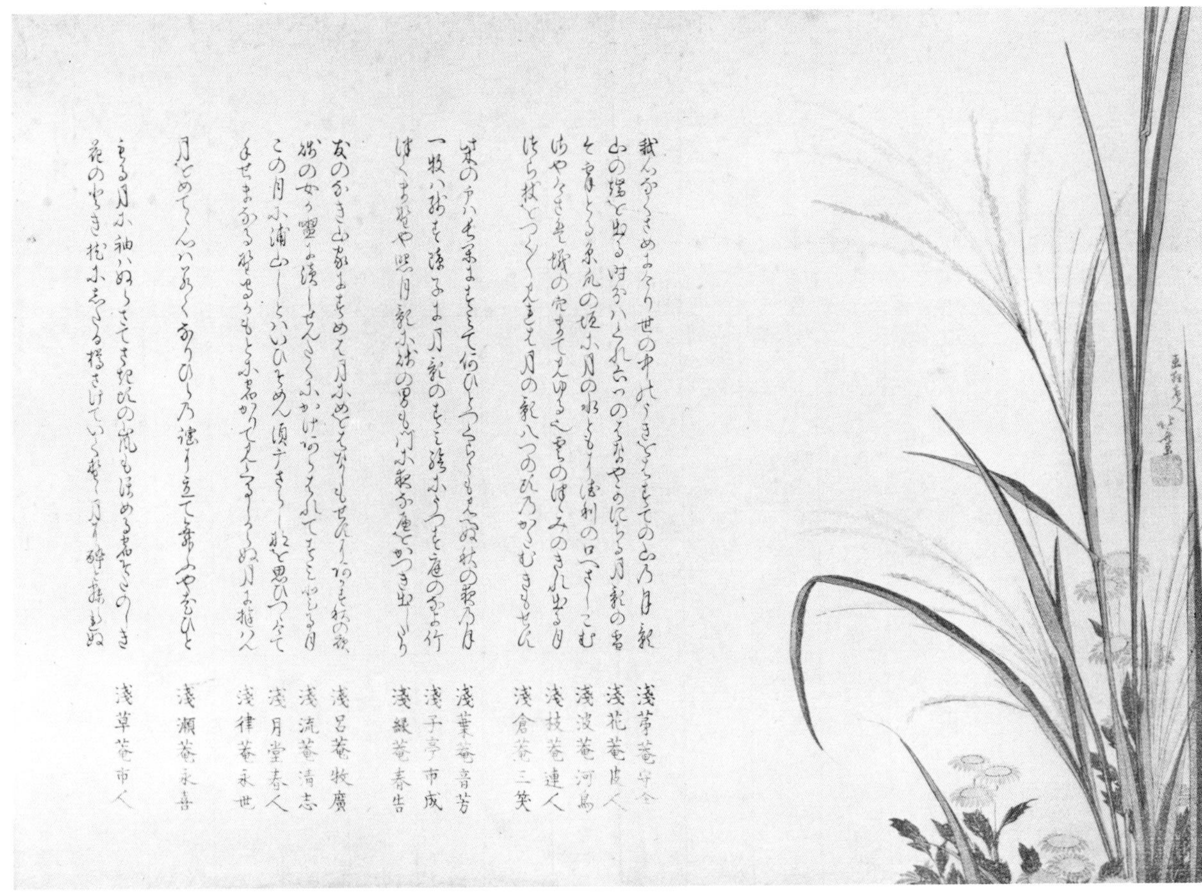

44

Asters and pampas grass
c. 1805
41.2 × 55.7 cm
signed Gakyōrōjin Hokusai ga
seal undeciphered
Beatty 987

The light of the moon is the subject of the
verses, and the flowers and grasses are printed
in pale colors as though seen by moonlight.
There is no prefatory note on the picture, but
the subject of all the poems is the moon so
they were probably composed during a moon-
viewing gathering in the autumn of the year.
Hokusai used the secondary name *gakyōrōjin*,
"old man with a passion for painting," on
several surimono designed in the middle of
the 1800s. The poets are all members of the
Asakusa Group, led by Sensōan Ichindo.
They include: Sembōan Shusha, Senkaan
Kawando, Sembaan Kawadori, Sengian
Tsurendo, Sensōan Sanshō, Sen'yōan
Otoyoshi, Senshitei Ichinari, Senrokuan
Harutsuge, Senroan Makihiro, Senryūan
Kiyoshi, Sengetsudō Harundo, Senritsuan
Nagayo, Sensean Nagaki, Sensōan Ichindo.

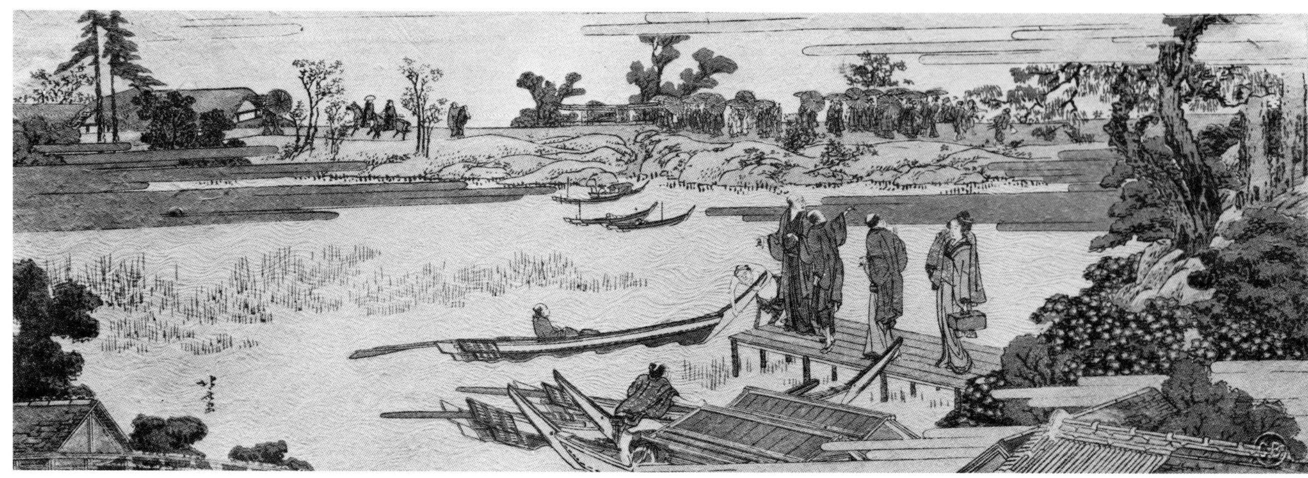

45
View of the Mimeguri Embankment
c. 1805
19.1 × 51.9 cm
signed Hokusai ga
Beatty 988

A group of men are standing on a pier on the
west bank of the Sumida River before em-
barking in rowboats, called *chokibune* or "boar
tusks" because of their shape. Across the
river, women are walking towards Mimeguri
Shrine, whose archway is visible above the
embankment. They carry umbrellas, perhaps
to honor the poet Kikaku, who ended drought
in 1693 by composing a poem for rain at
Mimeguri. The trees and the azaleas blossoming on Matsuchi Hill to the right also indicate
that Hokusai's print accompanied an announcement of some summer event. The design on the parcel on board the boat in the
center foreground may be the emblem of the
person or group that commissioned the picture. The arch of Imado Bridge appears in the
left corner of the print; the bridge crossed the
San'ya Canal, the route taken by the "boar-
tusk" boats to the licensed quarters of the
Yoshiwara.

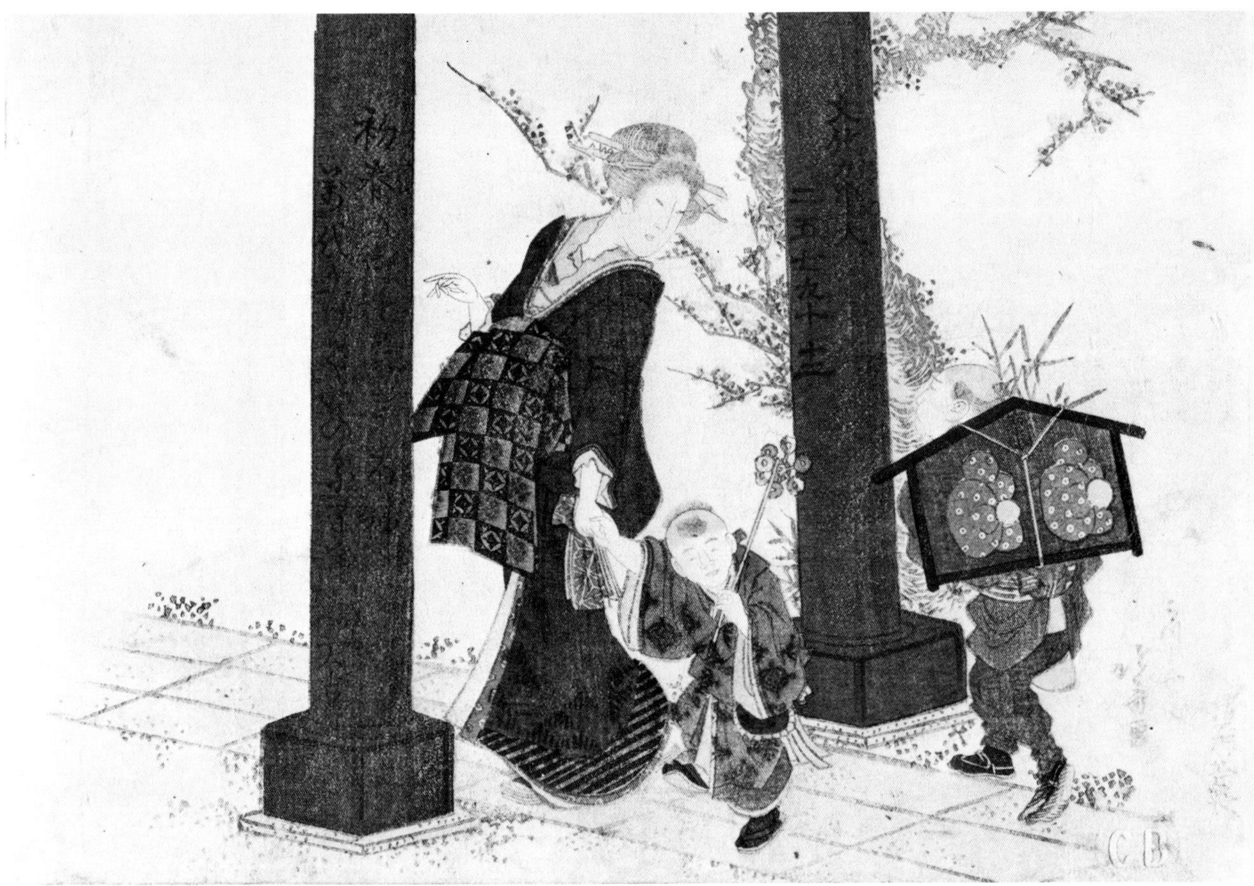

46

Mother and child at the gate of a shrine with
a young servant carrying a votive plaque
1812
13.3 × 18.6 cm
signed Katsushika Hokusai ga; printed by Surikō
Shinachō (?)
Beatty 500

This is a picture calendar; the date Bunka 9
(1812) and the numbers of the long months, 2,
5, 7, 9, 10 and 12 are printed in gold on the
right-hand stone post of the *torii* gateway.
The poem by Daikichi is also printed in gold
on the post on the left; much of it is indistinct. The boy to the right carries a votive
plaque decorated with two *kukurizaru*, cloth
dolls tied and folded into the shape of monkeys. This was included in the picture because 1812 was a Monkey Year. The colors in
this print are particularly delicate and beautiful. Although signed Hokusai, the picture
may have been designed by Hishikawa Sōri.

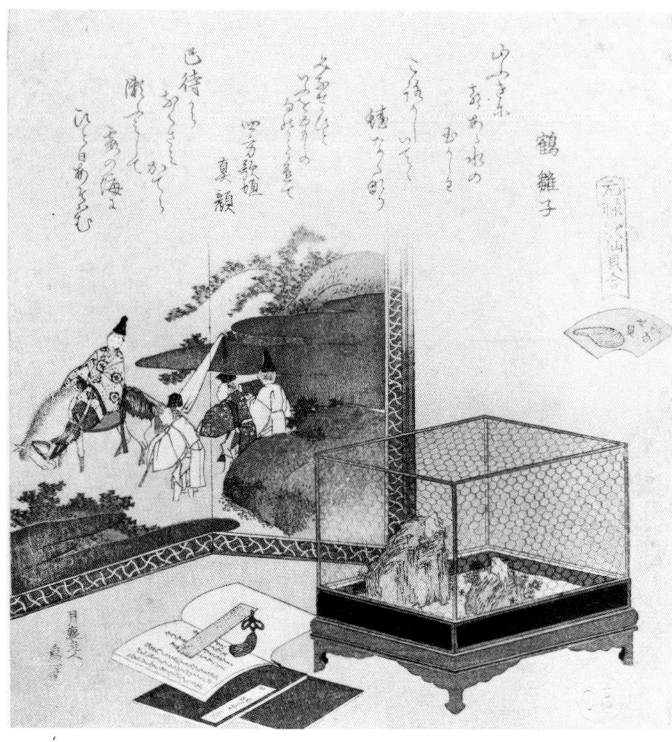

47

Minasegai, "The Dry-Shallows Shell"
series A Matching Game with the Genroku Poem
Shells
1821
19.9 × 17.9 cm
signed Getchirōjin Iitsu hitsu
Beatty 1420

Three thin books and a cage containing rocks
and two small frogs stand beside a painted
screen. The picture and the poems are based
on several associations with the name of the
shell. *Minase* means "dry shallows" and is illustrated by the dry sand and rocks in the
cage. It is also the name of a river near Kyōto
where, in 1488, the poets Sōgi, Sōchō and
Shōhaku composed a famous collection of one
hundred linked verses called *Minasegawa
sangin*, "Three Poets of the Minase River."
Their gathering is symbolized by the three
books in the picture. The Minase River was
also known as the Ide Tama River and was
famous for its yellow *yamabuki* flowers. The
poet Fujiwara no Shunzei (1114–1204) visited
the river on one of his journeys and composed
a celebrated verse about viewing the *yamabuki*
flowers as his horse stopped to drink in the
stream; this is the subject of the painting on
the screen in Hokusai's design. There is a
traditional association between frogs and
yamabuki in Japanese art and poetry; the artist

and poet may also have recalled that the Minase Shrine, beside the river, is dedicated to
the Emperor Gotoba (1183–98). Gotoba was
especially sensitive to sounds and once or-
dered the frogs in a pond at Amamura belong-
ing to his host, Shikekurō Chōja, to stop
croaking.

Magao's poem is an acrostic; that is to say,
each line of his verse begins with a syllable in
the name of the shell, *minase*. It begins with
the phrase *mimachi*, "waiting for the snake."
This was a practice among worshippers in the
Goddess Benten; they gathered at certain
shrines early on the day of the shrine's festival
(a Snake Day) and waited for the Hour of the
Snake (9:00–11:00 a.m.) when the goddess's
image would be displayed. For further information on this and other prints from the series, see Forrer and Keyes.

*Yamabuki ni koe aru mizu no tamagashiwa
korogashi idete kawazu nakunari*

"There are voices in the *yamabuki* flowers;
boulder in the water tumbles over and frogs
cry out" *Tsuru Hinako*

*Mimachi kara nagusami gatera sebumi shite kasumi
no umi ni hitoni asoban*

"Waiting for the snake: to beguile the time, I
wade through the shallows of the sea of mist
and enjoy the day" *Yomo Utagaki Magao*

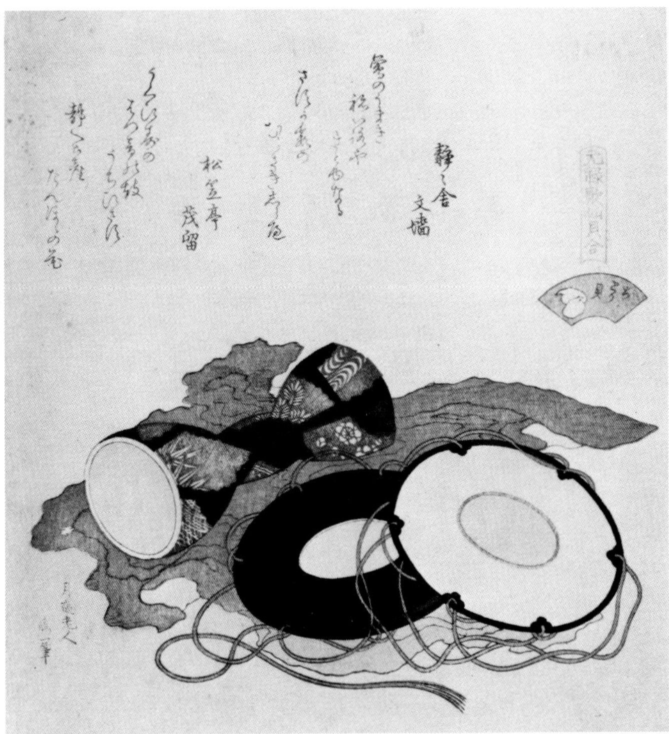

48

The plover shell
series A Matching Game with the Genroku Poem
Shells
1821
20.5 × 18.4 cm
signed Getchirōjin Iitsu hitsu
Beatty 1984

The painted lacquer body of a *tsuzumi*, or
hand drum, lies on a blue silk cloth next to
the two disengaged drum heads with their silk
cords. There is no mention of plovers in the
poems, but there is a mention of "the capital,"
and *uwachidori*, or "upper plover," was an al-
ternative name for *miyakodori*, the "Capital
Bird," a poetic word for the gulls that commonly floated among the waves on the
Sumida River and were celebrated in poetry.
Hokusai has drawn the shells in the cartouche
to look like floating gulls and he has suggested
a pair of gulls floating on blue silk waves with
the drum heads.

In the first poem there is a pun on *saki*,
which by itself means "first" but is also part
of *murasaki*, meaning "purple." *Uchihisasu*, a
poetic epithet for "capital," also contains the
word *uchi*, "to strike," which connects with
"drum"; *hisasu*, in this context, also means "to
make the sun shine." In the second poem, the
word *tampopo* (dandelion) is used to suggest
the sound of the hand drum.

*Uguisu no umaki neiro ya kikoyunaru sasuga
kasumi no murasaki shirabe*

"I hear the fine tone of the warbler; truly the
first song in the purple mist"

Seiseisha Fumigaki

*Uguisu no hatsune no tsuzumi uchihisasu miyako e
miyage tampopo no hana*

"The first song of the warbler that makes the
sun shine is a drum beat: *tampopo*, like dandelions taken as presents to the capital"

Shōryūtei Motome (or Shigeru)

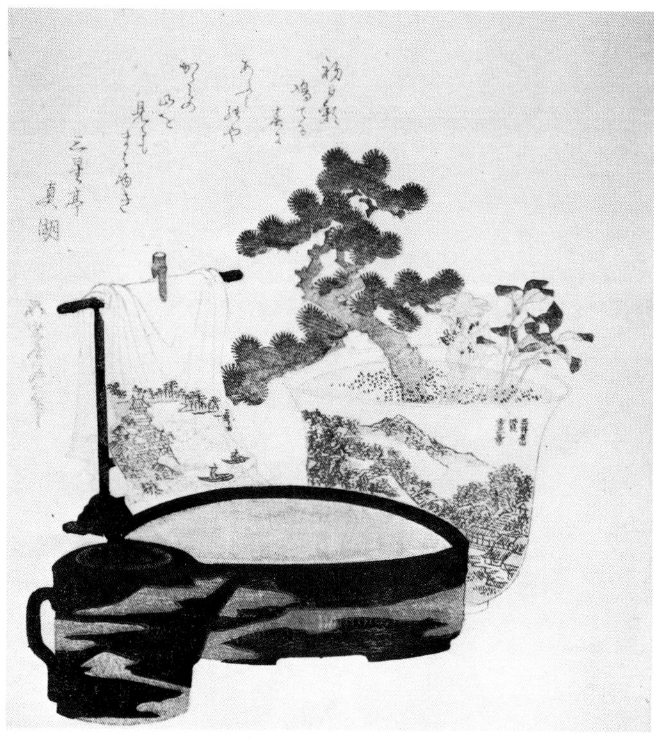

49

Porcelain bowl, towel rack, lacquer pitcher
and basin
series Horses
1822
20.8 × 18.3 cm
signed Fusenkyo Iitsu hitsu
Rose; Beatty 1982

In this quiet still life, Hokusai has combined
the traditional Eight Views of Lake Biwa and,
in the silver surface of water in the basin, a
reference to Mirror Mountain, a low hill near
Lake Biwa that is mentioned in the poem. Mt
Hira, Mii Temple and Ishiyama Temple are
painted on the porcelain planter and are identified in the short inscription at the right. The
floating temple on the side of the pitcher is
the Ukimidō at Katada; the Long Bridge of
Seta stretches across the side of the basin; the
building on the towel is the castle of Awazu.
Karasaki is represented by the miniature pine
tree. Yabase, which is always associated with
"returning sails," is suggested by the two
ships and the towel itself.

Some impressions of the print (Van Rappard-
Boon (1982), pl. 51) have a red gourd-shaped
stamp in the upper-right corner bearing the
series title and the picture title *mayoke*, which
literally means "talisman for driving off evil
spirits." In Hokusai's picture the talisman is the

mirror suggested by the silvery water in the
basin, and also mentioned in the verse.

*Hatsuhikage nioteru haru ni ōmi no ya kagami no
yama o miru mo mabayuki*

"In the first rays of the spring sun on Lake
Biwa, Mirror Mountain also glitters"

Sanseitei Maumi

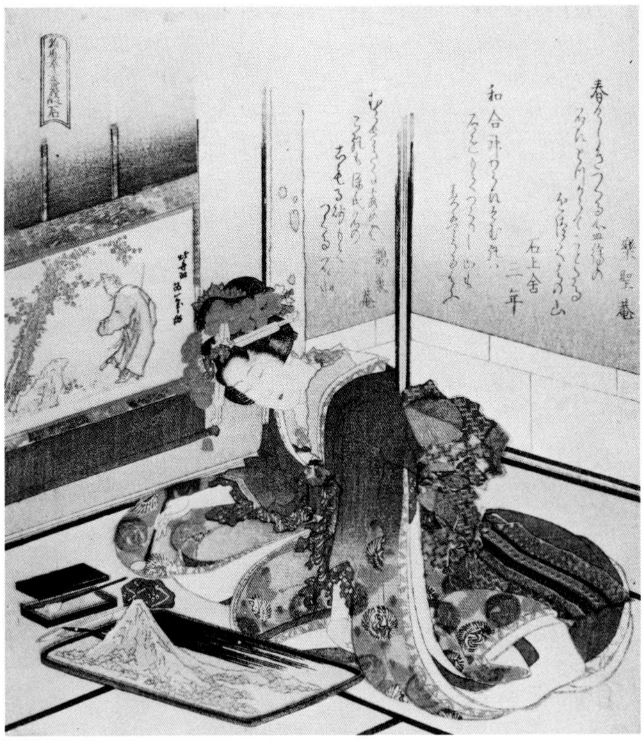

50

Stone

series Three Pictures for a Children's Hand Game
1823
21.5 × 18.3 cm
signed Hokusai aratame Iitsu hitsu (with *kakihan?*)
Beatty 1985

The young woman is painting the flat surface of a tray landscape, made with a mountain-shaped stone. A painting hangs in the alcove beside her. The subject of the painting is Huang Chuping, a Taoist adept who began life as a goatherd. At the age of fifteen, he found a cave and spent the next forty years there in meditation. When he emerged, he found that his goats had turned into blocks of white stone, but when he touched them with his staff they revived. This is another example of "Stone," the subject of the print, but also indicates that the print was published in the spring of 1823, a Goat Year.

Ken was a hand game played by children and adults, with many variations. The particular game that Hokusai chose to illustrate in this set is known in the West as "Stone, Paper and Scissors." The Stone subject was copied twice in the late nineteenth century; this is the only genuine impression presently known. Hokusai's design for Paper is a still life with red lacquer boxes of writing paper decorated with flying cranes; the third design, for Scis-sors, is a still life with a wooden chopstick container and a set of lacquer bowls.

The first poem mentions Mt Tsukuba near Edo, which had two peaks called Male and Female. The last poem contains a pun on Murasaki, which means "purple" but is also the name of the author of the *Tale of Genji*. There is another pun on Ishiyama, the temple near Lake Biwa where Murasaki wrote her novel. Ishiyama literally means "Stone Mountain."

Harugeshiki tsukuru bon-e no ishi hitotsu karade kototaru otsukuba no yama

"No need to borrow a single stone from the tray with the spring landscape: the Male peak of Mt Tsukuba is complete"   *Rakuseian*

Wagōjin waraisomureba ishi o mote tsukurishi yama mo haru wa uruou

"When the God of marriage smiles for the first time, the Spring and even the mountains made of stone soften"   *Sekijōsha Mitose*

Murasaki ni kasumeba kore mo genjina no komoru suna mote tsukuru ishiyama

"When the mist is purple, I make a Stone Mountain with the famous sand mentioned in the *Tale of Genji*"   *Shakusōan*

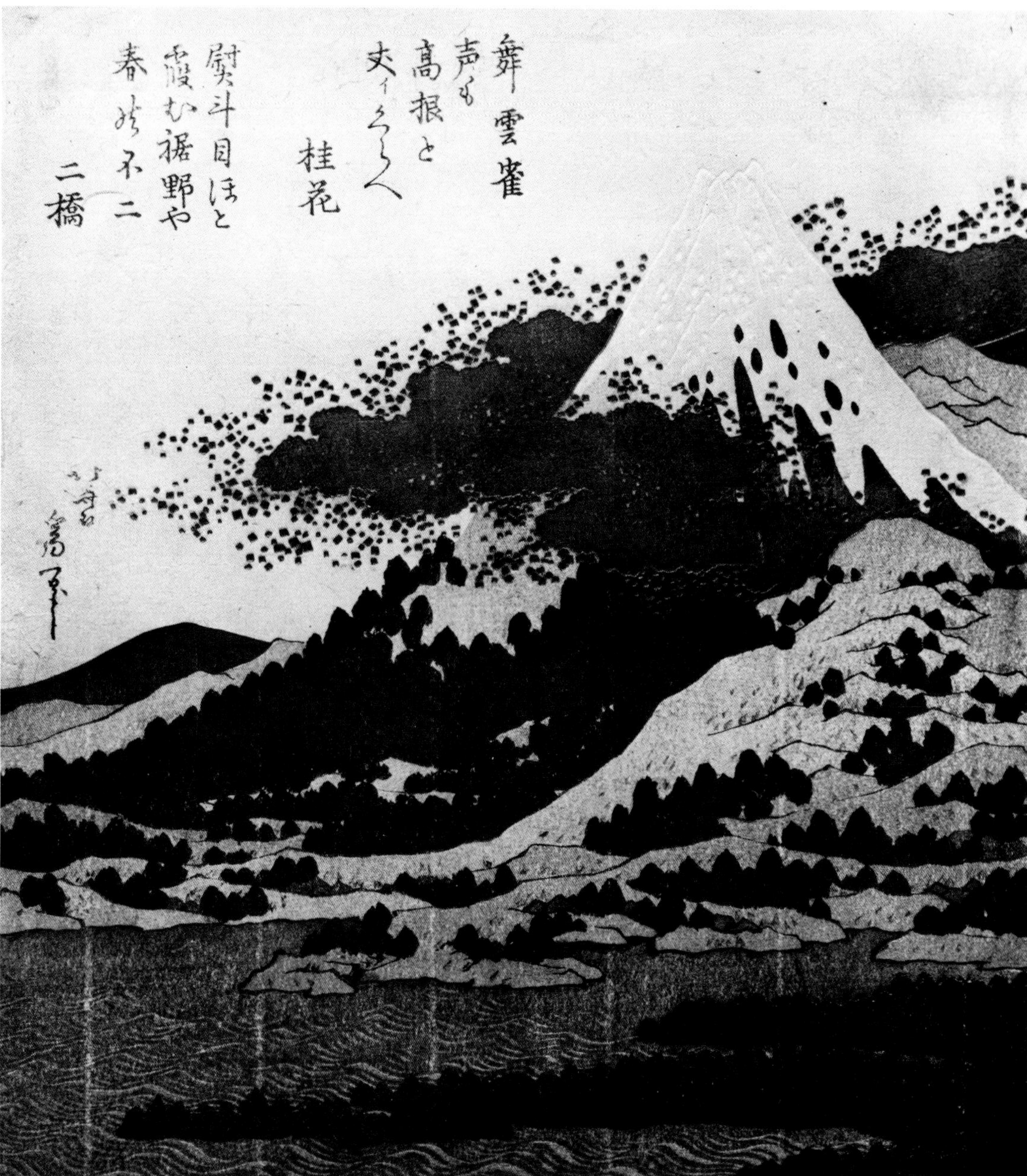

51

Mt Fuji from Lake Ashi in Hakone
c. early or mid 1830s
21.0 × 18.1 cm
signed Hokusai aratame Iitsu hitsu
Duret; Beatty 2027

Hokusai designed very few surimono after 1825. In the early 1830s, after the imported pigment Prussian blue began to be widely used on woodblock prints, he started to produce his series of *Thirty-six Views of Mt Fuji* for a commercial publisher; it was probably around then that he designed this print. Most surimono are inscribed with thirty-one-sylla-ble kyōka verse, but this picture bears two seventeen-syllable haiku. A *noshime* was a formal under-robe with a pattern of stripes around the waist.

Mai hibari koe mo takane to takekurabe

"The dancing skylarks compare the height of their voices to the tall peak"   *Keika*

Noshime hodo kasumu susono ya haru no fuji

"The foothills of Mt Fuji in the Spring are covered with mist like the pattern of a ceremonial gown"   *Nikyō*

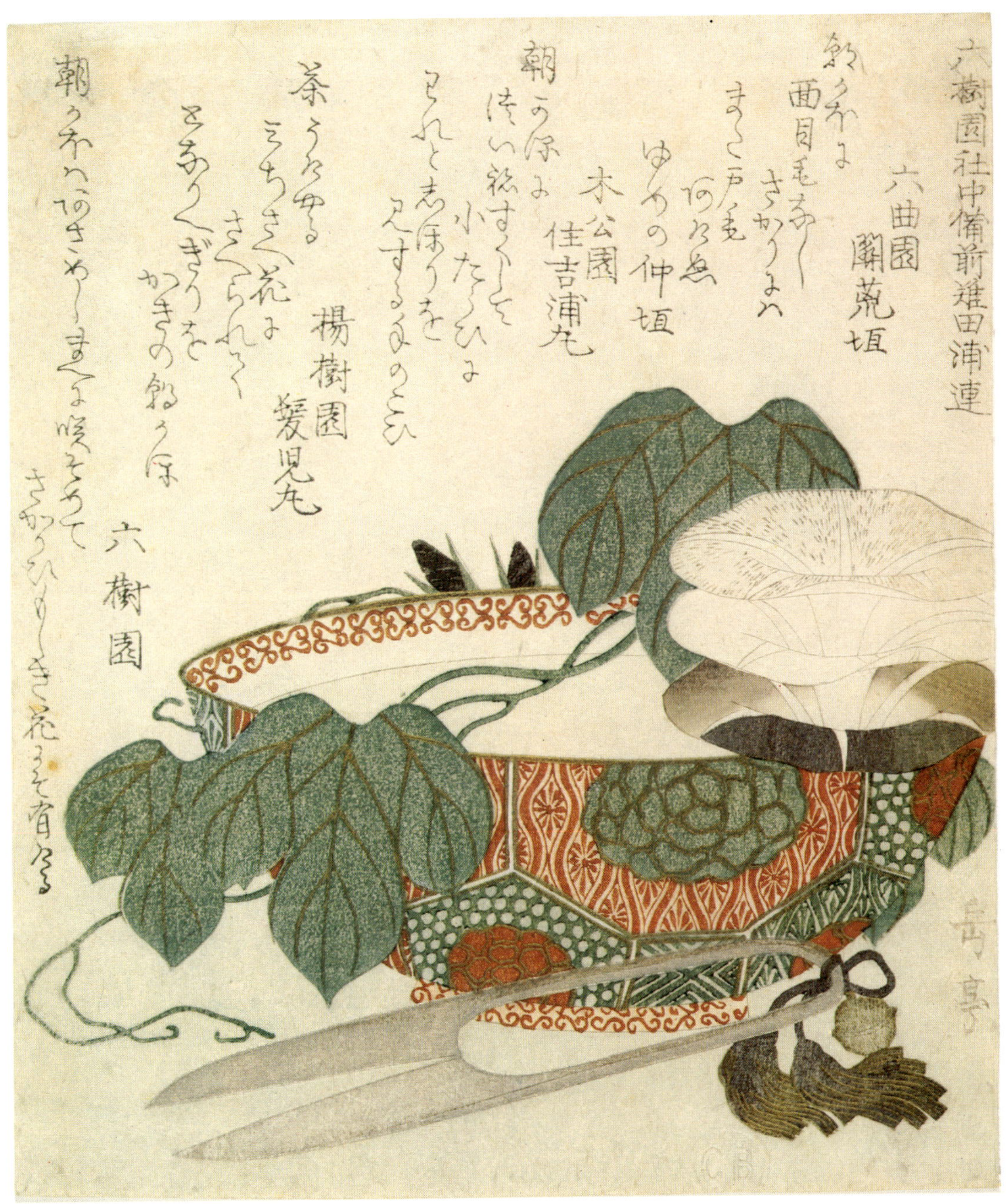

Gakutei, *Morning glories, scissors, and porcelain bowl*, cat. 9

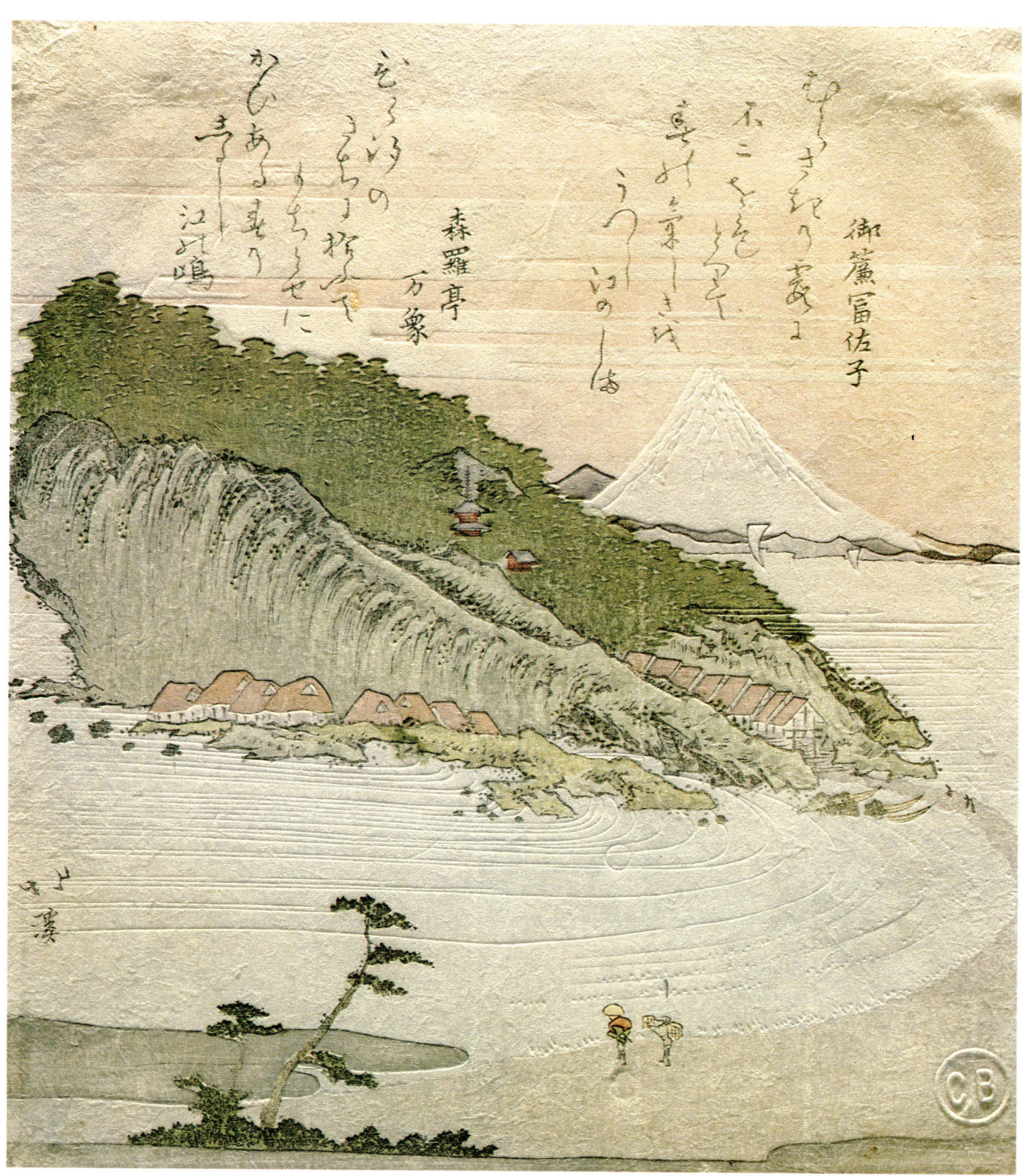

Hokkei, *Mt Fuji and the Island of Enoshima from Shichiri Beach*, cat. 24

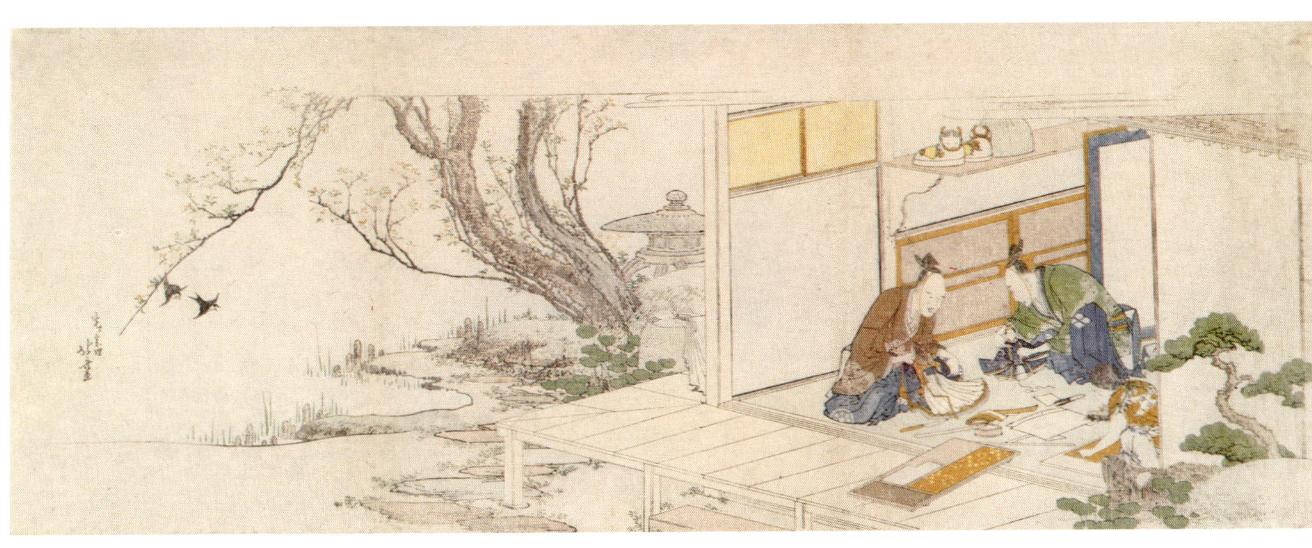

Hokusai, *Doll makers*, cat. 43

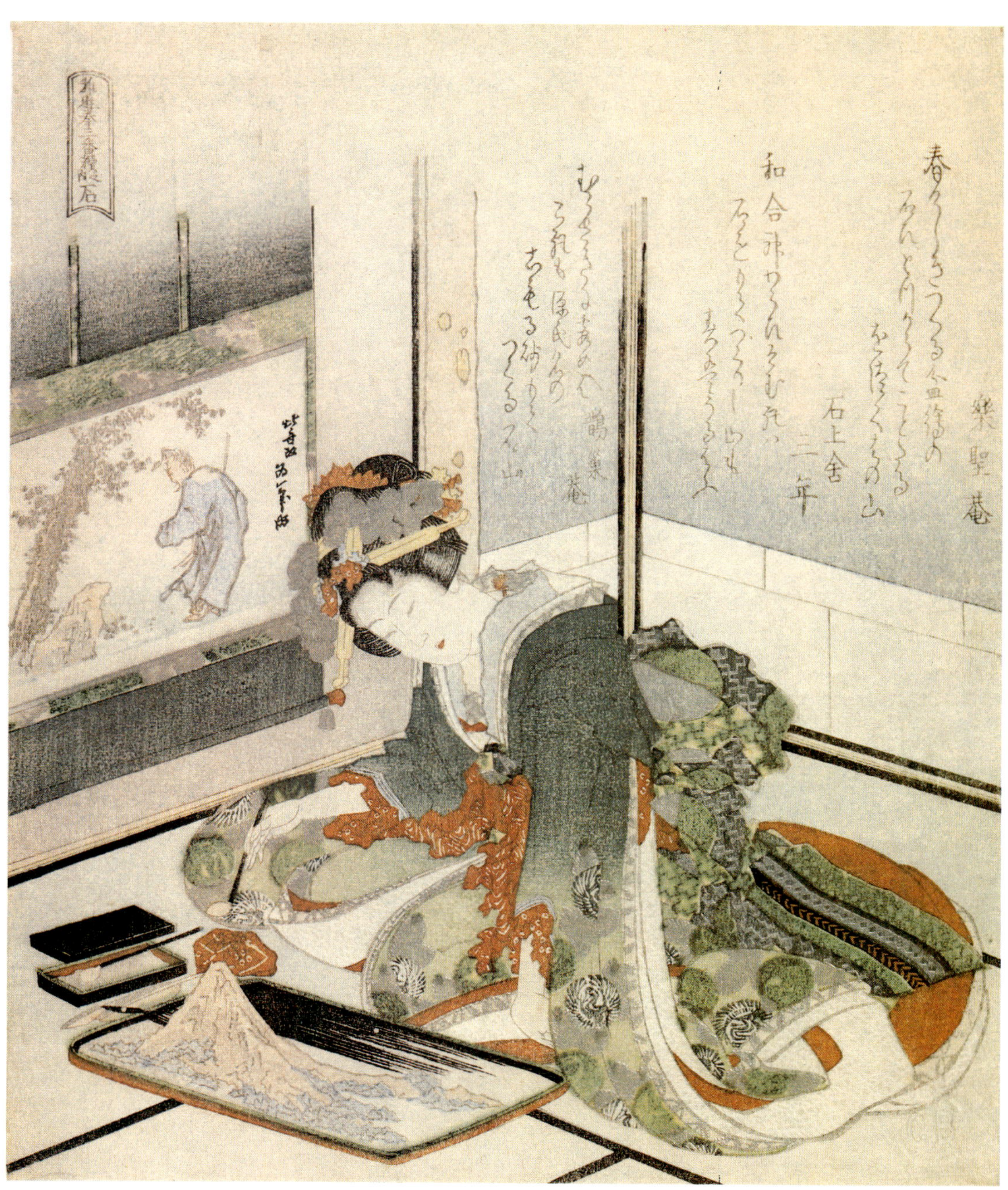

Hokusai, *Stone*, cat. 50

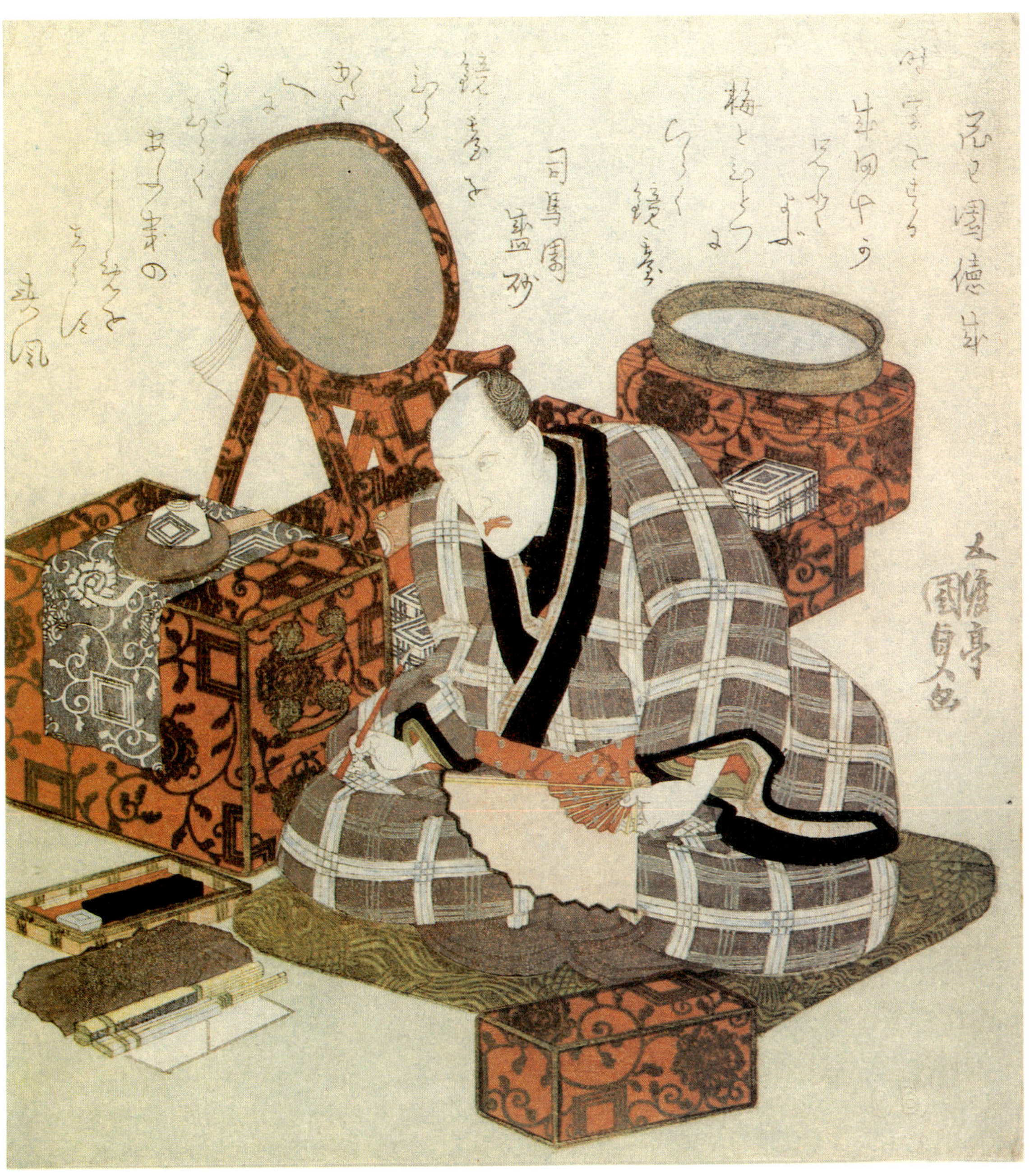

Utagawa Kunisada, *The actor Ichikawa Danjūrō VII preparing to inscribe a fan*, cat. 59

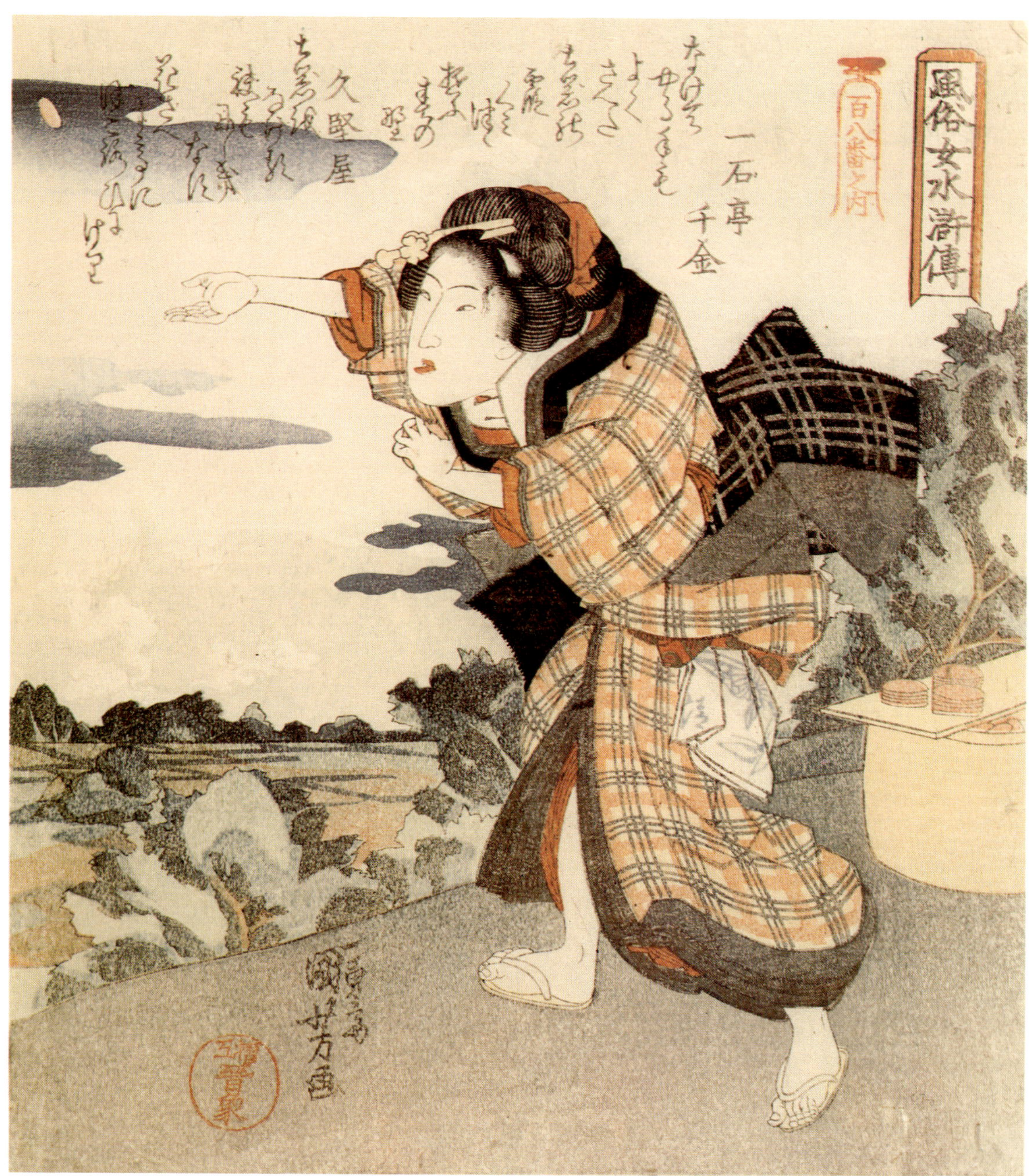

Utagawa Kuniyoshi, *Woman throwing clay dishes from Dōkan Hill*, cat. 60

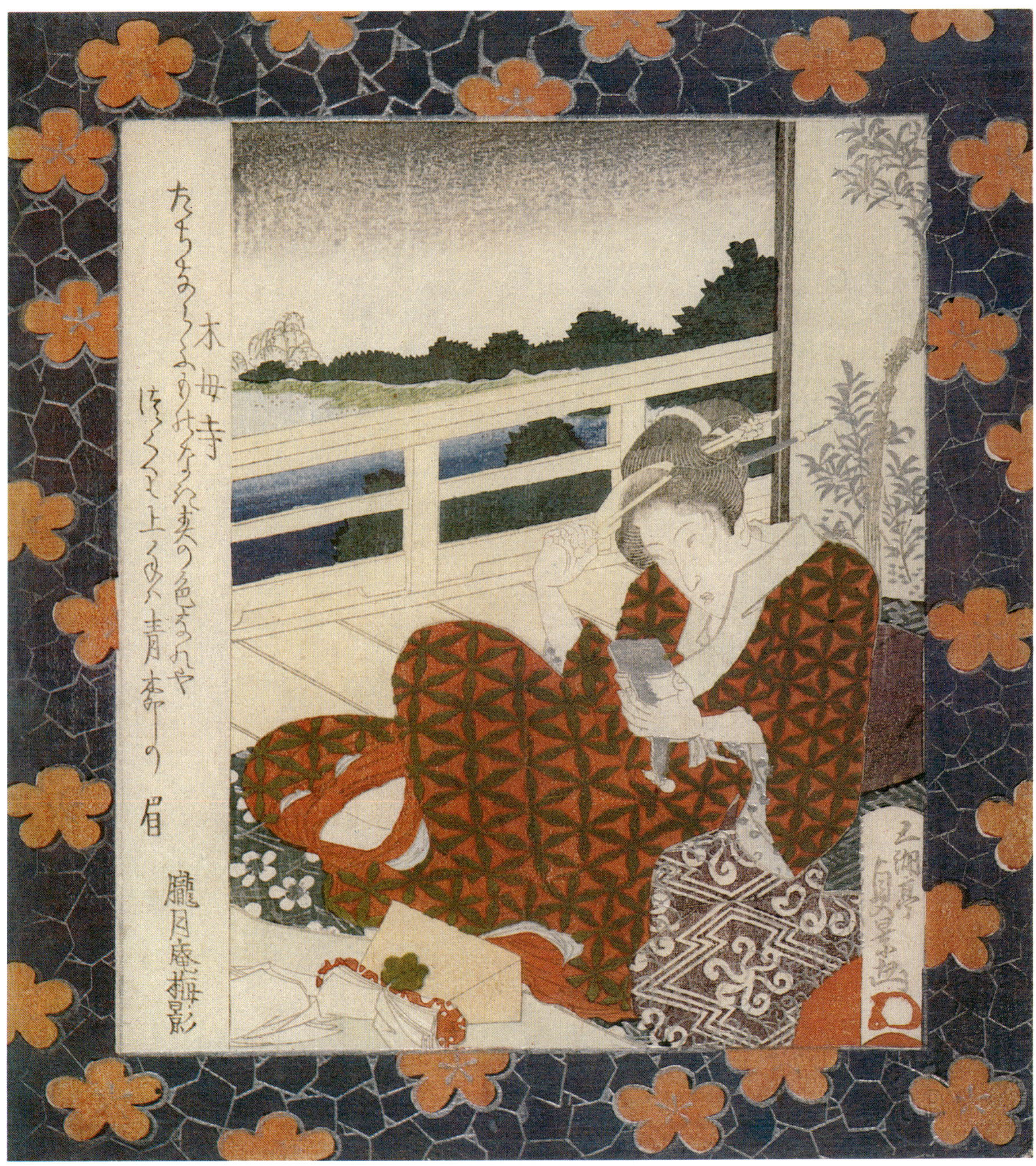

Utagawa Sadakage, *Geisha at a teahouse near Mokubo Temple*, cat. 63

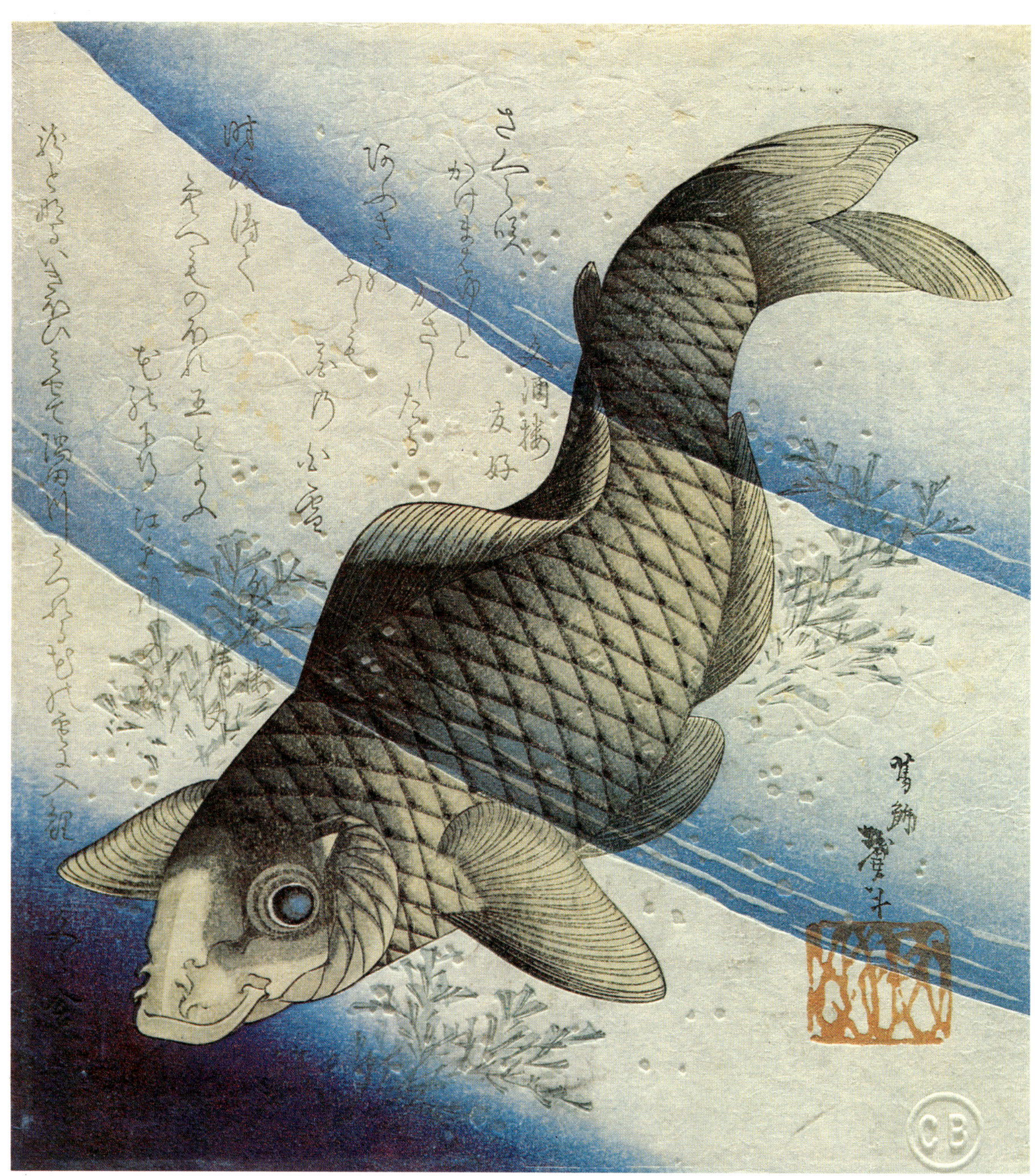

Katsushika Taito II, *Carp swimming among water weeds*, cat. 80

Ōkubo Ikkyū active *c.* 1840s

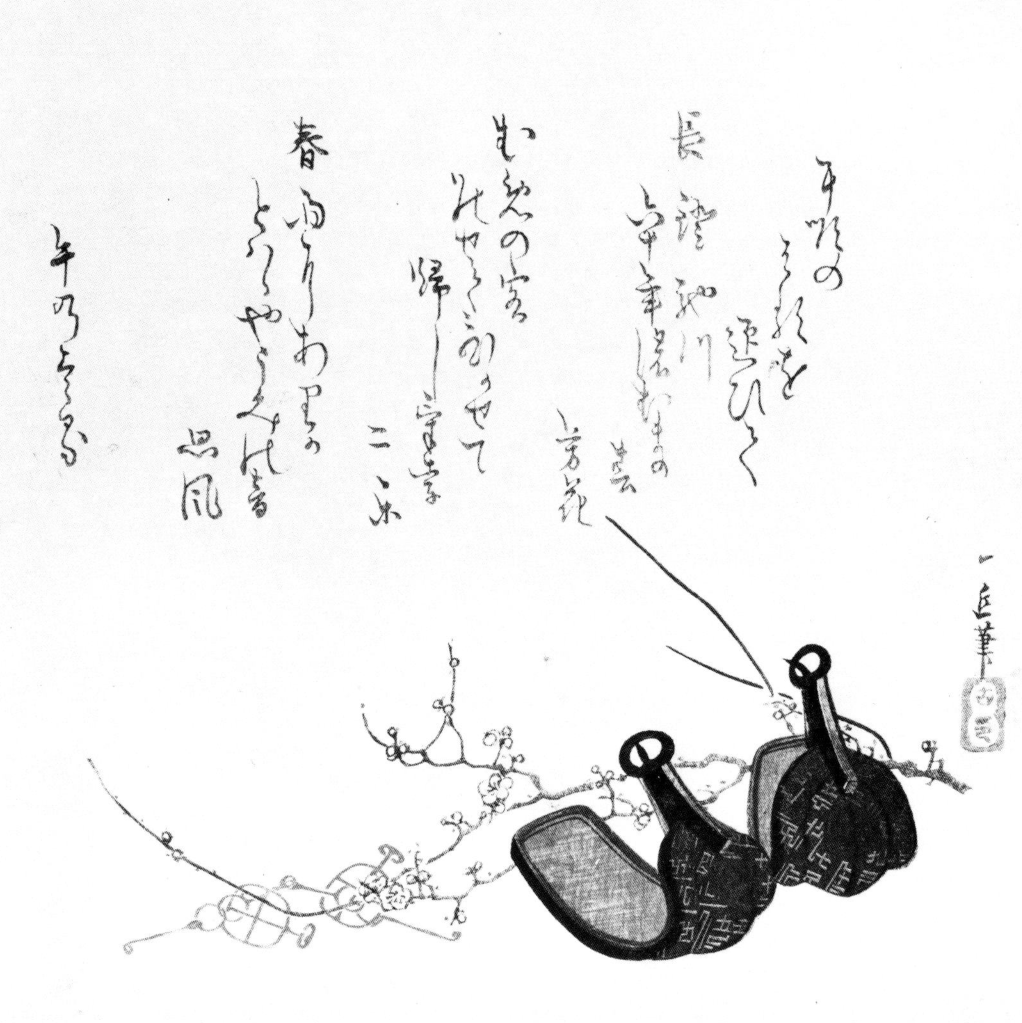

52

Stirrups, bridle bits and plum branch
1846
18.7 × 17.5 cm
signed Ikku hitsu
seal Ko in
Beatty 1017

This is a picture calendar for 1846, a Horse Year; the numerals for the long months 1, 3, 5, 6, 7, 9 and 11 are concealed in the pattern of silver inlay on the outside of the taller stirrup on the right; the numerals for the short months 2, 4, intercalary 5, 8, 10 and 12 are concealed in the pattern on the lower stirrup. Ikkyū (or Ikku) was probably an amateur artist. The print is square in format, but was published a decade after the vogue for suri-mono with thirty-one-syllable kyōka poems had ended. The three verses are seventeen-syllable haiku. The first links "long stirrups" with the spring of the Horse Year.

Nagaabumi hasetsu musoji no uma no haru

"Galloping with long stirrups for the sixtieth Spring, a Horse Year"   *Hōka*

Ume no kyaku nosete hikasete kaeshitari

"The guest at the plum viewing was put on a horse and led back home"   *Niraku*

Harusame ni arika towaru ya umi no oto

"The spring rain asks 'Where do you live?' to the sound of the sea"   *Shifū*

Ishikawa Kazan *active c. 1820s*

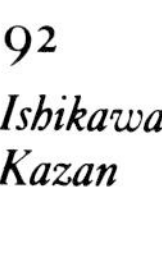

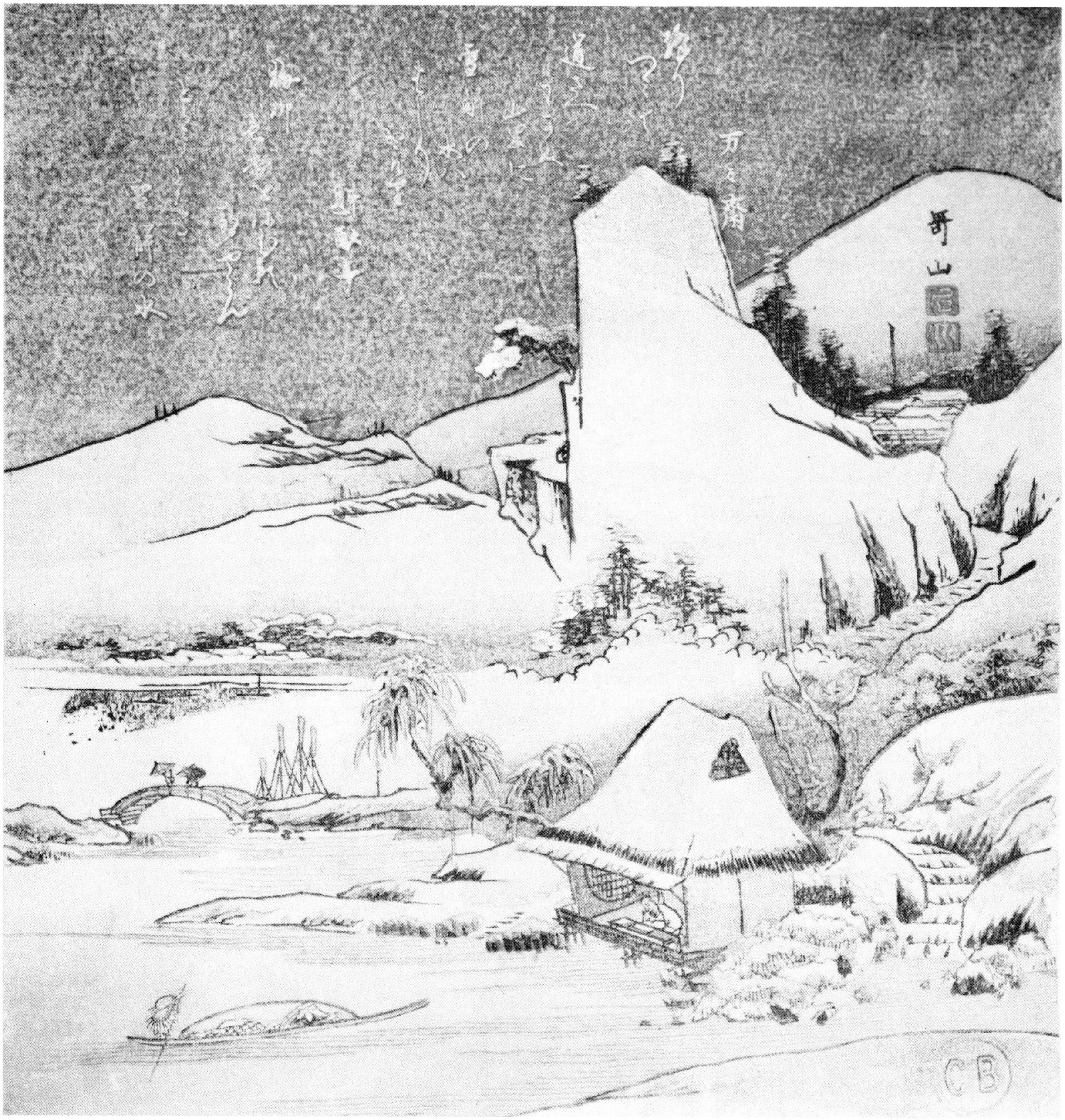

53

Snowy winter landscape
c. 1820s
18.6 × 17.2 cm
signed Kazan
seal Ishikawa
Beatty 1423

A plum tree blossoms by a scholar's hut and a light pink color brings the warmth of early spring to the winter landscape, which is printed in shades of gray and silver. The suri-mono is unusual because it is designed in the style of a Chinese painting, or rather, like a contemporary Japanese painting in the Chinese-inspired Nanga style. The poems are printed in silver and parts of them are indistinct; the first mentions a mountain village, the second mentions plum trees and willows; both speak of the water of melting snow.

Kōri no Michisube active *c.* 1810s

A kyōka poet and amateur designer

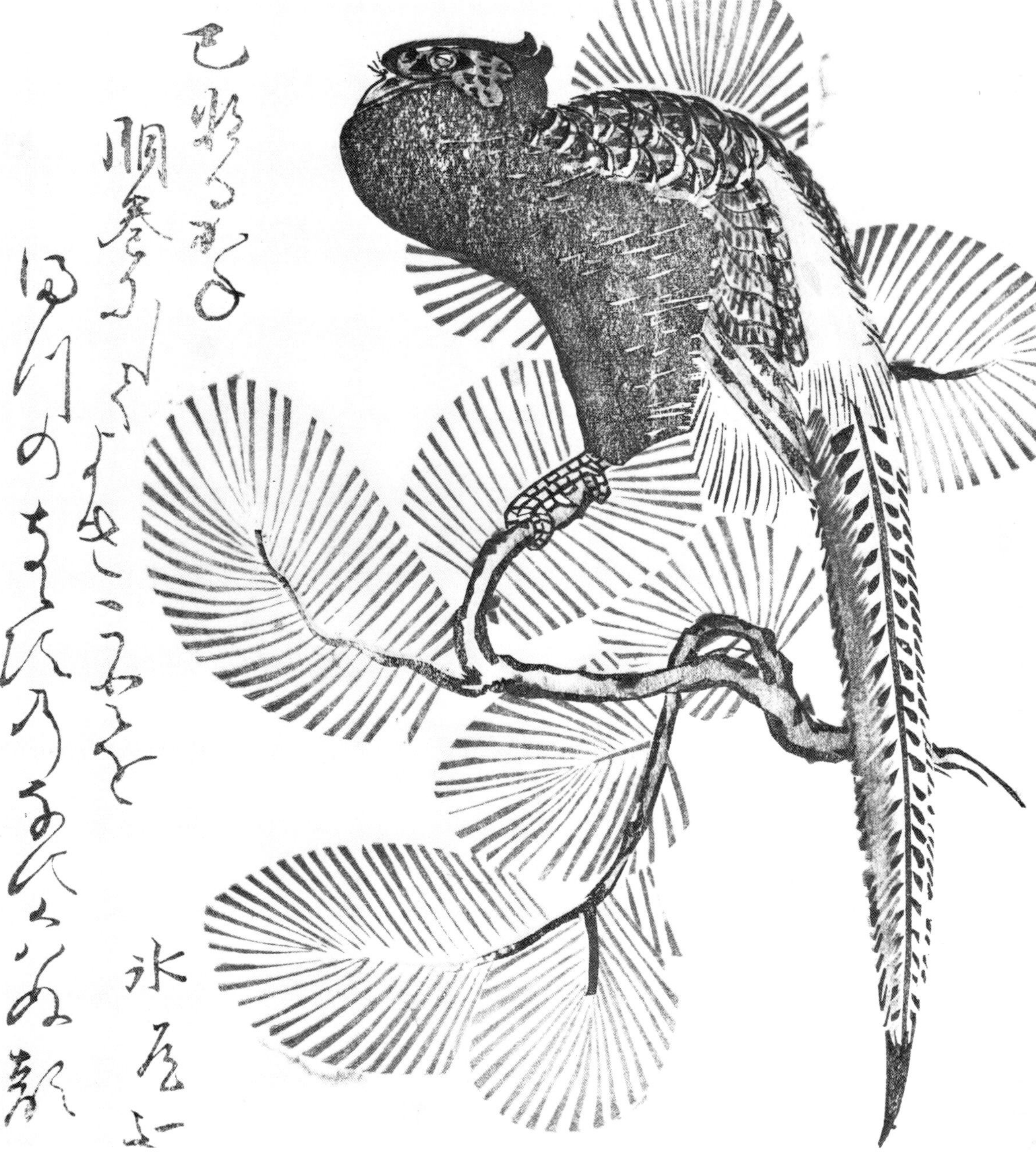

54

Pheasant on a pine branch
c. late 1810s or early 1820s
18.4 × 16.5 cm
signed Kōri no Michisube
Beatty 999

This rough, vigorous picture of a pine branch with golden needles and a pheasant with a golden tail is the work of an amateur artist, no doubt the poet, whose calligraphy is equally brisk and eccentric; his name means "Slip on the Icy Road." The opening phrase *mi naru* is written with characters meaning "become a snake," and the picture may have been pub-lished in 1821, a Snake Year. *Minarukane* are coins wrapped in paper and put away to in-crease one's prosperity on days in the almanac that combine the signs for snake (*mi*), action (*naru*) and the element Metal (*kane*). The cus-tom was based on the punning phrase *mi ni naru kane*, "the money which bears fruit."

Minarukane dōmaki ni shite yokikoto o matsu no kigisu no nani kuwanu kao

"The pheasant tucks its gold in its money belt and waits nonchalantly on the pine branch for something good to turn up" *Kōri no Michisube*

Isoda Koryūsai

Koryūsai began his career as a designer of commercial woodblock prints of women. He may have been a pupil of Suzuki Harunobu, as his earliest prints are similar in style and are signed Haruhiro. In the 1770s he designed a number of prints in the narrow upright *hashira-e*, "pillar-picture," format, as well as many striking pictures of animals, birds and flowers. In 1781 he is said to have been awarded the honorary title *hokkyō*, and around that time he retired largely from print design to devote himself to painting, much of it in the academic Kanō style. He is said to have been a *ronin*, or unemployed samurai, formerly in the service of the Tsuchiya clan whose residence was in the Koishikawa district of Edo. If this is true, he was one of the few professional ukiyo-e artists who came from the ranks of the warrior class.

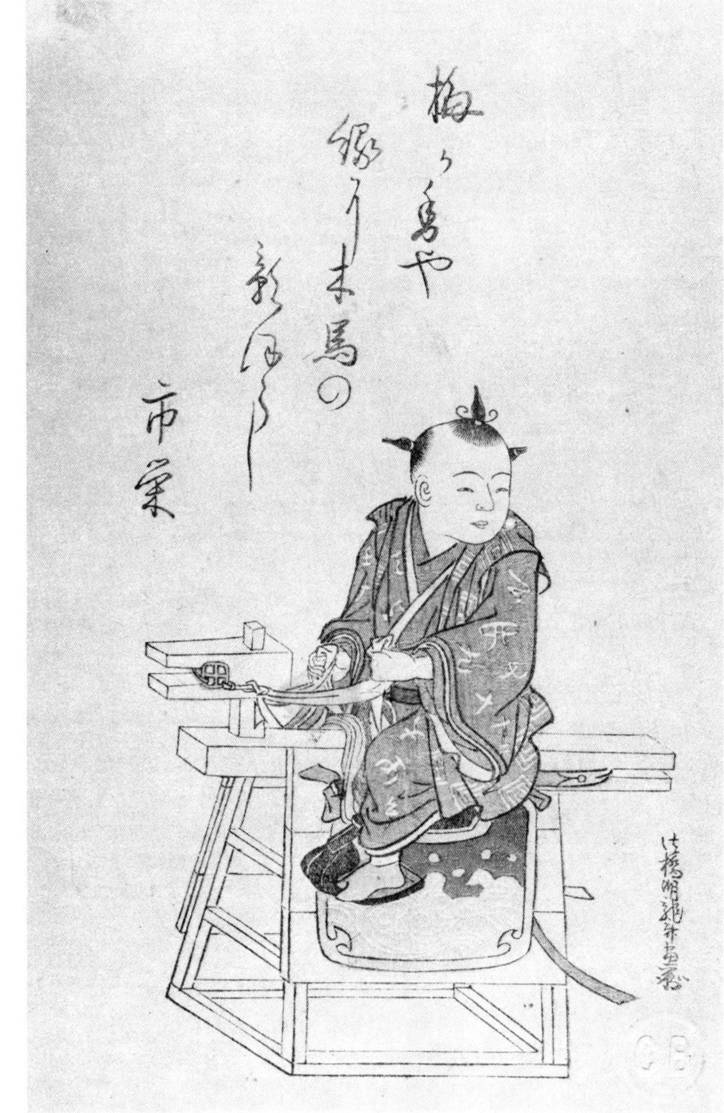

55

Child on the wooden hobby horse
1786
17.5 × 10.7 cm
signed Hokkyo Koryusai ga
seal kakihan
Beatty 2215

This is a picture calendar for 1786, a Horse
Year. The character *dai*, meaning "large" or
"long," the two cyclical signs for the year and
the numbers for the long months 2, 4, 7, 9,
10, intercalary 10 and 12, appear on the boy's
robe. The poem is a seventeen-syllable haiku.

Ume ga ka ya en ni mokuba no kagebōshi

"The fragrance of plum blossom and the
shadow of a wooden horse on the veranda"
Shiei

Utagawa Kuninao 1793–1854

Kuninao was born in Shinano Province. He is said to have studied Chinese painting before he arrived in Edo and studied with Toyokuni. He painted pictures of women in ukiyo-e style, designed a number of woodblock prints, mostly of women, and a few surimono.

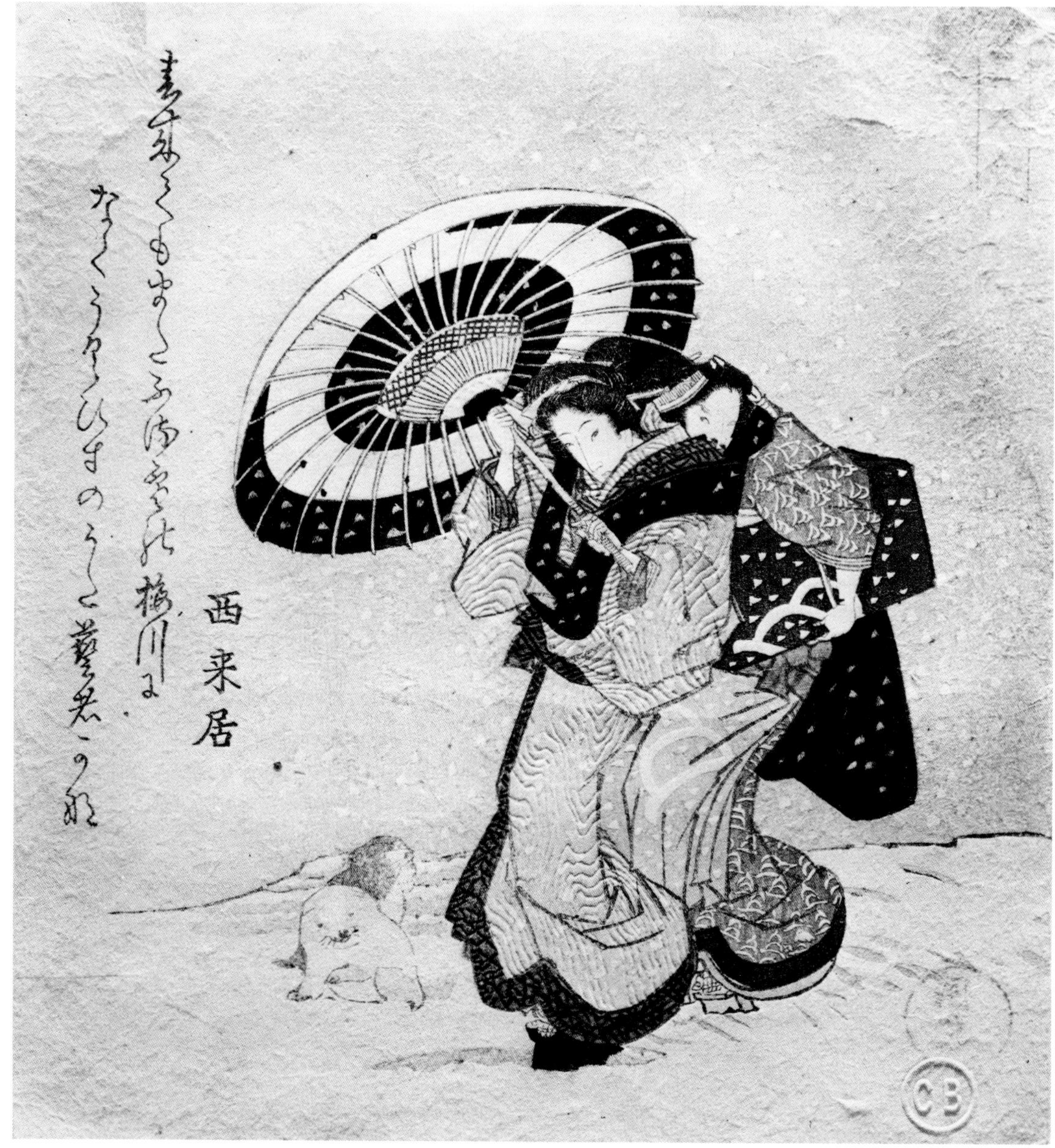

56

Geisha and attendant walking along an embankment in the snow
series Beautiful Women
early or mid 1820s
21.2 × 18.9 cm
seal Kuninao
Gonse; Beatty 1860

A geisha holds an umbrella to protect herself and her attendant from the falling snow; her attendant carries the geisha's samisen. The box's cloth wrapping and the attendant's robe and apron are all decorated with the poet's emblem. The poem mentions Umegawa, "Plum River," the name of a restaurant and teahouse near Yanagi Bridge in Edo; Yanagi ("Willow") Bridge crossed the Kanda River near its intersection with the Sumida River. Geisha were commonly hired to perform in restaurants and the woman in Kuninao's print is either walking to work along the riverbank in the snow storm or returning home. The two puppies on the left are intentionally printed in pale colors to contrast with the bright, clear figures of the women.

Haru kite mo mada furu yuki no umegawa ni naku uguisu no uta geisha kana

"Spring comes, but snow falls still; the warbler singing by the Plum River is a geisha"

Sairaikyo

Kunisada was born in the Honjo district of Edo, where his father, Shōbei, managed the Itsutsume ferry on the Tatekawa River, near the Five Hundred Rakan Temple. He became a pupil of Toyokuni at the age of fifteen in 1801, and began to design book illustrations and single-sheet prints around 1807. His genius was first recognized about 1815, when he designed a group of seven half-length portraits of actors with mica backgrounds; after that he became a celebrity and was on close terms with many of the leading actors, writers and artists of the period. It was probably this personal contact that brought Kunisada so many commissions to design surimono of actors for poets and groups who shared his special interest in the kabuki theater. Many of his surimono were portraits of his friend, the kabuki actor Ichikawa Danjūrō VII (1791–1859). Kunisada also designed many surimono of beautiful women. His surimono were mainly in the square format and range in date from the early 1810s to the mid 1830s, although most of them seem to have appeared in the decade between the late 1810s and the late 1820s. The majority were separate designs, but some were published as sets or extended compositions of two or more panels. Kunisada probably designed between two and three hundred surimono, a large number in itself, but small by comparison with his total output of over ten thousand single-sheet woodblock prints (some writers suggest a figure as high as twenty-five thousand), not to mention the paintings and his numerous book illustrations.

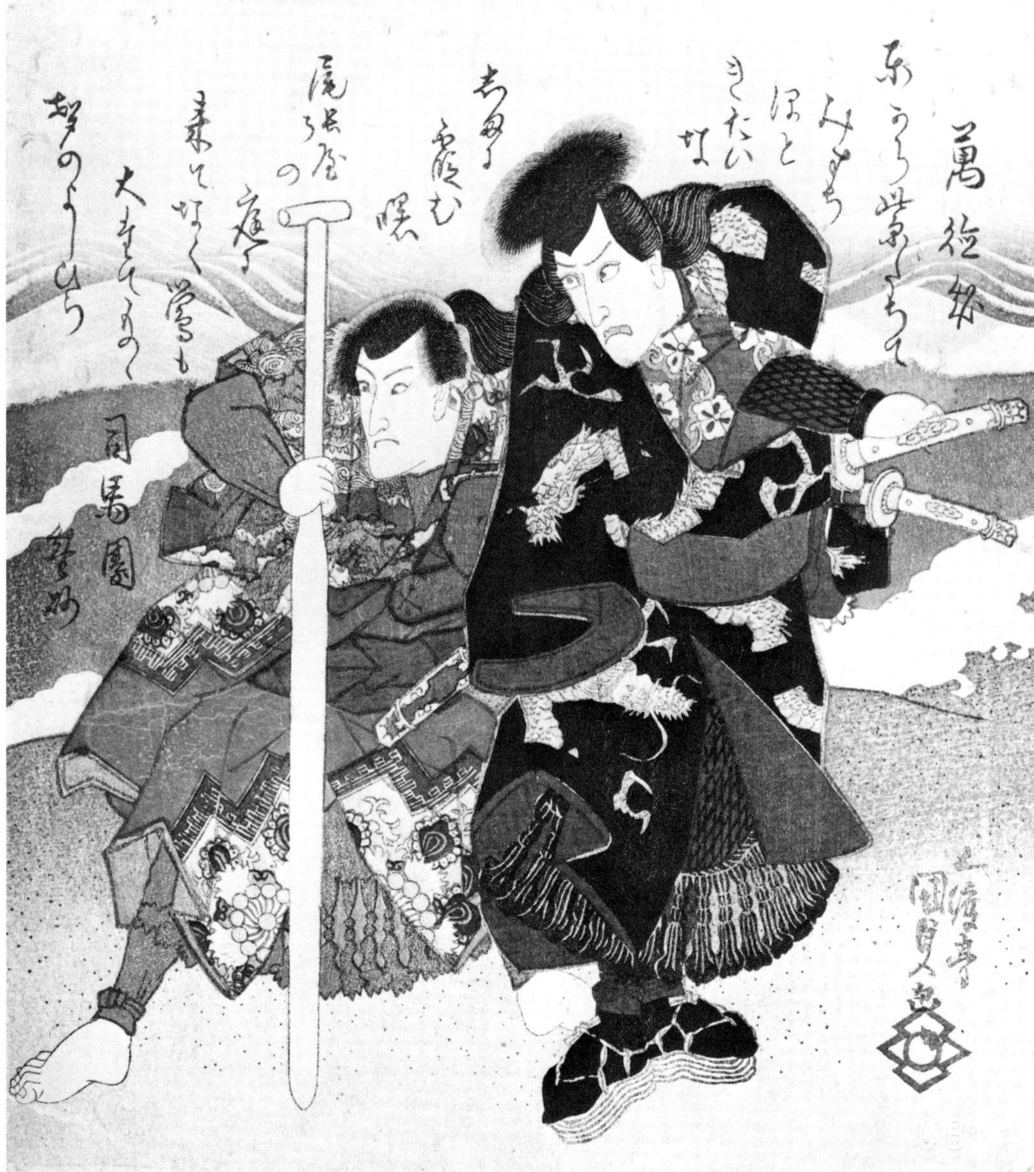

57

Ichikawa Danjūrō VII and Seki Sanjūrō II
probably 1823
21.8 × 19.1 cm
signed Gototei Kunisada ga
seal *toshidama* in angular cartouche
Meade; Beatty 2303

Ichikawa Danjūrō VII is dressed in a black
robe over a coat of mail and wears a bushy
wig; these features identify him as the Taira
warrior Akushichibyōe Kagekiyo. Seki
Sanjūrō II used the *yagō*, or "house name," of
Owariya and his role is identified in the second poem as Akugenta Yoshihira. The two
actors appeared together at the Ichimura
Theater in 1/1823 in the play *Yaegasumi soga no
kumiito*, "The Soga Clan Interwoven like

Bands of Mist," a plausible data for the print,
although the published theatrical records omit
the role of Yoshihira for Sanjūrō.

*Higashi kara murasakidachite misuji hodo kitai na
shima ni kasumu akebono*

"From the east, purple rises in three bands
covering the strange island with mist at dawn"
          Yorozu Tokunari

*Owariya no niwa ni kite naku uguisu mo
ōdatemono no koe no yoshihira*

"The warbler which comes to sing in Owariya's
garden has a fine voice, like a great actor in
the role of Yoshihira"   *Shibaen Morizuna*

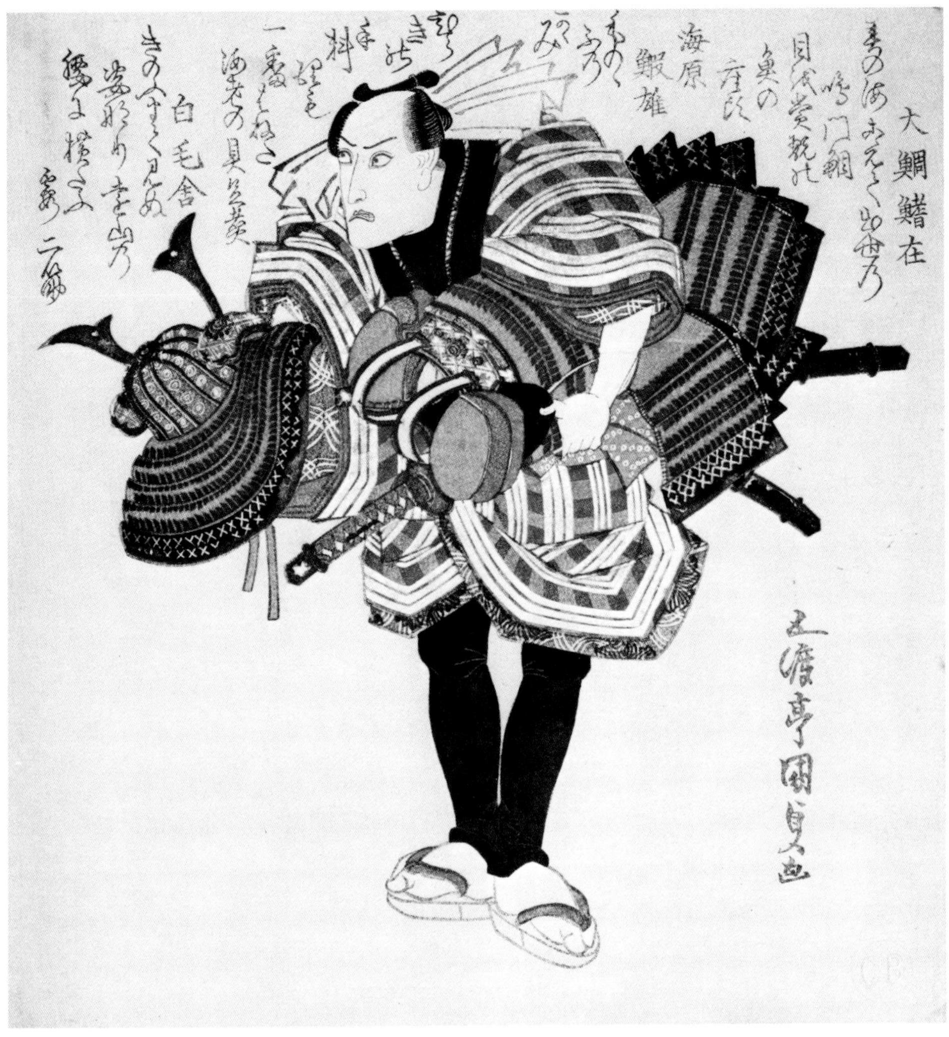

58

The actor Ichikawa Danjūrō VII as a towns-
man, holding a helmet and a suit of armor
mid 1820s
21.5 × 19.3 cm
signed Gototei Kunisada ga
Meade; Beatty 2302

The first poem speaks of a sea bream with
remarkable eyes; Danjūrō had conspicuously
protruding eyes and was the leader of a theatrical troupe. One of his emblems was a
shrimp and the second poem speaks of a
shrimp dish called "armor stew." This connects with the armor in the picture, so the
reference to cooking in the poem may suggest
that Danjūrō is performing the role of a chef.
The meaning of the last verse is somewhat
unclear. It may mean that the picture was
published at the end of 1824 or the beginning
of 1825, soon after Danjūrō returned from a
trip to the mountainous province of Kai. The
names of the first two poets, "Great Bream

with Fins" and "Shrimp of the Sea Plains,"
are based on the actor's eyes and emblem.

*Haru no umi koete shusse no narutodai me o shōgun
no uo no zagashira*

"Crossing the spring sea, the bream from
Naruto with the remarkable eyes has risen in
the world to become the leader of the troupe
of fish"
Ōdai Hireari

*Mononofu no kagamibiraki no teryōri mo ichiban
haneda ebi no gusoku ni*

"When a warrior cuts a mirror cake, the best
dish is shrimp from Haneda in an armor
stew"
Unabara Ebio

*Kinō made minu sugata nari tōyama no koshi ni
yokotau kasumi futasuji*

"Until yesterday I had never seen the flanks
of the distant mountains of Toyama bounded
by two bands of mist"
Hakumōsha

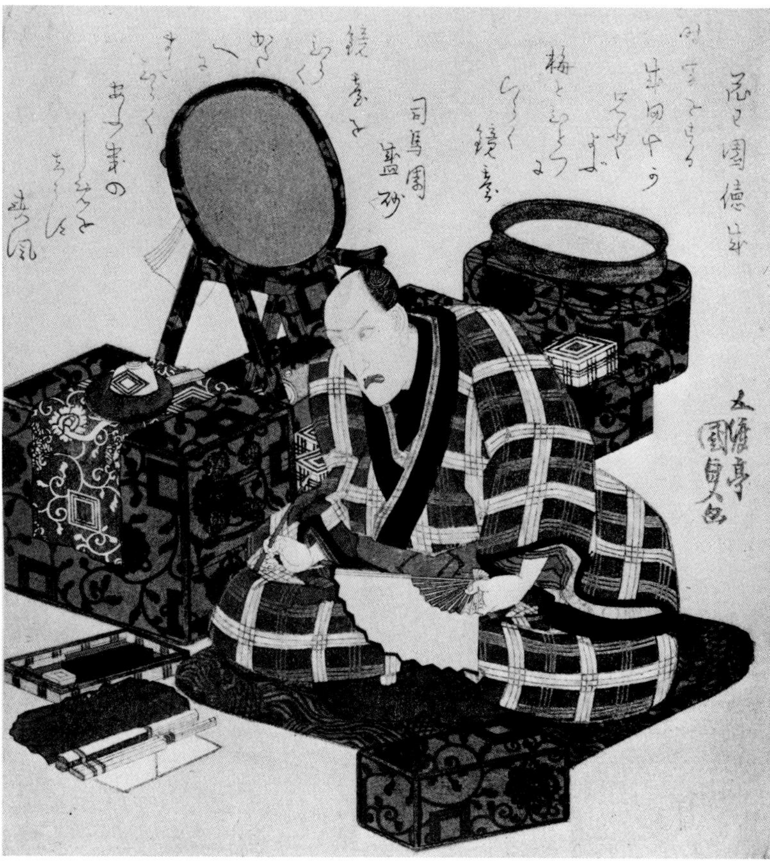

59

The actor Ichikawa Danjūrō VII preparing to
inscribe a fan
mid 1820s
21.2 × 18.7 cm
signed Gototei Kunisada ga
Meade; Beatty 2304

The actor is seated in his dressing room; his
towel and lacquer make-up stand are decorated with the pattern of three concentric
squares, the crest of the Ichikawa clan of actors, and the peony, one of Danjūrō's personal
emblems. His gold cushion is decorated with
swimming carp, another personal emblem.
Danjūrō was the leading male kabuki actor of
the mid-nineteenth century. He was also a
poet and calligrapher and so was often asked
to inscribe fans as mementos for patrons, ad-
mirers and literary friends. The cover of his
writing box rests beside him in the foreground; the base of the box with brushes,
inkstone and water dropper lies to his right.
On the floor in front of him are two more
fans closed with paper bands, a square poem
sheet and a parcel wrapped in purple silk,
which may contain yet further fans. As the
actor has been appearing in the role of Gorō

Tokimune, the younger of the Soga brothers,
both poems contain a pun on *kyōdai*, which
means "brothers" and "mirror stand." Both
poems also speak of "opening," a word linked
with fans and the blossoming of flowers.
Naritaya was the *yagō*, or house name, of
Danjūrō. The print cannot be dated by the
role because Danjūrō acted the role of Gorō
every spring in the 1820s, except 1820, 1824
and 1829; but the reference to the "Elder-
Brother" plum may refer to the reconciliation
between Danjūrō and Onoe Kikugorō in 1822.

*Tokimune o suru naritaya ga ani to yobu ume to
hitotsu ni hiraku kyōdai*

"Naritaya acts the role of Tokimune; one
flower of the plum tree called the 'Elder
Brother' blooms as he opens the mirror stand"
Kaōen Tokunari

*Kyōdai o hiraku katae ni mata hiraku ōgi no shime
o chirasu harukaze*

"He opens the mirror stand and, like flowers
on a branch, the spring wind scatters a sheaf
of fans"
Shibaen Morizuna

Utagawa Kuniyoshi 1798–1861, active from 1814

Kuniyoshi was born on the fifteenth day of the eleventh month of the ninth year of the Kansei period (January 1798 by the Western calendar). His father was a dyer in Edo. He entered Toyokuni's studio at the age of fourteen in 1811 and his first signed work appeared three years later. Probably because of his youth he was unable to compete with Toyokuni's many pupils for commissions. It was only in 1827, after his teacher's death, that he gained public recognition for a set of pictures of the heroes of the Chinese novel *Suikoden*, "All Men Are Brothers," whose faces he is said to have copied from sculptures of the Five Hundred Arhats at a temple in the Honjo district of Edo. The success of this set led to some private commissions for surimono; Kuniyoshi probably designed forty surimono in the square format in the late 1820s and early 1830s. Afterwards he designed a few surimono in larger formats, including two handsome prints published around 1849, which he produced with Shibata Zeshin.

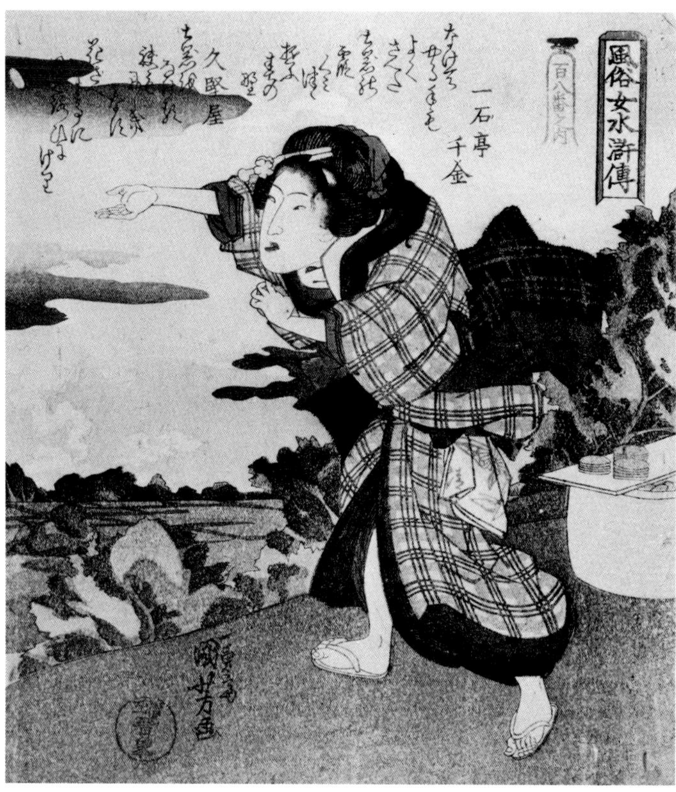

60

Woman throwing clay dishes from Dōkan Hill
series Modern Women as the One Hundred and
Eight Heroes of the *Suikoden*
c. 1830
21.1 × 18.5 cm
signed Ichiyūsai Kuniyoshi ga; printed by Surikō Shinzō
Meade; Beatty 2305

The young woman is throwing unfired earth-
enware dishes from a hilltop: a basket full of
the dishes rests on the ground behind her.
This pastime was popular at three hills in
Edo: Asuka, Atago and Dōkan; the empty
rural landscape in the distance shows that this
is Dōkan Hill, near Nippori village on the
northern outskirts of Edo. In this set, Kuniyoshi places women against backgrounds
which are, for the most part, landscapes
drawn and printed with chiaroscuro in a
Western style. Just as there is a contrast between the modern woman and the "foreign"
landscape, there is a further association in
each print between the woman's pose or activity and a hero in a "foreign" book, *Shui
huchuan*, "All Men Are Brothers" (*Suikoden* in
Japanese), a Chinese novel of the late Yuan or
early Ming Dynasty, which was translated
into Japanese at the beginning of the nineteenth century. *Shui huchuan* is the story of a
group of outlaws who banded together to correct the abuses of the corrupt national government. Kuniyoshi's picture alludes to the following episode. When the band attacked the
city of Tungbing, they found it defended by a
warrior named Zhang Jing, who in one day
disabled fifteen of their best fighters by
throwing stones at them. The following day,
when the heroes conquered the city and cap-
tured Zhang Jing, they treated him with such
courtesy that he joined their band. The
Hisakataya Group chose Zhang Jing as a subject for this print because the poet Senkin
used the secondary name Ikkokutei, which
means "One Rock." Both poems mention
throwing. "Mist," in the first poem, is a eu-
phemism for wine. There is a pun in the
second poem on *hokorobi*, which means "rip"
and "blossom."

*Nagete yaru te mo yoku saeta kawarake no kasumi
kumitsutsu asobu haru no no*

"The hand that throws the earthen cups with
such skill is just as good at dipping misty
wine with them on an outing in the spring
fields"
Ikkokutei Senkin

*Kawarake o nageru tamoto mo nishiki nasu hana
sae ude ni hokorobinikeri*

"As she throws the earthen cups her sleeve
rips and flowers of brocade blossom on her
arm"
Hisakataya

Shinsui Michikazu (or Tsūen)

An amateur artist active in the late 1790s

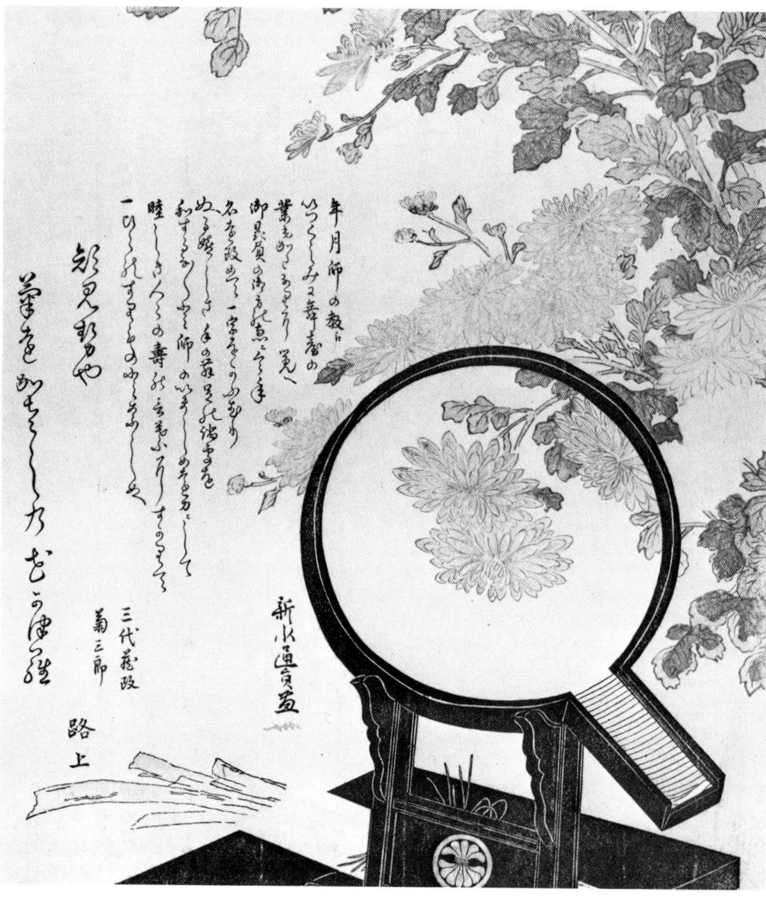

61

Mirror stand with mirror reflecting
chrysanthemums
1797 or earlier
36.6 × 31.6 cm
signed Shinsui Michikazu [or Tsūen] ga
seal *kakihan*
Beatty 2241

Segawa Kikusaburō (1784–1839), an important
actor of female roles in the beginning of the
nineteenth century, began his career as a child
actor using the name Anegawa Minato and
changed his name to Segawa Miyozō in
11/1789. This print commemorates a second
change of name, to Segawa Kikusaburō. The
date of this name change is uncertain, but the
name Kikusaburō begins to appear in the published records of kabuki theater in 1/1798, so
the latest date that the surimono could have
been published is autumn of the previous
year. The word *kiku* in the actor's name
means chrysanthemum and the flower reflected in the mirror on the dressing table thus
symbolizes the actor, whose family crest, a
bundle of cotton wadding within a circle, is
painted on the lacquered mirror stand. The

bundle of long, uneven strips that rests behind the mirror on the stand is *noshi*, dried
strips of abalone, which were used to decorate
gifts on special occasions. The long inscription
and the seventeen-syllable verse were composed by the actor, who signs them with his
poetry name, Rojō.

He praises his teacher, commends himself
to his patrons and concludes with the words
*mutsumajiki hitobito no kotobuki no kotoba ni
sugarite hitohira no surimono to nashinu* (relying
on the kindly words of friendly people, I have
made a single surimono). This indicates that
the actor himself commissioned and distributed the print. *Kaomise* were the kabuki performances given during the eleventh month of
the year. Additional poems by other actors
may have been trimmed at the left; no other
pictures by Michikazu have been recorded and
no other impression of the present print is
known.

Kaomise ya kiku o kazashi no hanakatsura

"For the *kaomise* performances: an actor's wig
decorated with chrysanthemums"   *Rojō*

Utagawa Sadakage

A pupil of Kunisada who designed a number of commercial prints and surimono, mostly of women.

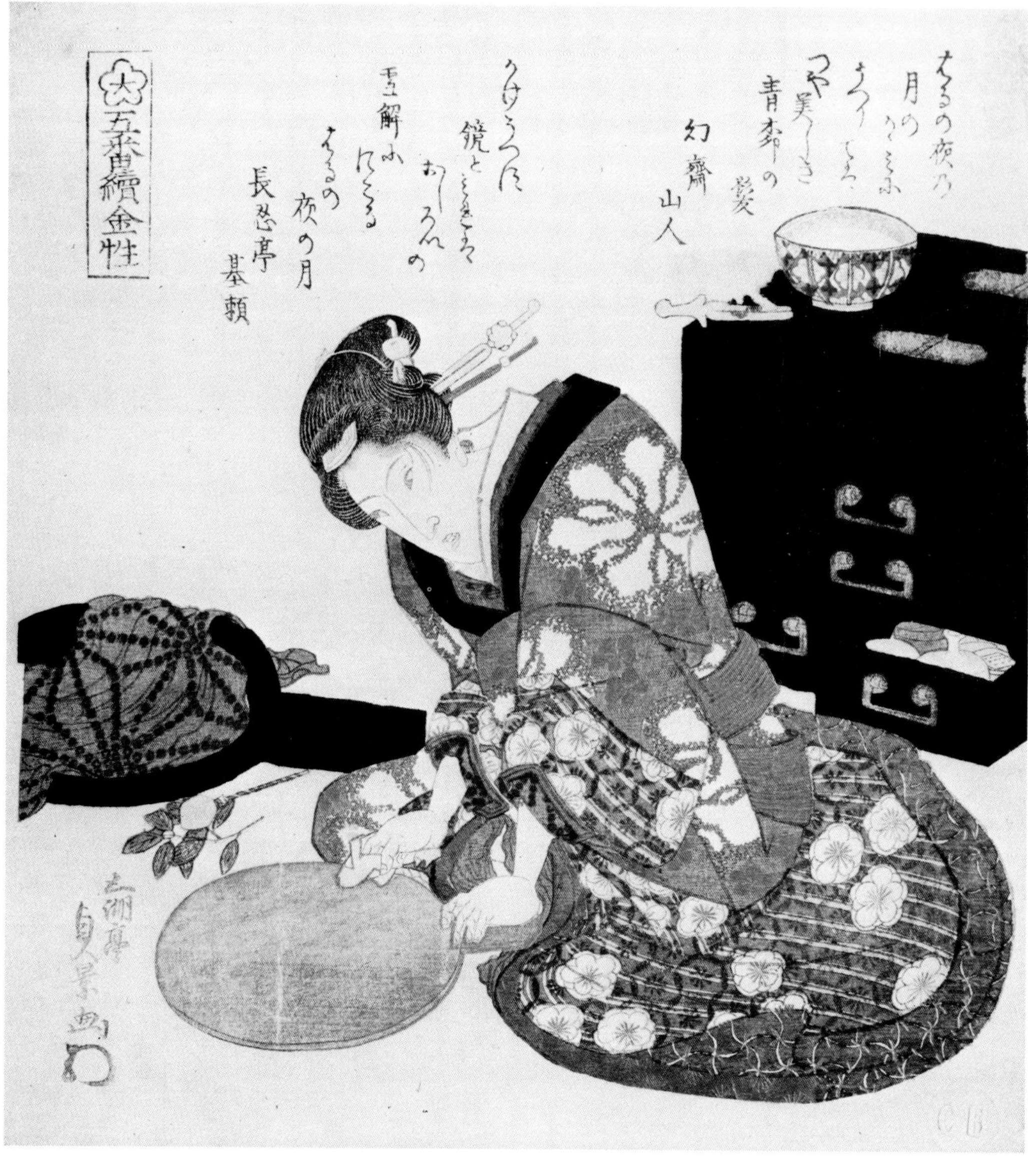

62

Metal
series A Set of Five
c. mid 1820s
21.5 × 19.0 cm
signed Gokotei Sadakage ga
seal kakihan
Beatty 919

The set was designed for a group led by the poet Shakuyakutei, whose plum-blossom emblem appears at the top of the title cartouche. The set illustrates personality types associated with the Five Elements: Wood, Fire, Earth, Metal and Water. The woman is kneeling beside a lacquer chest of drawers and polishing a metal mirror; a lacquer mirror case rests on the floor beside her on the left. The cloth-covered stick probably contains a polishing

substance and the leaves were undoubtedly used for the same purpose. The element Metal was associated with the color white and this may be the reason that *oshiroi* (white face powder) is mentioned in the second poem.

Haru no yo no tsuki no kagami ni utsurite wa tsuya utsukushiki aoyagi no kami

"Reflected in the mirror of the moon on the spring night, the beautiful glossy green hair of the willow"   *Gensai Sanjin*

Kage utsusu kagami to mireba oshiroi no yukige ni nigoru haru no yo no tsuki

"When she looks at her reflection in the mirror, the melting snow of her powder clouds the spring evening moon" *Chōnintei Motoyori*

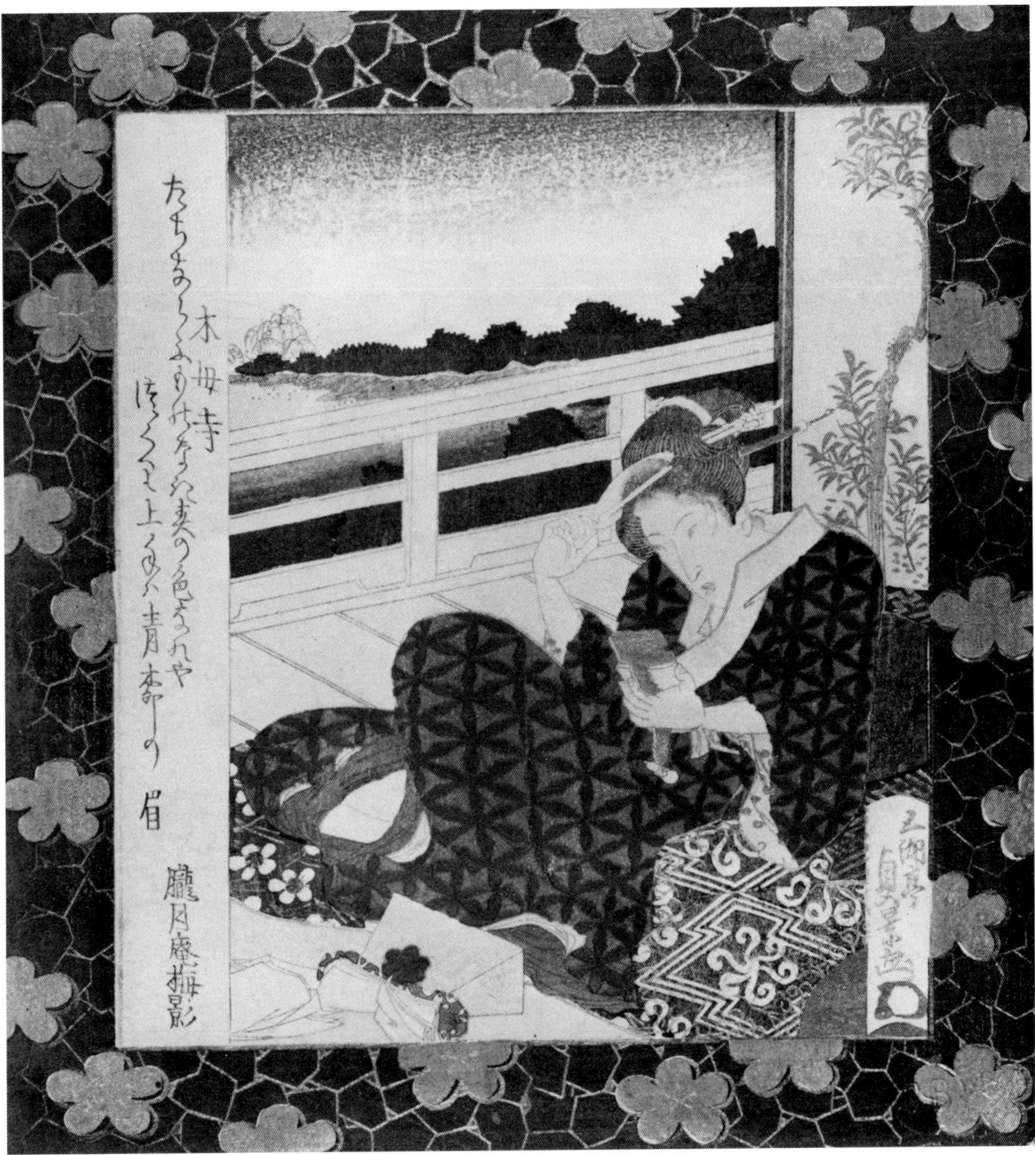

63

Geisha at a teahouse near Mokubo Temple
from an untitled series of famous places in
Edo
c. mid 1820s
20.9 × 18.5 cm
signed Gokotei Sadakage ga
seal kakihan
Beatty 918

A geisha leans against a box wrapped in purple cloth; this may be her samisen case. She
looks at her reflection in a hand mirror and
adjusts her hairpin. Her robe is open, her red
crepe under-sash is loose and her pillow is
overturned, as though she has just entertained
a lover. Outside, a light rain falls on the
Sumida River. The place name is given to the
right of the poem on each print in the series.

The pattern of plum blossoms and cracking
ice on the border indicates that the set was
designed for the poet Shakuyakutei and his
circle. In the poem there is a pun on *iro*,
which means "color" and "love."

Tachinarabu mono naki haru no iro nare ya
tsukuri jōzu wa aoyagi no mayu

"Is there anything to equal the colors of love
in Spring? She is skillful at putting make-up
on her green willow brows" *Rōgetsuan Umekage*

Yanagawa Shigemasa

A pupil of Yanagawa Shigenobu; cat. no. 64 is the artist's only recorded surimono.

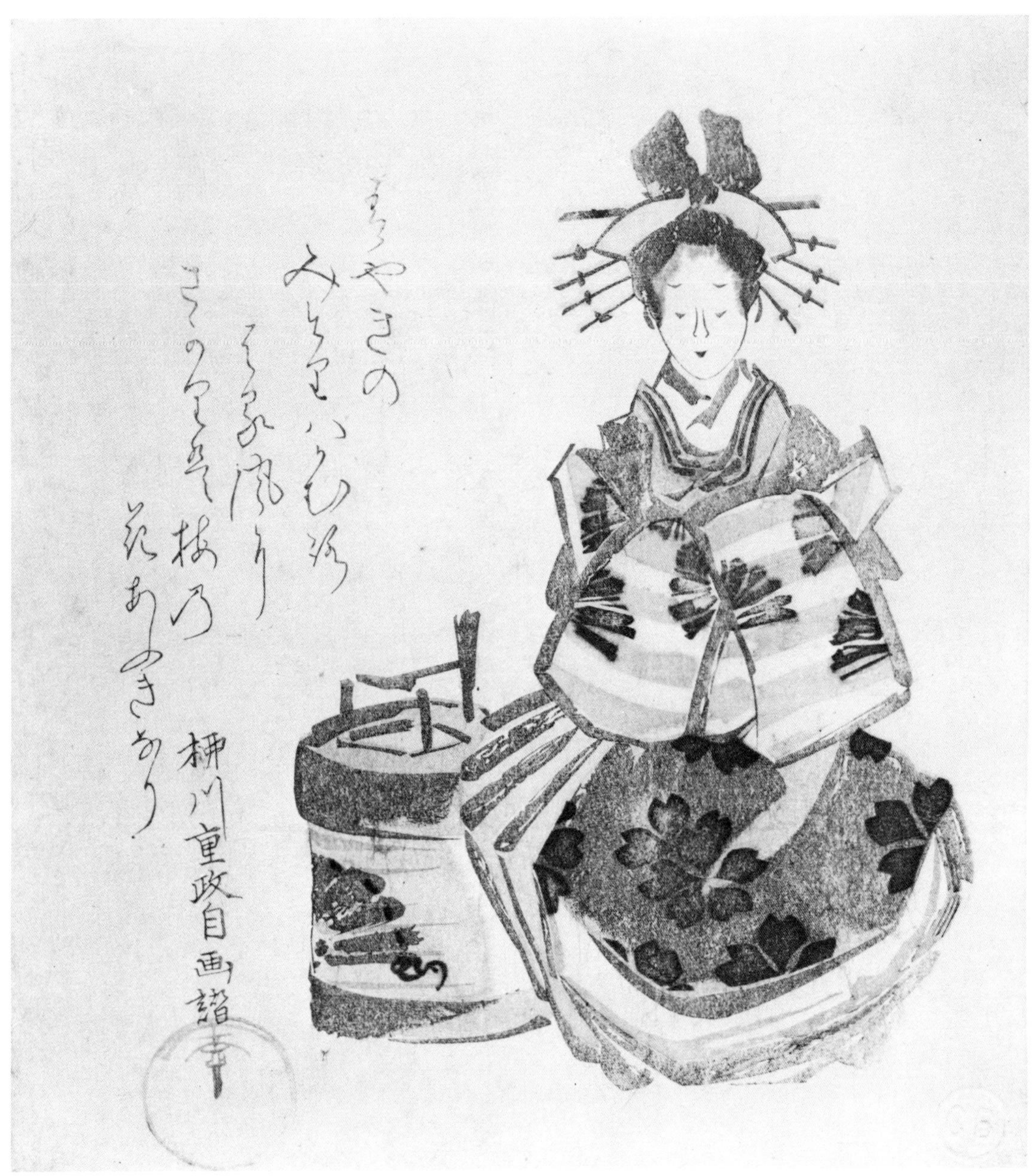

64

The courtesan Hanaōgi standing beside a
lantern
c. early 1820s
20.8 × 18.0 cm
signed Yanagawa Shigemasa Jigasan
seal Yana
Beatty 2030

Hanaōgi was the name used by one of the
highest ranking courtesans at the Ōgiya, or
"Fan House," in the Yoshiwara district of
Edo. Each high-ranking courtesan in the
Yoshiwara was attended by two child understudies called *kamuro*, who wore costumes
with the same pattern as their mistress and
had short, poetic names. One of Hanaōgi's
kamuro was named Midori, or "Green." There
is a pun in the artist's verse on *hana*, which
means "flower" and which is also the beginning of the name Hanaōgi. The picture is
engraved and printed to reproduce the effect
of a free, sketchy, informal brush painting.

*Aoyagi no midori wa kamuro harukaze ni sakari
wa ume no hanaōgi nari*

"The Green of the willow is a *kamuro;* what
flowers in the spring breeze is plum blossom
and Hanaōgi"   *Shigemasa*

Yanagawa Shigenobu II

active 1824–60

Shigenobu is said to have been the third son of Shiga Risai (1762–1840), a samurai, poet, scholar and government official in charge of financial administration in Ōsaka. If this is true, then he must have met his teacher, Shigenobu, when Shigenobu visited Ōsaka in 1822. His first work, an anthology of verse on the Musashi Plain, edited by Sensōan Ichindo and published in 1824, was signed Tanishirō Yanagawa. Another book of verse with illustrations signed Yanagawa Juzan was published the following year. Juzan assumed his teacher's name in the spring of 1833, after Shigenobu's death. He designed a number of surimono in the mid 1830s and was active as an illustrator of popular fiction until 1860.

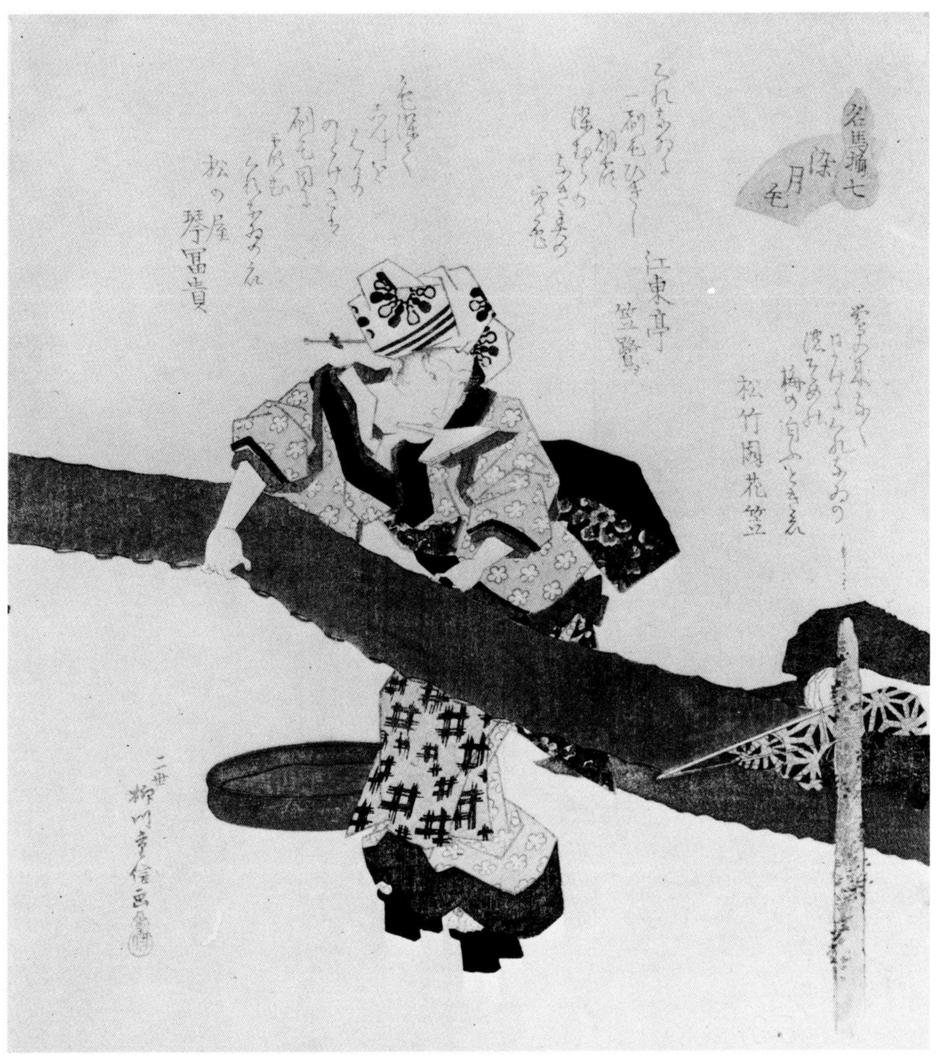

65

Number seven: Applying dye
series Famous Horses
1834
20.5 × 17.6 cm
signed Nisei Yanagawa Shigenobu ga
seal Shigenobu
unidentified Japanese collector's seal on verso;
Beatty 2029

The woman has applied a brilliant red dye to a piece of silk with the brush that she holds in her mouth; she has stretched the cloth between two posts to dry. A metal vat of dye rests on the ground beside her and several more rolls of fabric are piled on a mat to the right. There is a pattern of wood grain on the stretched fabric, perhaps because the marks of the dyer's brush are mentioned in two of the verses. In the first poem *tokiginu* is a garment whose material has been unstitched to wash it, or in this case to dye it, more easily. In the last poem there is a pun on *haru*, which means "spring" and "to stretch."

Uguisu no kinaku hikage ni kurenai no kozome no ume no niou tokiginu

"When the warbler comes and sings, the sun's rays dye deep red the perfuming plum blossoms and the unsewn robe" *Shōchikuen Hanagasa*

Kurenai ni hitohake hikishi asagasumi somemura no naki haru no sora iro

"Red, with one stroke of the brush, is the morning mist; no dye blotches in the color of the spring sky" *Kōtōtei Kasasagi*

Iro somete shinji o haru no nodokesa wa hakeme ni kasumu kurenai no kinu

"On a calm spring day they stretch the dyed material for padding; the brushmarks are like mist on the red silk" *Matsunoya Kotobuki*

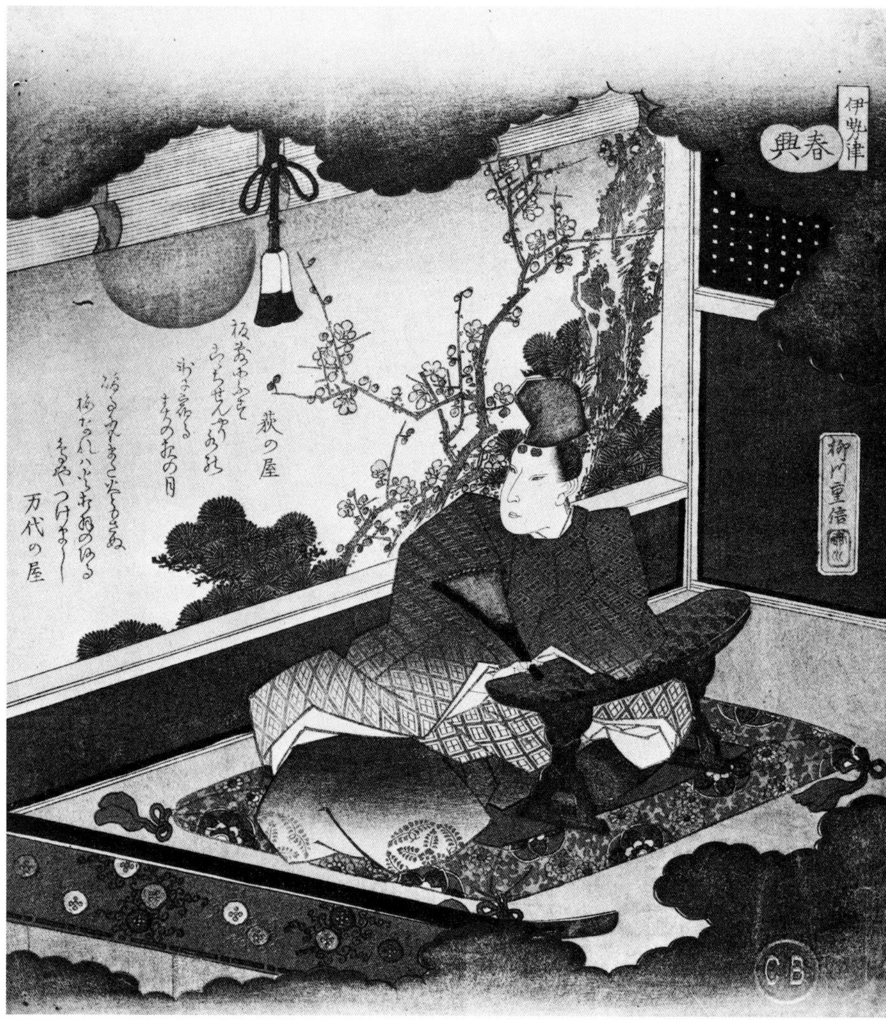

66

Spring at Ise Harbor, the mood of Spring
1835
21.1 × 18.5 cm
signed Yanagawa Shigenobu
seal Yanagawa
Beatty 2035

A court nobleman leans against an armrest
and looks out of his window at the plum
blossom and full moon. In front of him is a
lacquered frame, from which a curtain is suspended as a room divider; gold clouds sur-
round the border of the picture on three sides.
This is the second state of the right-hand
panel of a diptych. In the first state both
prints are subtitled *kinoto hitsuji*, the cyclical
signs for 1835, rather than *shunkyō* as here.
The left panel shows a woman standing beside a *koto*. An example of the complete diptych is in the Fogg Art Museum.

Shunkyō, "the mood of Spring," is a common subject for poetry; Ise Harbor may refer
to an episode in classical literature. In the
second poem, the poet has a plum branch
with unopened buds. He wants to send a
hawk with it because the lowest feathers on a
hawk's wing are called *hiuchiba*, "feathers that
light a fire." These will make the branch
"burst into flame" by making the buds
blossom.

*Itajiki ni fusu kokochi sen yarimizu no kōri ni
yadoru haru no yo no tsuki*

"As though it were lying on a wooden floor,
the moon of the spring night lodges on the ice
of the stream in the garden"   *Oginoya*

*Okuru nimo mada hi tomosanu ume nareba
hiuchiba no aru tori ya tsukemashi*

"I want to send a plum branch to a friend,
but its fire is still not lit; I will send along a
hawk with flintstone feathers" *Yorozuyonoya*

Ryūryūkyo Shinsai active 1799–1823

Shinsai was an early pupil of Katsushika Hokusai. His first work was a humorous illustrated book *Keiseikai neko no maki*, "A Cat Visits the Prostitutes," published in 1799, the year Hokusai gave up the name Sōri and established himself as an independent artist. The name Shinsai, "Dragon Studio," is apparently derived from Hokusai's auxiliary name Tatsumasa (or Shinsei). Shinsai specialized in surimono and privately commissioned works. The *Ukiyo-e ruikō* says that he never designed commercial prints, but this is not true: he designed two sets of landscapes in Western style and at least two triptychs, one of the Gissharō Teahouse in the town of Furuichi near Ise, the other a landscape, which identifies him as coming from, or living in, Gumma Prefecture.

Shinsai's *gō*, Ryūryūkyo, also indicates an early relationship with Hokusai because that name was used by Hokusai's predecessor, Tawaraya Sōri I. In the early 1800s Shinsai designed prints in small formats; in the mid 1810s he began working in the square format, which he used almost exclusively in his late work. Shinsai was one of the first surimono designers to explore the still life. He was also one of the first artists to design large sets of surimono on a common theme, the first and largest being *Kasen awase*, a collection of pictures designed for the Yomo Group in 1809 on the theme of the Thirty-six Shells.

There is a gap in the sequence of Shinsai's prints around the mid 1810s and there is some indication that the artist traveled to the Kyōto–Ōsaka area then.

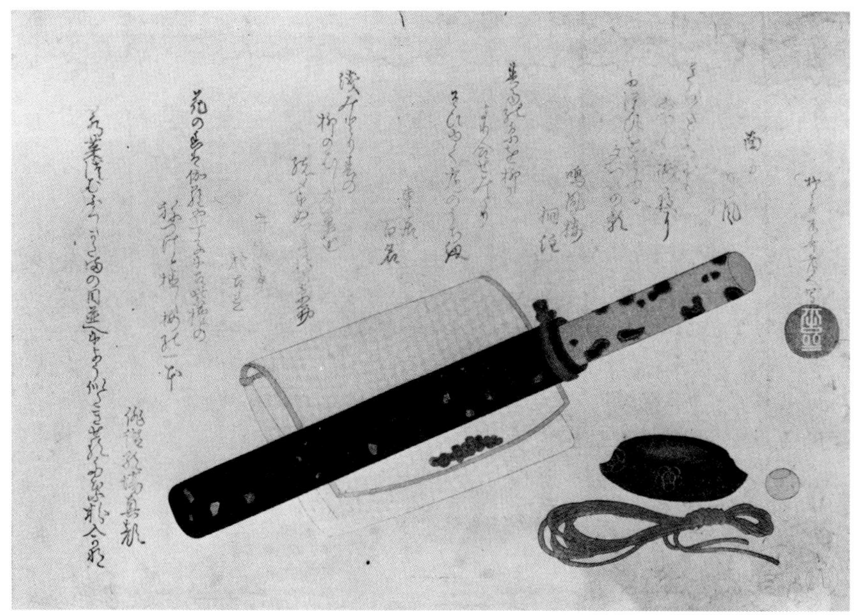

67

Pipe case, tobacco pouch, *netsuke, ojime* and cord
c. early 1810s
20.8 × 28.0 cm
signed Ryūryūkyo Shinsai rōjin sha
seal Shinsai
Beatty 873

The opalescent spots on the black pipe case
are actual flakes of mother-of-pearl, which
have been fixed to the surface of the paper
with lacquer or animal glue; the number, size
and position of these flakes varies greatly from
impression to impression. The mottled orange
cover of the case reproduces the texture of
tortoiseshell. The dark-brown circular object
is a *kagamibuta netsuke,* a carved button that
kept the cord of the case attached to a man's
sash when it was worn; it is made of *shitan,* or
red sandalwood. Each of the five poems refers
to one of the five objects in the picture. The
first refers to the pipe case indirectly by men-
tioning the glittering light of *yūzutsu,* Venus,
or the Evening Star. The *ojime* mentioned in
the third verse is the small bead that was used
to adjust the length and tightness of the cord
between the pipe case and the fastener, or
netsuke; these beads were often made of
mushinosu, a material with a pitted surface like
an "insect nest." In the last poem, the beaded
texture of the tobacco pouch reminds the poet
of rows of jewels.

Shinsai adds the word *rōjin,* or "old man,"
to his signature here. He rarely signs surimono this way, but this name does appear in
a poetry anthology he illustrated in 1813.

Other impressions of the print are in the Rijksmuseum voor Volkenkunde, Leiden, and in
the Heinz Kaempfer collection in The Hague.

*Kirakira to mizu tomo shizuku ume ga e ni nioi o
souru yūzutsu no kage*

"Glittering, the drops of water on the plum
branch are more fragrant by the light of the
Evening Star"   *Nampōgaki Makaze*

*Harusame ni ito o yanagi ni yoriawase midori
soiyuku niwa no uchihimo*

"Threads of willow and spring rain twisted
together make a green cord for the garden"
        Meihōrō Kirizumi

*Asamidori haru no yanagi no mushi no su o ojime
ni nukeru eda no itosuji*

"Through buds like insect nests on the light-
green willow, as through an *ojime,* strands of
branches pass"   *Azumai Hyakumei*

*Hana no ka wa kyara ya chōji ni Koshitan shitan
no netsuke to ueshi ume wa ippon*

"Its flowers have the fragrance of aloes, clove
and a sandalwood *netsuke;* only the plum"
        Shushintei Okotaru

*Wakana tsumu fugushi ka tama no menarabe ni yō
nita kiseru tabakoire kana*

"The tobacco pouch looks like rows of jewels;
the pipe is like a trowel for picking spring
herbs"   *Haikai Utaba Magao*

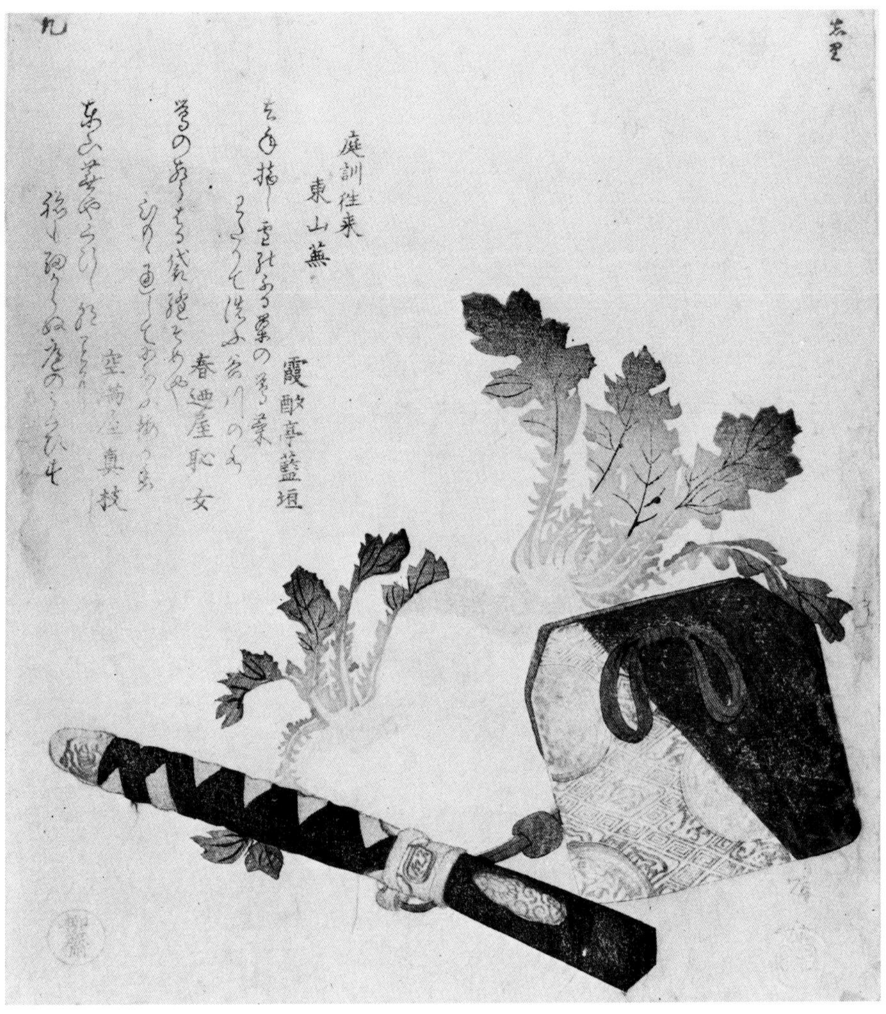

68

A turnip from Higashiyama
late 1810s
21.0 × 17.9 cm
signed Shinsai; engraved and printed by Ryūsai
Beatty 870

The dagger, the radishes and brocade pouch
are probably taken from one of the didactic
model letters in the fourteenth-century anthology *Tekin ōrai*, "The Communication of
Household Wisdom." All three poems mention the warbler; one of them mentions turnips and two of them mention the cord on the
pouch. There is an appealing contrast between the embossed, snowy, cloud-like shapes
of the turnips and the distinct outlines and
vivid colors of the dagger and pouch. The
small, red, hand-written characters in the upper corners of the print read "9" and, possibly, "Masato." A similar script, with different
words and numbers, appears on other surimono by Shinsai. In the first poem, *uguisuna*,
the "warbler plant," is a poetic name for the
plant called rape, or *Brassica napus;* there is a
pun on *tsumu*, which means "to pick" and "to
pile"; also on *furu*, which means "old" and "to
fall."

*Kozo tsumishi yuki no furusu no uguisuna watarite
arau tanigawa no mizu*

"Last year snow fell on the old nest of the
warbler; I pick the warbler plant and cross the
valley stream to wash it"   *Kashakutei Aigaki*

*Uguisu no koe haru fukuro nuizome ya himo mo
tōshite niou ume ga ka*

"The warbler's voice is like a pouch sewn in
the Spring: the fragrance of plum blossom
escapes the cord"   *Harunoya Hajime*

*Higashiyama kabura ya kuishi asagoto ni ne mo
hosokaranu niwa no uguisu*

"Has it eaten a radish from Higashiyama? Every morning the voice of the warbler sounds
full"   *Soramitsuya Maeda*

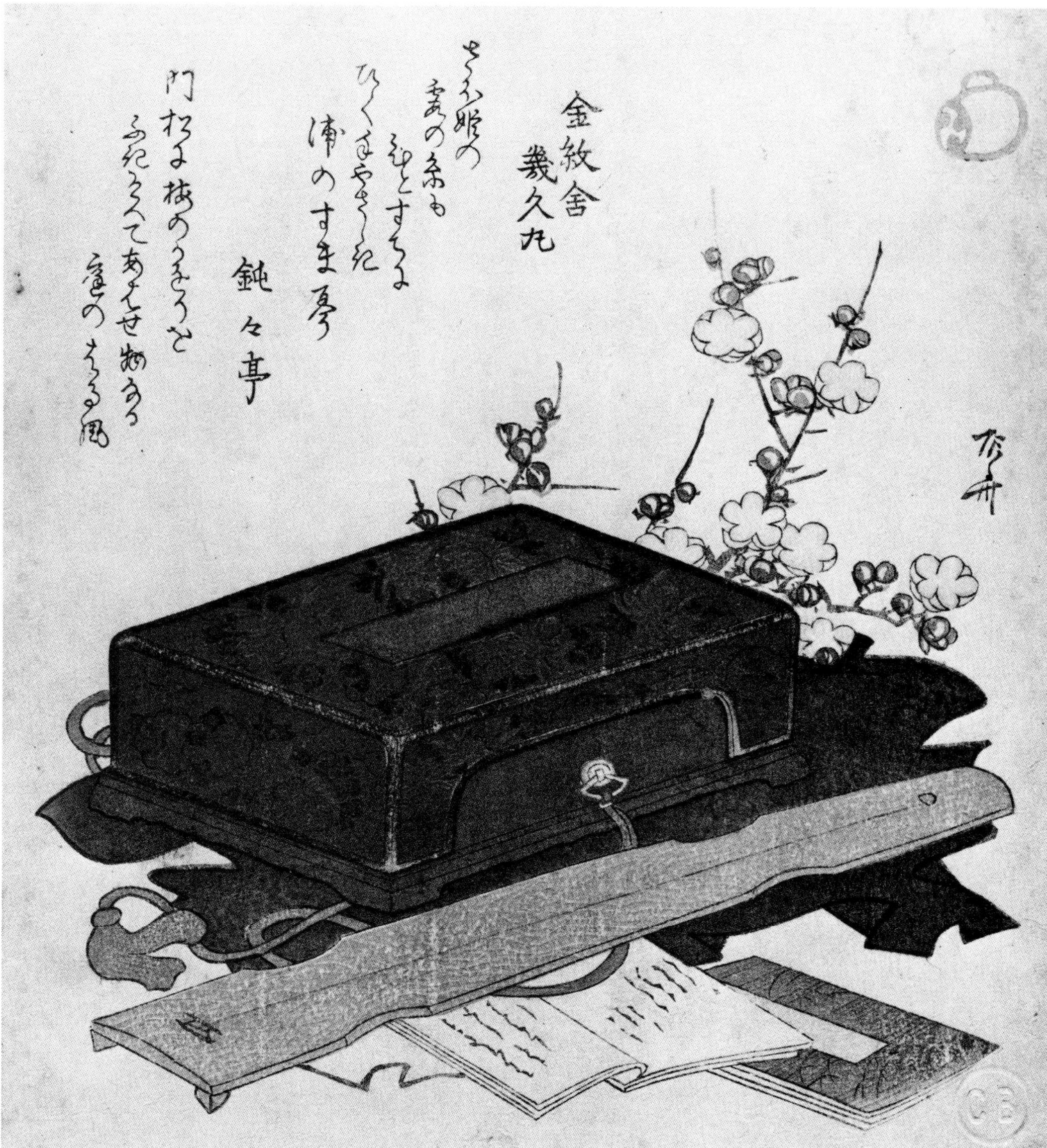

69

Lacquer bookcase, books, plum blossom and
one-stringed harp
late 1810s
20.7 × 18.2 cm
signed Shinsai
Beatty 2246

The single-stringed harp, or *ichigen kin*, was
also called a *sumagoto* or "Suma zither" because the courtier Ariwara Yukihira is said to
have fashioned one during his exile on the
Bay of Suma. The normal *sumagoto* was a
little over one meter in length and had note
markings along its length; on it, one could
play melodies of great intricacy and subtle
beauty. The instrument in Shinsai's picture
seems to be a miniature; a pattern of wood
grain has been engraved on its body and a
pattern of silver chrysanthemums is printed
on the brown box lid. There is a pun in the
first poem on *yasashiki*, which means "easy"
and "elegant."

*Saohime no kasumi no ito mo hitosuji ni hikute
yasashiki ura no sumagoto*

"The Goddess of Spring, on one strand of
mist, plays with easy elegance the harp of
Suma Bay"   *Kimmonsha Ikumaru*

*Kadomatsu ni ume no kaori o fukisoete awasemono
naru niwa no harukaze*

"When the fragrance of plum blossom is
blown to the pine-tree decorations at the gate,
they are joined: a spring breeze in the garden"
                                        Dondontei

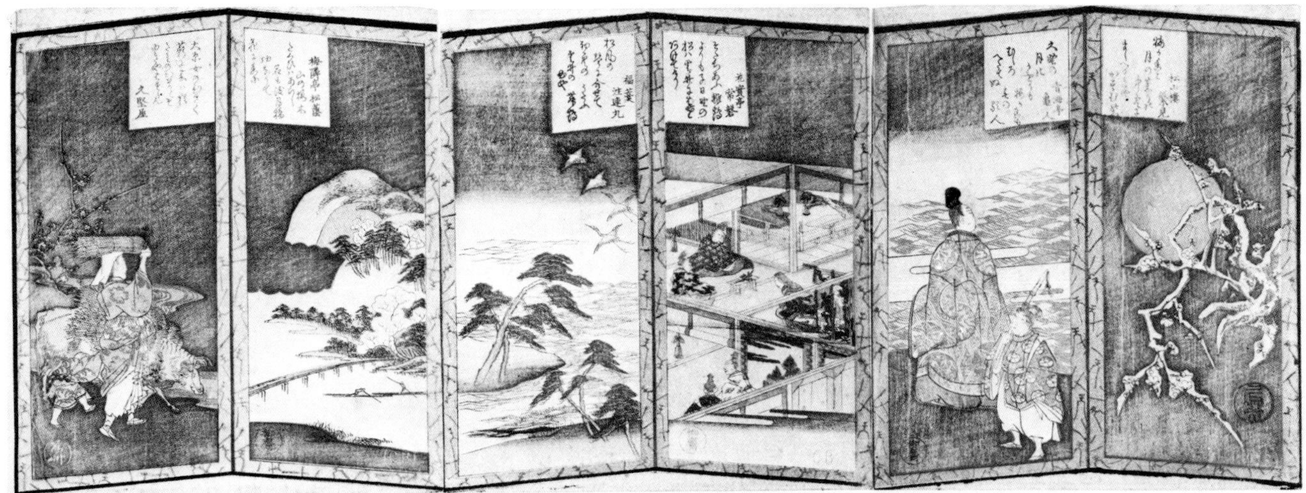

70

Screen for the Hisakataya Group
late 1810s
20.8 × 54.9 cm
seal Shinsai
engraved and printed by Ryūsai
Beatty 834

Each of the three sheets contains two pictures, with gold backgrounds and tan borders, bearing the emblem of the Hisakataya Group; surrounding the borders is a black wooden frame. Each picture is drawn at a slight angle as though it were the panel of a standing screen. Shinsai's seal appears on the two outer panels and the hand-stamped seal of Ryūsai, the engraver or printer, appears on each sheet. The six pictures are of conventional subjects in classical painting; none of them is drawn or composed in an ukiyo-e style. From right to left the subjects are:

Full moon and snowy plum branch; the moon is printed in silver.
Court poet and young attendant standing beside the sea.
Bird's-eye view of a palace with courtiers examining a young pine shoot.
Beach with pine trees and flying cranes.
Cherry trees in blossom by Togetsu Bridge at Arashiyama in Kyōto.
Peasant woman from Ōhara, near Kyōto, with bundles of twigs, an ox and a child.

The complete set of six prints forming a pair of six-panel screens is illustrated in Van Rappard-Boon (1982), pls. 97–102. In the third poem there is a pun on *ha* which means "pine needles" and "wings." In the fifth poem there is a pun on *araji*, "there is none," and Arashi-

yama, the area west of Kyōto famous for its cherry trees.

Ume ga ka to tsuki no kaori no nakazora ni majieru iro ya kasumu murasaki

"The scent of plum blossom and the fragrance of the moon blend in the sky into a misty purple color"
Shōzanrō Shigemi

Hisakata no tsuki no kaori mo ume ga ka mo mushiro hedatenu haru no utabito

"The fragrance of the moon and the scent of plum blossom share the same seat with the spring poet"
Seikaitei Kamendo

Sodachiau hinazuru yori mo ne no hi no no matsu wa kumoi ni ha o agetekeri

"Higher than the growing cranes, the pine tree on the Rat Day in the field raises its branches to the sky"
Kajitsutei Tokiwa

Matsukaze no koto ni awasete hatsuzora no kumoi no tobu ya utau maizuru

"Joining the music of the wind in the pine trees, flying among the clouds, cranes dance and sing in the New Year sky"
Fukuwara Tsuzuremaru

Hana ni ka ni kō narite na mo togetsukyō tagui wa araji yama no sakuragi

"For its fragrance and blossoms and famous Togetsu Bridge, incomparable: Arashiyama with its cherry trees"
Bairintei Matsukage

Oharame no hisagu takigi ni haru wa nao tami no kamado zo nigi ya wasuran

"With the firewood the maidens of Ohara sell, Spring makes the people's stoves even busier"
Hisakataya

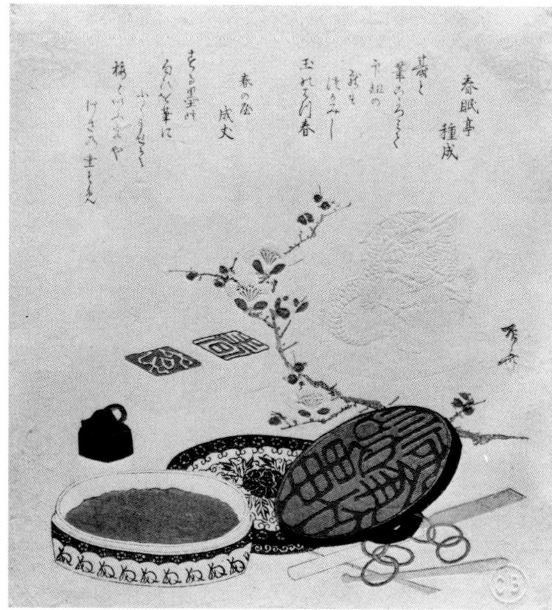

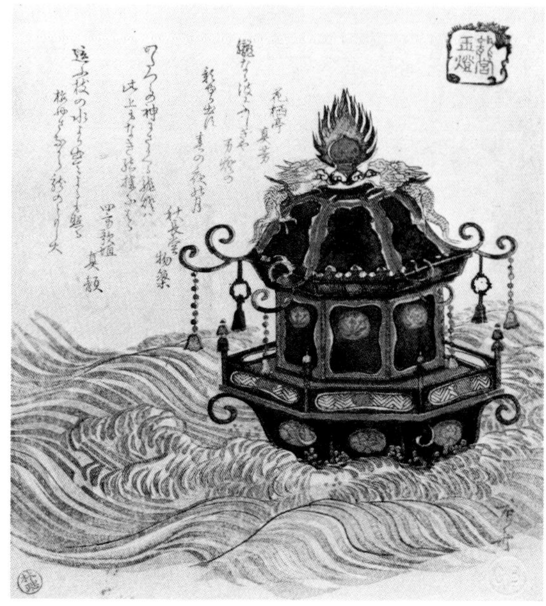

71

Seals, carving tools, porcelain ink box and
plum branch
1820
21.6 × 18.9 cm
signed Shinsai
Beatty 2114

The embossed dragon on the stone seal in the
background and the mention of a dragon in
the first poem indicate that the print was published in 1820, a Dragon Year. The inscription on the large seal reads *tsurukame shōchiku*,
"crane and turtle, pine tree and bamboo," all
symbols of long life and felicity. The double
seal in the background seems to read *haru no
mado* or *shunsō*, "spring window." It must be
the personal seal of the poet Harunoya, a
judge in the Honchō Group, since the edge of
the porcelain ink box is decorated with a row
of rabbit-like emblems formed from the characters of his personal name, Naritake.

*Kotobuki to fude kokoromite inchu no tatsu mo
tsukamishi tama no hatsuharu*

"As I began to write the character for 'long
life' on New Year's Day, the dragon on the
seal knob seized the brush, as if it were a
spring jewel"   *Shummintei Tanenari*

*Suru sumi no nioi o fude ni fukumasete ume to iu
hi ya kesa no kakizome*

"I fill my brush with the fragrance of fresh
ink and write the character for 'plum tree' this
morning as my first calligraphy"
                          Harunoya Naritake

72

The jewelled lantern
series The Palace of the Dragon King
1820
20.2 × 17.6 cm
signed Shinsai
Hayashi; Beatty 2109

Phosphorescent algae on the surface of the
ocean sometimes glow like torches at night
and Japanese sailors called them *ryūtō*, or
"dragon lanterns." During the day, mirages
may also form, in which the Japanese imag-
ined they could see towers like this one, of
the Dragon King's palace. The tower-like lantern in Shinsai's print has indigo side panels,
red trim, and silver and bronze balustrades.

*Oboronaru nami ni fushigi ya mandō no kage
yuriidasu haru no yo no tsuki*

"How strange, that on the misty waves ten
thousand lanterns shimmer in the spring night
with the moon"
             Kaseitei (or Hanazumitei) Mayoshi

*Watatsumi no kami ni sasaguru ryutō wa kono ue
mo naki kekkō na haru*

"There is nothing finer than the dragon lanterns presented to the God of the Sea"
                          Shūchōdō Monoyana

*Hau eda no mizu yori idete yoru mo teru ume ya
sanagara tatsu no tomoshibi*

"Its branches creep out of the water and the
plum tree shines at night like dragon lanterns"
                          Yomo Utagaki Magao

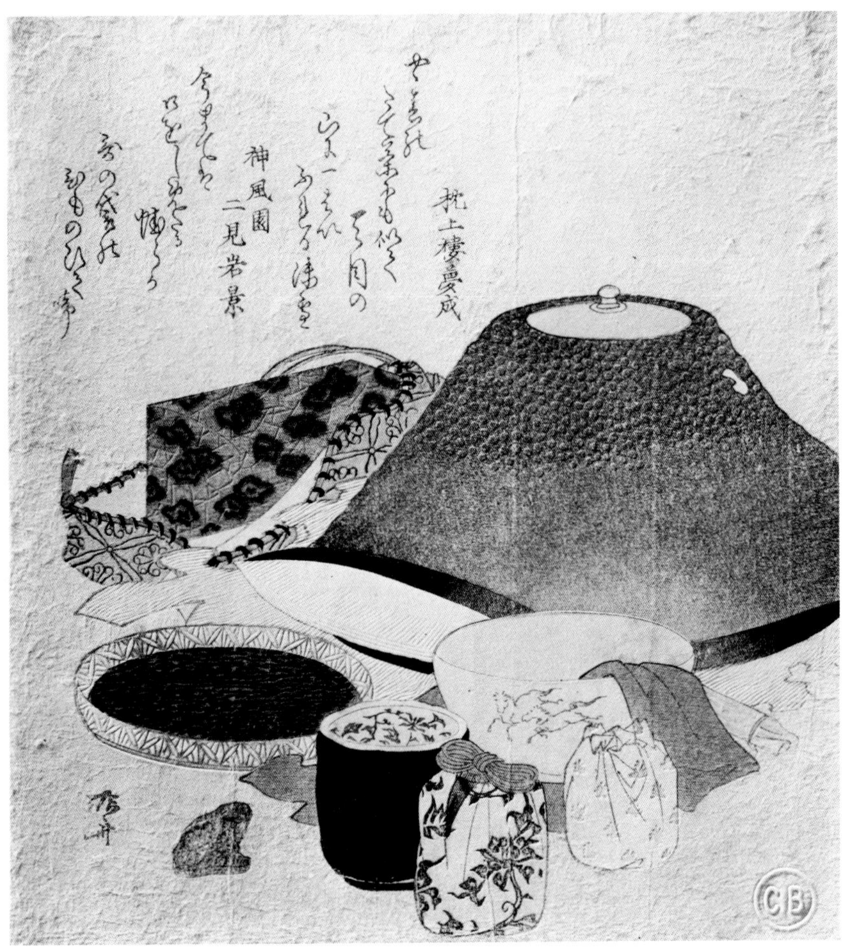

73

Iron kettle and implements for the tea
ceremony
c. 1820
20.8 × 18.2 cm
signed Shinsai
Beatty 1037

Beside the iron kettle there is a lacquer box
decorated with a pattern of plovers and in
front of it is a feather for fanning the fire
which heats water for tea. The tea bowl is
decorated with two running horses, beside it
are a black cup with a painted interior and
two tea caddies in brocade bags. The circular
dish with the silver rim is probably a plate for
serving sweet cakes during the tea ceremony.
The first poem joins the image of light snow
in early spring on Mt Tianmu with a cup of
tea served in a *temmoku* bowl. *Temmoku* (the
Japanese pronunciation of Tianmu) was a
dark-glazed Chinese stoneware of the Song
Dynasty, which was often used in the tea
ceremony. No *temmoku* ware appears in the
picture, but the kettle with its uneven surface
partially resembles a mountain lightly covered
with snow; *awayuki* (light snow) was also the
name of a sweet cake that could be eaten
during the tea ceremony. *Utabukuro* (or *uta no
fukuro*) is the word for a poem pouch and for
the part of a frog's throat that swells when it
croaks; these images probably led Shinsai to
include the small metal paperweight in the
shape of a frog and the many cloth pouches in
his design.

*Yaya haru no tatecha ǹi mo nite temmoku no yama
ni ippai fureru awayuki*
"Just like a ceremonial cup of tea in early
Spring: on Mt Tianmu, light snow falling"
Chinjōrō Yumenari

*Ima made wa kuchi o shimetaru kawazura ga uta
no fukuro no himo no hikunaki*

"Till now, the mouth of the poem pouch and
the frog's throat have both been closed; when
the string is open, they sing"
Jimpūen Futami Iwakage

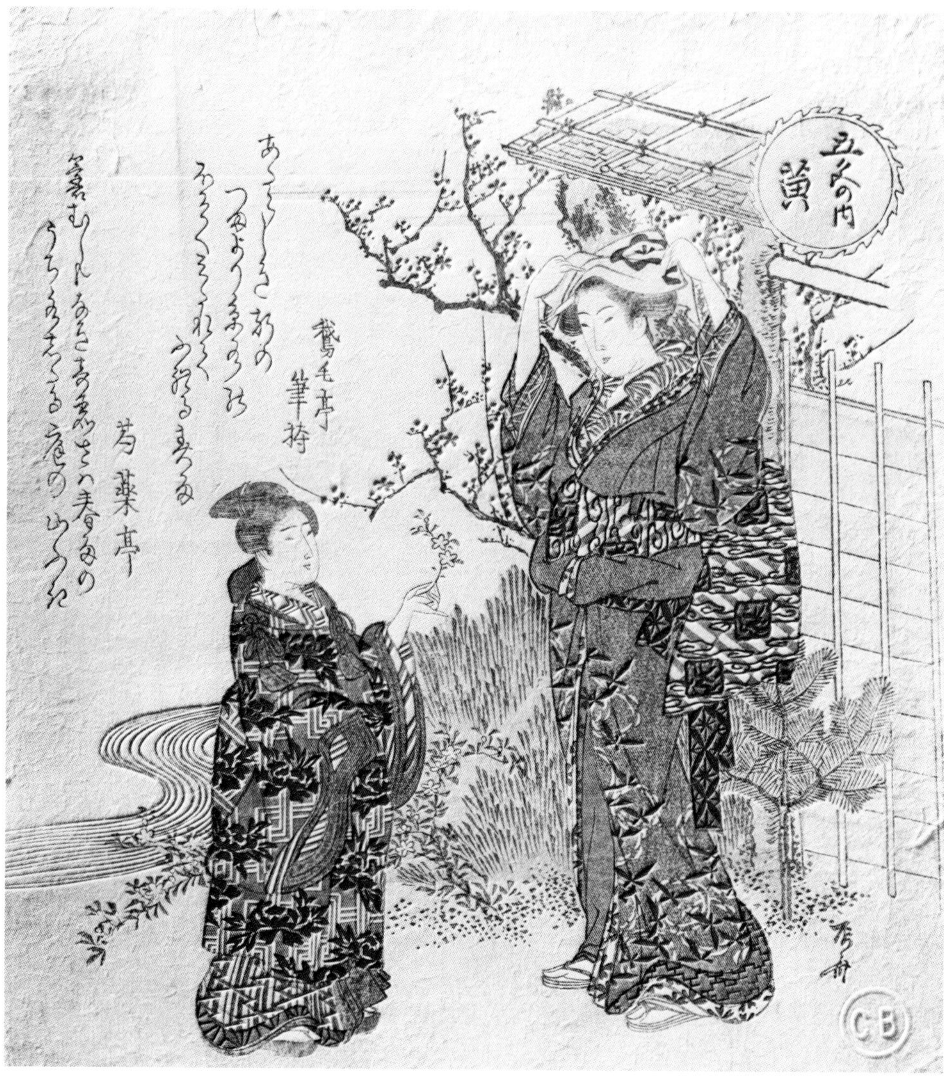

74

Yellow
series Five Colors
c. 1820
21.1 × 18.6 cm
signed Shinsai
Beatty 2104

A young boy from a wealthy family presents his mother with a spray of yellow *yamabuki* flowers. The *yamabuki* plant did not bear fruit, and both the picture and the poems allude to the story of Prince Kaneakira, a tenth-century poet who presented a spray of the same flowers to someone who had asked to borrow a raincoat, since *mino nashi*, "no raincoat," also means "no fruit." The story was repeated in the fifteenth century when the general Ōta Dōkan asked a young peasant girl for a raincoat and was handed a spray of *yamabuki*. At first he was angered, but when her gesture was explained to him, he marvelled at her knowledge and resolved to master classical poetry.

The plum blossom on the woman's headdress is the emblem of the poet Shakuyakutei. The second poem suggests that *minomushi*, or "rain-coat bugs," would keep the bushes in the garden dry.

Atarashiki noki no tsuma yori itomizu no hosoku midarete fureru harusame

"From the edge of the new eaves, the spring rain falls in thin, tangled threads"

Gamōtei Fudemochi

Minomushi mo naki kireisa wa harusame no uchimizu shitaru niwa no yamabuki

"It is lovely when there are no 'raincoat bugs' and the spring rain falls on the *yamabuki* in the garden" *Shakuyakutei*

Kubo Shumman

Born in Edo, Shumman originally studied with Kitao Shigemasa and the poet Katori Nahiko. He began designing woodblock prints in the 1780s. During this period he studied kyōka verse with Rokujuen, becoming a judge and leader of the Bakuro Group. He then gave up commercial print design and devoted himself to painting, the production of poetry albums and surimono. Shumman was skilled in metal inlay, shell craft and lacquer. There is also some evidence that he engraved, and possibly printed, surimono. The figure drawing in his early surimono was influenced by Hokusai and Tsutsumi Tōrin. His earliest surimono seem to have been designed in the long horizontal format and many of them were announcements for musical performances. In the late 1790s he began to design more surimono in small formats and in 1809 he was responsible for some of the first square surimono. In the last decade of his life, the 1810s, he was one of the most prolific, original and sophisticated surimono designers. He seems to have conceived the first sets of surimono on themes related to classical Japanese literature, and he was among the earliest print artists to explore the still life.

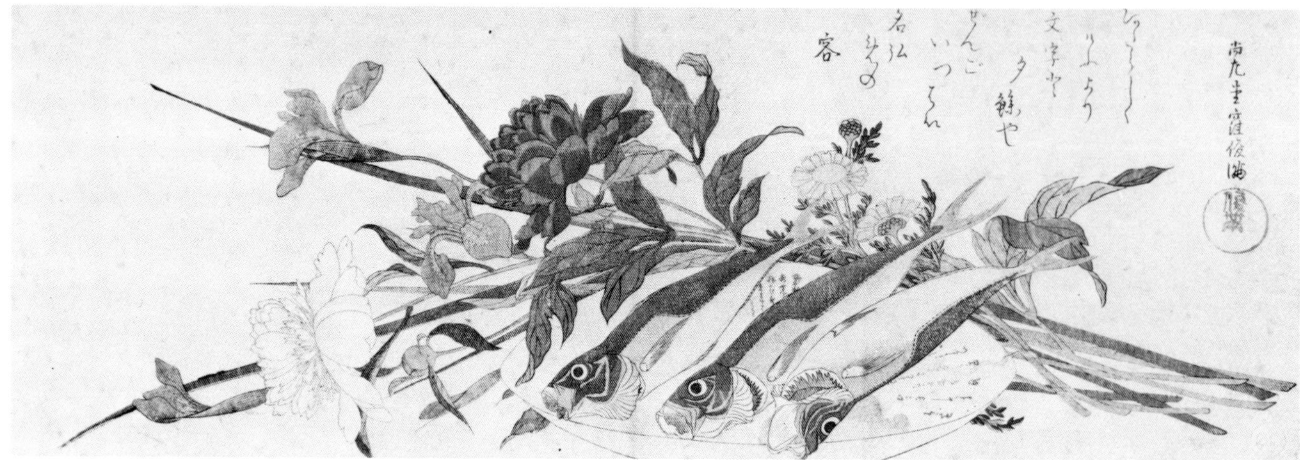

75

Iris, dandelions, peonies and three mackerel
on porcelain plate
late 1790s or early 1800s
17.9 × 49.0 cm
signed Shōsadō Kubo Shumman
seal Shumman
Beatty 1019

Long surimono were often published as invitations to musical events or to commemorate special poetry gatherings. Occasionally they announced a change of name and that seems to have been the purpose of this exquisite still life.

The irises indicate that the picture was published in early summer. The red writing on the porcelain plate is indistinct; mica is printed on the fishes' scale. The print may have been published to announce the change of name and reopening of a restaurant. It is more likely, however, that the print announced a musician's change of name. Singers of the Tokiwazu clan often began their name with the syllables *moji*, and Tokiwazu Rinnosuke was given the name Komojidayū, "Little Mojidayū" (he was eight years old at the time), in the sixth month of 1799, just before the death of the clan leader Tokiwazu Mojidayū II a month later. This may well be the name change commemorated by the print, although, according to Jack Hillier, the printed text that accompanied the picture was a "long list of kyōka clubs and their members, one of them being the Shumman club" (Hillier, 1960, pp. 110–11). Unfortunately, no printed text accompanies this impression.

The poem contains a series of puns on words related to fish and eating. *Aji* means "mackerel" and "taste"; *zengo* means "before and after"; *zeigo* are the spiny fins on a mackerel; *ippai* means "one cup (of wine)" and "full"; *moji* means "words," but also "fish trap"; *yū* means "evening" and *iu* means "to be called."

*Atarashiku kyō yori moji to yū aji ya zengo ippai
nahirome no kyaku*

"From today Moji is the new name for the mackerel, full of spines; all evening from beginning to end delicious drinks for the guests at the announcement party"   *Shumman*

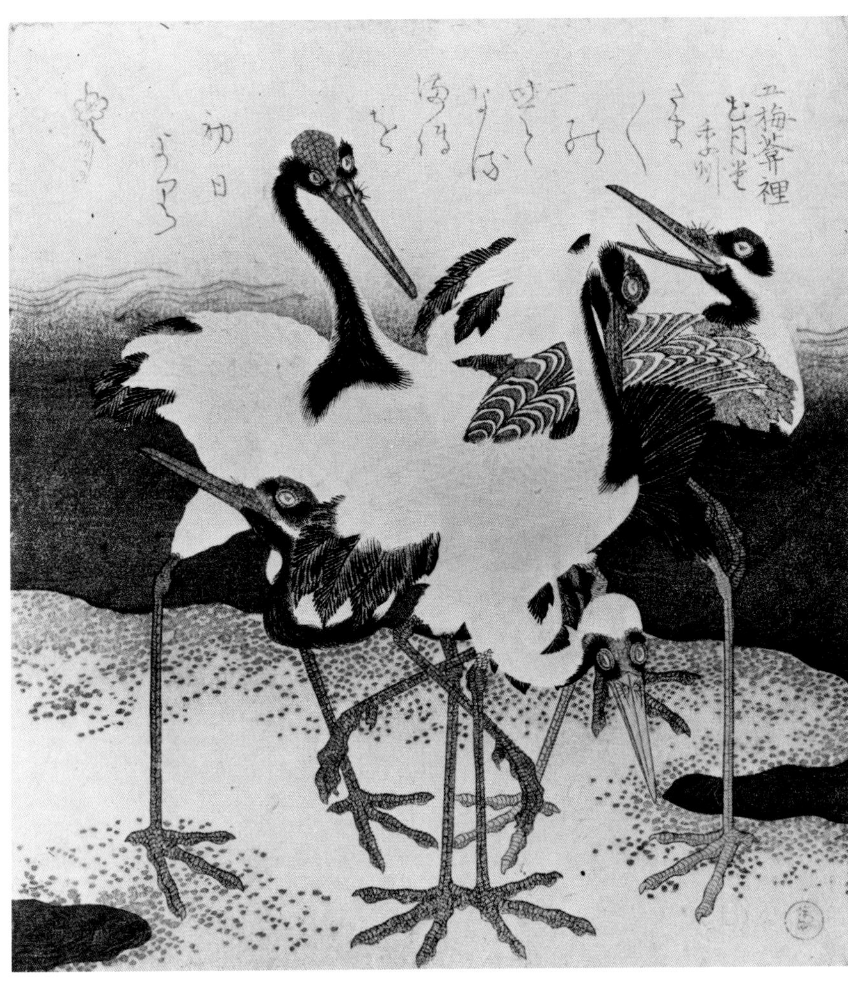

76

Five cranes on a spit of sand

series Three Petals

probably 1816

21.3 × 18.5 cm

seal Shumman

engraved and printed by Shumman

Rose; Beatty 2064

There are actually six prints in this set, three of birds and three of flowers. One is a picture of a plum branch beside a metal seal shaped like a rat, indicating that the set was published in 1816, a Rat Year. There are two states of this picture of cranes. In the first state, the poem ends with the phrase *hatsu hiyori*, written with characters meaning the "first good weather of the New Year." An impression of this state is illustrated in color in Van Rappard-Boon (1979), p. 39. In the second state, the phrase is corrected to *hatsuhi yori*, "from the first day of the New Year," by changing the last character to syllabic script. Most impressions of the print belong to this state.

Kagetsudō Kishū was a haiku poet; that is to say, he wrote seventeen-syllable verse rather than the thirty-one-syllable kyōka usually found on surimono. One of his names was Gobaian, "Hut of Five Plum Trees"; this may have been the poetic name he chose for his actual residence, in which case the five cranes in Shumman's picture may be a graceful allusion to the five trees. The series title is written on a poem slip hanging from a plum branch; this is probably another allusion to the poet's name and could even be his personal emblem. The title *Three Petals* may also derive from the flowering plum trees, although *hira* can mean a flat object like a sheet of paper, or a woodblock print. The five cranes with their embossed white feathers and odd poses suit the idea of a various world conveyed in the poem.

Samazama no yo to naru made o hatsuhi yori

"Various things to happen in the world; all start with the first sunrise"

Gobaian uchi Kagetsudō Kishū

Katsukawa Shunshō

1726–1793, active 1768–92

Shunshō's first woodblock prints were published in the spring of 1768. Most of his prints were portraits of kabuki actors, although he designed some pictures of women, calendar pictures and surimono. He designed a number of outstandingillustrated books, including those produced in collaboration with Bunchō (1770), Shigemasa (1776) and Shun'ei (1790). He was also one of the most accomplished painters of the ukiyo-e school and it has been suggested that he studied with Miyagawa Chōshun, Katsukawa Shunsui and Kō Sukoku. Nothing factual is known about his life, however, before the appearance of his first prints and it is even uncertain whether he was born in Edo or in the Kyōto–Ōsaka area. His first prints are unsigned and bear only a jar-shaped seal inscribed with the character *hayashi* (forest). This is said to have been the business seal used by Hayashiya Shichiemon, Shunshō's landlord at the time. Shunshō reverted to the seal from 11/1785 to 11/1786, when his friend, the actor Nakamura Nakazō I, changed his name to Nakayama Kojūrō. Shunshō retired from print design in 1787, after apparently accompanying Nakayama Kojūrō on a tour to Ōsaka. He resumed work around 1791, after the paralysis of his eldest pupil Shunkō, but died soon afterwards on the eighth day of the twelfth month of the fourth year of the Kansei period (19 January 1793 by the Western calendar).

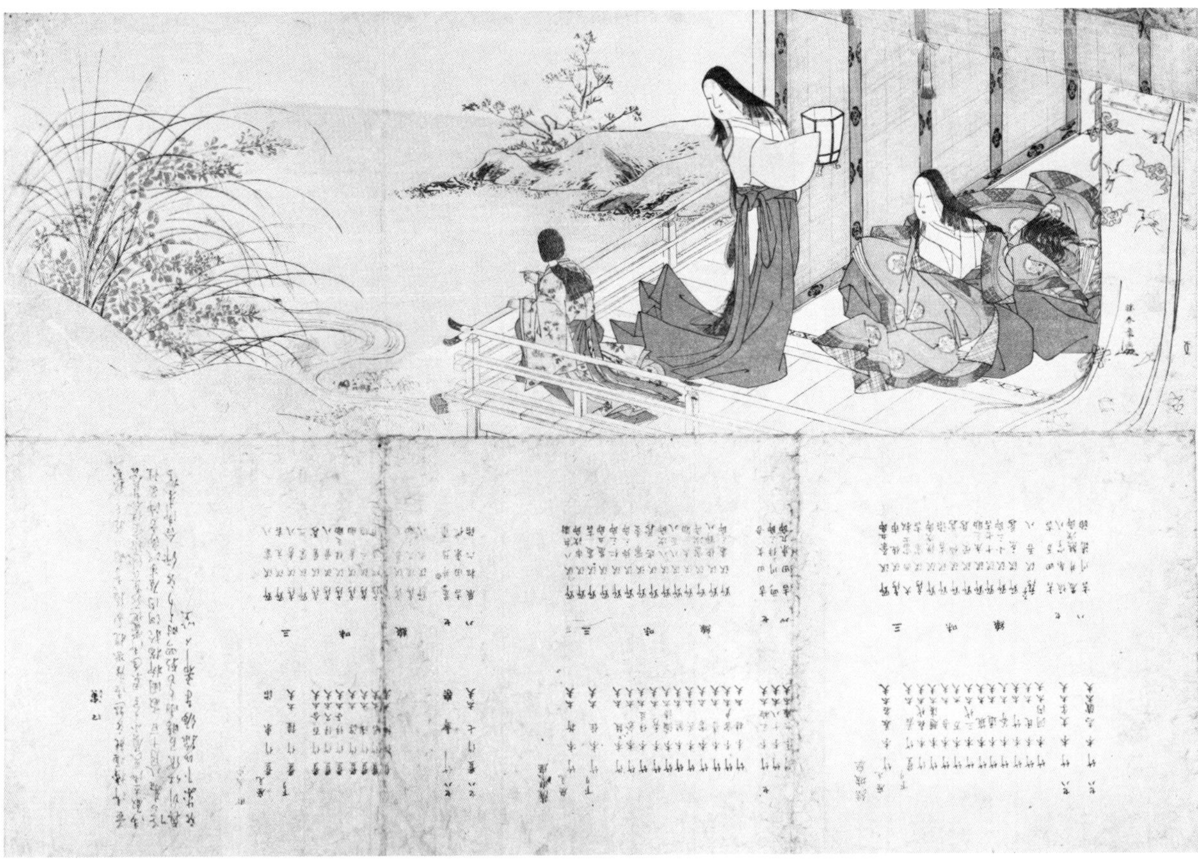

77

Court ladies on balcony by pond
probably 1772
40.5 × 55.7 cm
signed Katsu Shunshō ga
seal kakihan
Beatty 92 j

The inscription on the lower-left corner of the sheet announces a performance of *jōruri*, the chanted accompaniment to the puppet theater, to be held "rain or shine, at 9:30 in the morning of the eleventh day of the eighth month at the theater of Kawachiya Hanjirō at Yanagi Bridge in the Ryōgoku district" of Edo. The remainder of the text lists the chanters and samisen accompanists engaged at the three major Edo puppet theaters, the Hizen, the Satsuma and the Yūki, who are to appear at this performance. One performer at each theater is described as *kudari*, that is, as having "come down" to Edo from Ōsaka; the Ōsaka chanter performing at the Hizen theater is identified as Toyotake Kanedayū I. Kanedayū was born in Ōsaka in 1731 and died there in 1779; his only visit to Edo began in 1772 and he returned to Ōsaka in the third month of 1774. Since the word *kudari* was usually pre-

fixed to the names of performers who had recently arrived from the Kyōto–Ōsaka area, the print was probably published soon after Kanedayū's arrival in 1772.

Although Shunshō is best known for his actor portraits, in the early 1770s he designed a series of color prints illustrating scenes from the *Tales of Ise.* The court ladies in those pictures were drawn in much the same style as the women in this print and the square, formal script of the signature on those prints is like Shunshō's signature on the surimono.

The extra soiling along the folds in the textual area indicates that the surimono was presented with the announcement side facing out. When the sheet was turned and opened, the viewer first saw the bush clover by the water; further unfolding revealed the women in the house. The lantern held by the standing woman throws a ray of light to the left side of the print above an area in shadow. It is one of the earliest examples of this effect in Japanese prints. The print is also the earliest dated example now known of a picture announcing a particular event and is therefore one of the earliest surimono.

Katsukawa Shuntei

1770–1820, active from late 1790s

A pupil of Katsukawa Shun'ei, he designed a number of book illustrations and single-sheet prints of warriors, women, actors and Western-style landscapes; he also designed a few surimono.

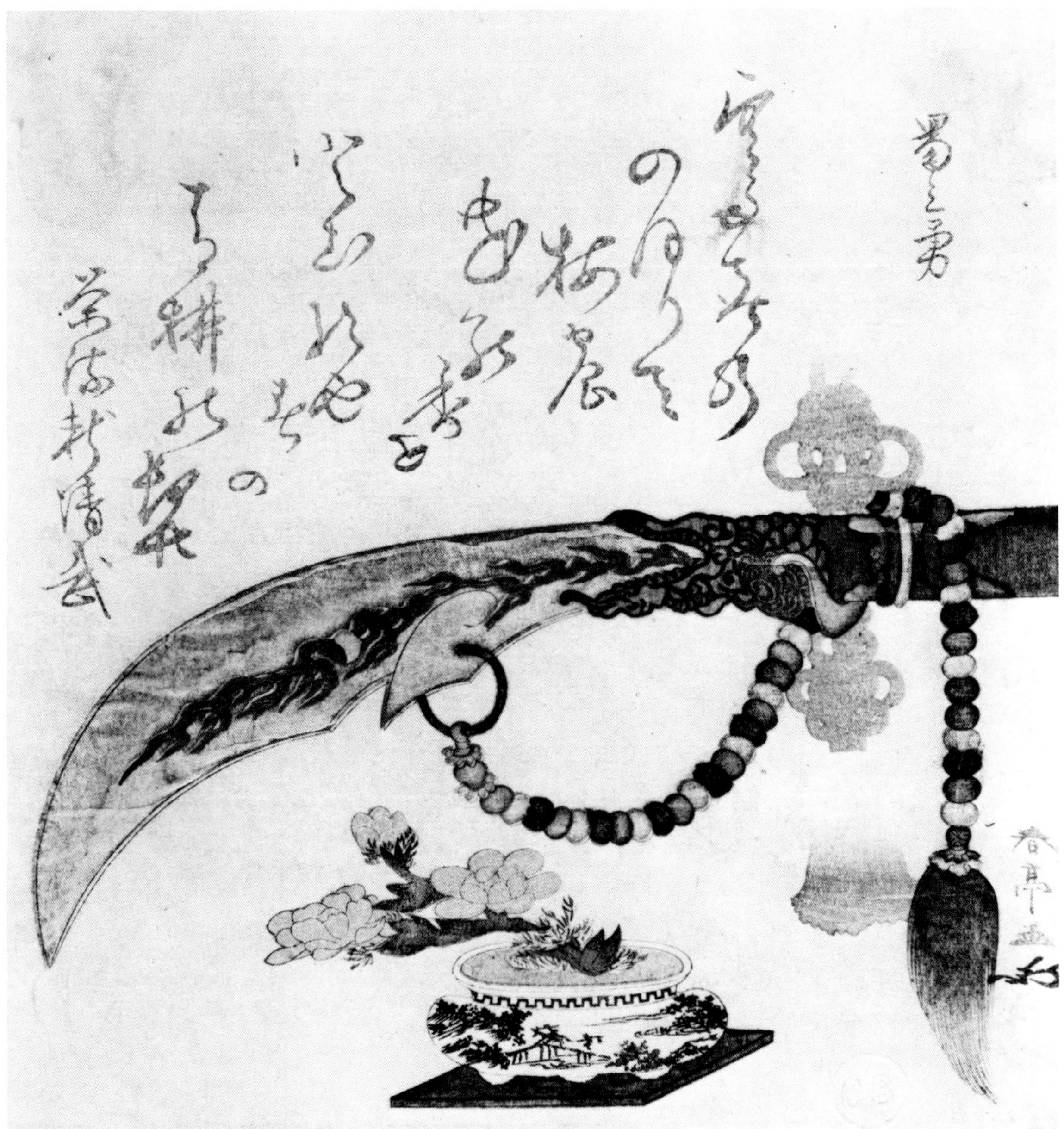

78

	Halberd, flowering adonis and knotted cord
series	Three Heroes of the State of Shu
	c. mid or late 1810s
	19.5 × 18.2 cm
signed	Shuntei ga
seal	kakihan
	Beatty 1009

The magnificent halberd, with its blade emerging from the hilt like a fiery breath from a dragon's mouth, is a symbol of Guanyu, one of the Three Heroes of the State of Shu during the second century AD. Guanyu's exploits are described in the Chinese novel, *Romance of Three Kingdoms;* he was tall and powerful and had a long black beard. The poet compares the beard to the branches of a spring willow; the "singing voice" belongs to a warbler. Shuntei probably designed two more prints with symbols of Zhang Fei and Liu Bei, the other heroes of the state of Shu. The calligraphy on this print is bolder and the gray ink is paler than on most surimono.

Utagoe no noborite ume no hana no ka o tomuru ya haru no aoyagi no hige

"The singing voice rises with the fragrance of the plum blossoms and rests in the beard of the green spring willow"   *Saryūken Kiyotake*

Hishikawa Sōri

active 1797–*c.* 1813

When Hokusai gave up the name Sōri in 1798, it was adopted by one of his early pupils, Rinsai Sōji. After Hokusai changed his name to Taito in 1810, Sōri may have taken the name Hokusai and designed a few surimono, the latest being for the spring of 1813 (see cat. no. 46).

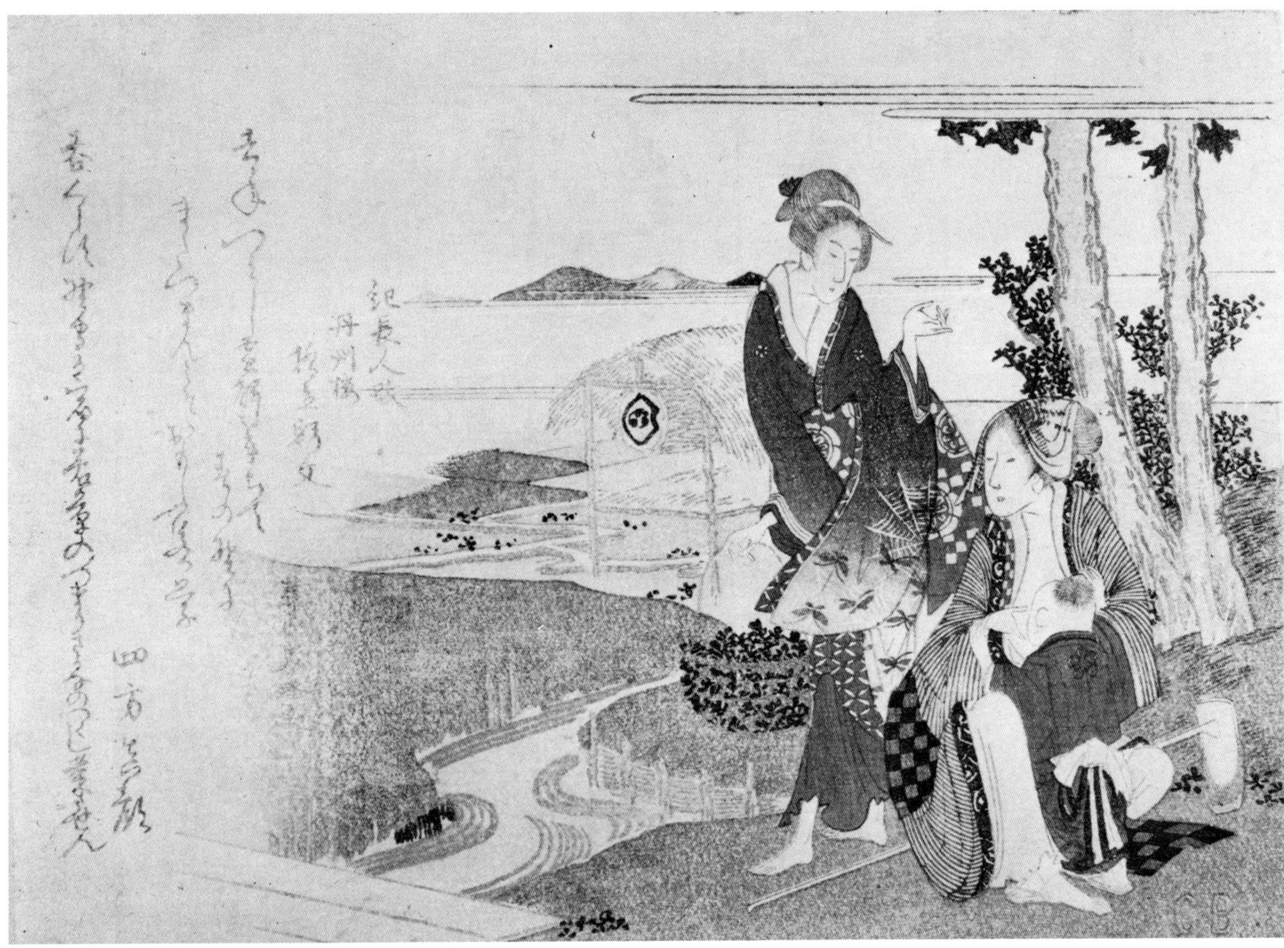

79

Two women beside a stream
1800–05
13.8 × 18.6 cm
signed Hishikawa Sōri ga
Beatty 2245

A peasant woman kneels beside her mattock
and nurses her child as a barefoot woman in
more elegant town robes stands beside her
with a basket of spring herbs. Behind them is
a temporary structure built in the rice fields;
hanging from one end is a plaque with the
emblem of the Yomo poetry group. The print
announces that Ki no Nagando is changing his
name to Tanshūrō Hashidate Mifumi. He
must have been a provincial poet, because the
first two characters in his secondary name,
Tanshū, mean the "province of Tan," that is
to say Tango, a coastal region on the western
side of Honshū. Hashidate is an abbreviation
of Amanohashidate, the most famous scenic
spot in Tango Province. His personal name,
Mifumi, means "honorable letter," and is
taken from a celebrated classical poem by

Koshikibu no Naishi which mentions
Amanohashidate.

Both poems mention *wakakusa*, the first
young grass of spring. There are puns in the
second poem on *nomi* (drink) and *nomori*, the
man whose duty it was to watch and protect
the rice fields; and on *tsuma* (wife) and *tsumu*
(to pick). It is not clear why she should cook
horsetails to go with his fish.

*Kozo tsumishi yukige o machite haru no no ni mata
tsuman tozo omou wakakusa*

"As I wait for last year's snow to melt, I think
of being in spring fields again picking young
grass"
　　　　　Tanshūrō Hashidate Mifumi,
　　　　　formerly Ki no Nagando

*Nomi kurasu nomori ga yado ni wakakusa no
tsuma ka sakana no tsukushi nisasen*

"Drinking away, the watchman of the fields
stays at home, with a wife like young grass;
can he make her cook some horsetails to go
with his fish?"
　　　　　Yomo Magao

Katsushika Taito II

active mid 1810s–*c.* 1850

Taito was a samurai of the Toyooka clan, who originally lived in Yamashita in Kōzuke Province. He seems to have met Hokusai in Nagoya in the mid 1810s and collaborated with him on the second volume of *Hokusai manga,* "The Hokusai Sketchbooks," which was published there in 1815. He moved to Edo and took the name Taito II in or after 1820, when Hokusai changed his own name to Iitsu. He designed a few square surimono around the late 1820s and early 1830s and sometime afterwards moved to Ōsaka. His last dated work was an illustrated book published in 1850. Although it may only be coincidence, the first two characters in the *gō* Toenrō, which Taito used in 1815, make up the name of the engraver and printer Toen, whose seal appears on calendar pictures designed by Hokusai and others in the mid 1790s.

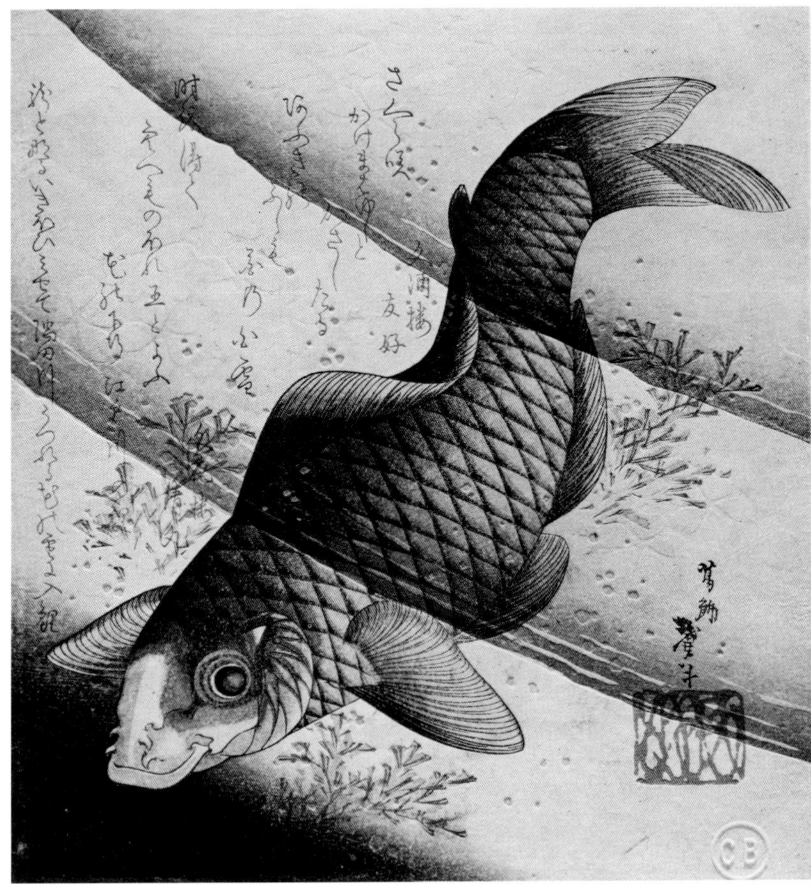

80

Carp swimming among waterweeds
probably 1832
20.8 × 18.4 cm
signed Katsushika Taito
seal undeciphered
Gonse; Beatty 2235

This striking print, one of Taito's finest surimono, seems to have been based on a surimono by Gakutei published around the middle of the 1820s. Taito's carp is more supple
than Gakutei's and has a more humorous
expression. The sketchy rendering of the
waterweeds gives the fish more prominence in
Taito's print; the colored bands of water give
more drama to the picture; the embossed
cherry blossoms contribute an effect of trans-
parency to the water and give the picture a
remarkable depth.

   Since the last poem recalls the legend of the
carp changing into a dragon, the print may
have been published in 1832, a Dragon Year.
The surimono probably predates Taito's finest
commercially published print, a large upright
sheet in the *ōban* format with a picture of a
carp swimming upwards through waterweeds

on the right and a panel of calligraphy on the
left. In the first verse, the poet holds a fan
painted with a view of Mt Fuji. In the second
poem, the carp is compared to cherry blossoms, king of the flowers. The third poem
may have prompted Taito's design.

*Sakura saku kage mabayushi to kazashitaru ogi no
fuji mo hana no shirayuki*

"Cherry trees in bloom so bright I raise my
fan: its Fuji, too, is covered with a white
snow of flowers"   *Bunshūrō Tomoyoshi*

*Toki o ete sora e mo nobore o to yobu hana no
shitayuku edogawa no koi*

"Seize the time, climb even to the sky, oh
carp, moving beneath the kingly flowers on
the Edo River"   *Bunkaro Kiyomaru*

*Tatsu to naru ikioi misete sumidagawa utsureru
hana no kumo ni iru koi*

"It turns into a dragon, shows its strength,
the carp that enters the cloud of flowers reflected in the Sumida River"   *Bumbunsha*

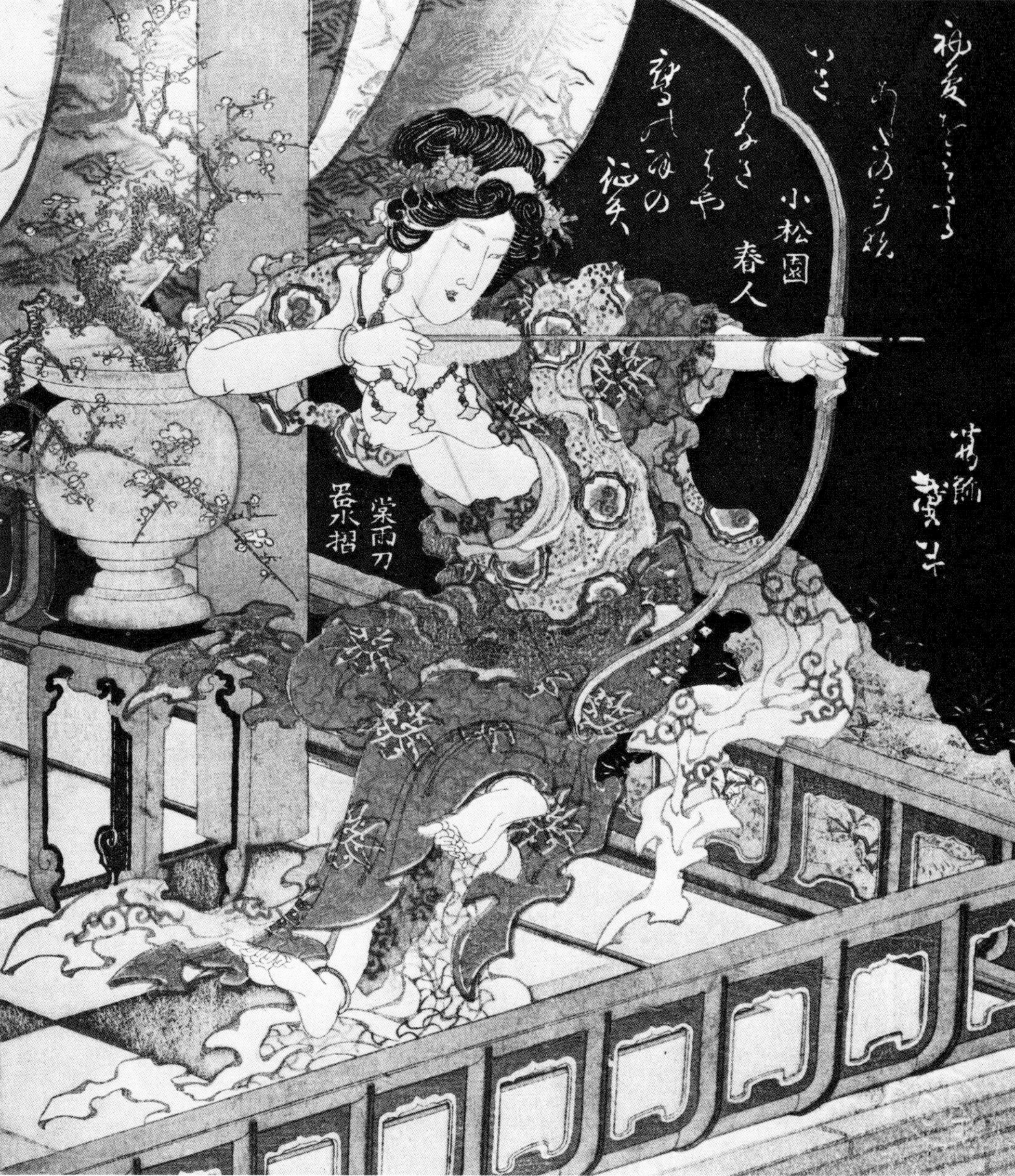

81

Seated woman with a bow
perhaps 1832
21.4 × 18.3 cm
signed Katsushika Taito; engraved by Tōu tō;
printed by Kisui suri
Tuke; Beatty 282

As the woman's elaborate costume and jewelry are neither Chinese nor Japanese, she is probably meant to represent Kayō Fujin, the consort of Prince Hanzoku in tropical India. Kayō Fujin was the first incarnation of a magic nine-tailed fox who appeared successively as a consort to rulers in India, China and Japan. In Japan, the fox appeared as

Tamamo no Mae and disrupted the imperial court until it was exorcised by the court astrologer, Abe no Seimei. A dragon is printed in silver on the curtain in the background and the print may have been published in 1832, a Dragon Year. The falcon-feathered arrow is mentioned in the poem because the falcon was one of the Three Lucky Dreams of the New Year.

Hatsuyume o mitaru ashita no yumi no tsuru iza hanasabaya taka no ha no soya

"In my dream I saw it: in the morning I will string my bow and shoot the falcon-feathered arrow"   *Shōshōen (Komatsuen) Harundo*

Tsutsumi Tōrin

Tōrin III was active from the 1790s until the first quarter of the nineteenth century. When he died in the early 1830s, he was over eighty. He designed a certain number of album sheets, surimono, *harimaze* (cut-out) sheets and fan prints, but he was principally famous during his lifetime as a masterly decorative painter of votive pictures, festival lanterns and banners; he also received numerous commissions to paint buildings at shrines and temples. He was a master of shell work and other crafts, organizing public exhibitions of wicker sculpture and other forms of decorative art. He was greatly admired for his technical skill, particularly among craftsmen; practically every decorative painter of the period, in the Kyōto–Ōsaka area as well as in Edo, was either his direct pupil or imitated his style.

One of the artist's earliest paintings is a votive picture of Hanshin at Sensō Temple in Asakusa, on which he announces a change of name from Shūgetsu to Tōrin III. From the mid-nineteenth century onwards, all biographers of the Tsutsumi artists have known of this painting and its signature. Since they assumed that the founder of the Tsutsumi school had been Tōrin I, they reasoned that there must have been another artist active at the end of the eighteenth century named Tōrin II. But the founder of the Tsutsumi school did not call himself Tōrin I and no works have ever appeared, as far as I know, that can be attributed to a late eighteenth-century Tōrin II.

A more reasonable explanation of Shūgetsu's claim to be the third artist to use the name Tōrin lies in his bold claim, also documented in the middle of the nineteenth century, that he was the thirteenth-generation descendant of the great ink painter of the fifteenth century, Sesshū. The only way an artist of the Edo period could legitimately claim descent from Sesshū was through association with the Unkoku school, which in the late sixteenth century had achieved official recognition of its artistic descent from him. Indeed, the first painter to use the name Tōrin was an early eighteenth-century painter of the Unkoku school. There is no documented relation between this artist, a pupil of Tōchaku and a native of Naruto, and the Tōrin who founded the Tsutsumi school, but Tōrin III did not need to be able to prove a relationship between the two in order to claim one. Until contradictory evidence comes to light, I think we should consider the Unkoku-school artist as Tōrin I and the founder of the Tsutsumi school as Tōrin II. Tōrin III had a daughter named Fuki, who designed a long surimono signed Saki no Tōrin musume Fuki; this reference to the "former Tōrin" suggests that for some time the artist worked under another name.

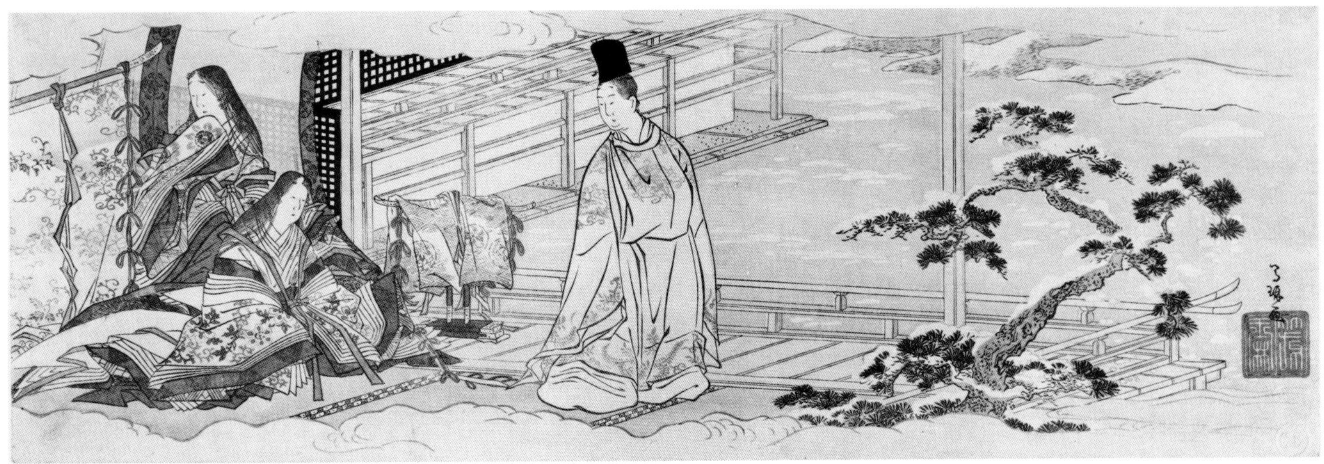

82

Courtier and two court ladies

c. 1790s

18.5 × 51.8 cm

signed Tōrin ga
seal Tōrin

Beatty 1236

The picture is designed like a section of a painted handscroll; yellow clouds edged with light brown frame the scene. A courtier of the Heian court looks down at a kneeling woman dressed in full court robes; outside the room, snow remains in patches on the light green ground of the courtyard and caps the branches of the pine tree. The colors of the print are delicate and mica is used on the seated woman's robes. Tōrin very rarely drew classical subjects; most of his prints are of peasants or workmen and are drawn in a deliberately awkward style.

Utagawa Toyoharu

1735–1814, active 1770s

Chiefly remembered as a designer of *uki-e*, or "perspective prints," Toyoharu had a far-reaching influence on ukiyo-e as the teacher of Toyokuni and Toyohiro, and the founder of the Utagawa school. He was born either in Toyooka in Tajima Province, or in Usuki in Bungo Province, studied with the Kanō-style painter Tsuruzawa Tangei in Kyōto and, later, under the name Toyofusa, with Toriyama Sekien in Edo. He may also have been influenced by the ukiyo-e print designers Nishimura Shigenaga and Ishikawa Toyonobu. He seems to have based his artistic clan name, Utagawa, on the name of the district in Edo where he lived, Udagawachō.

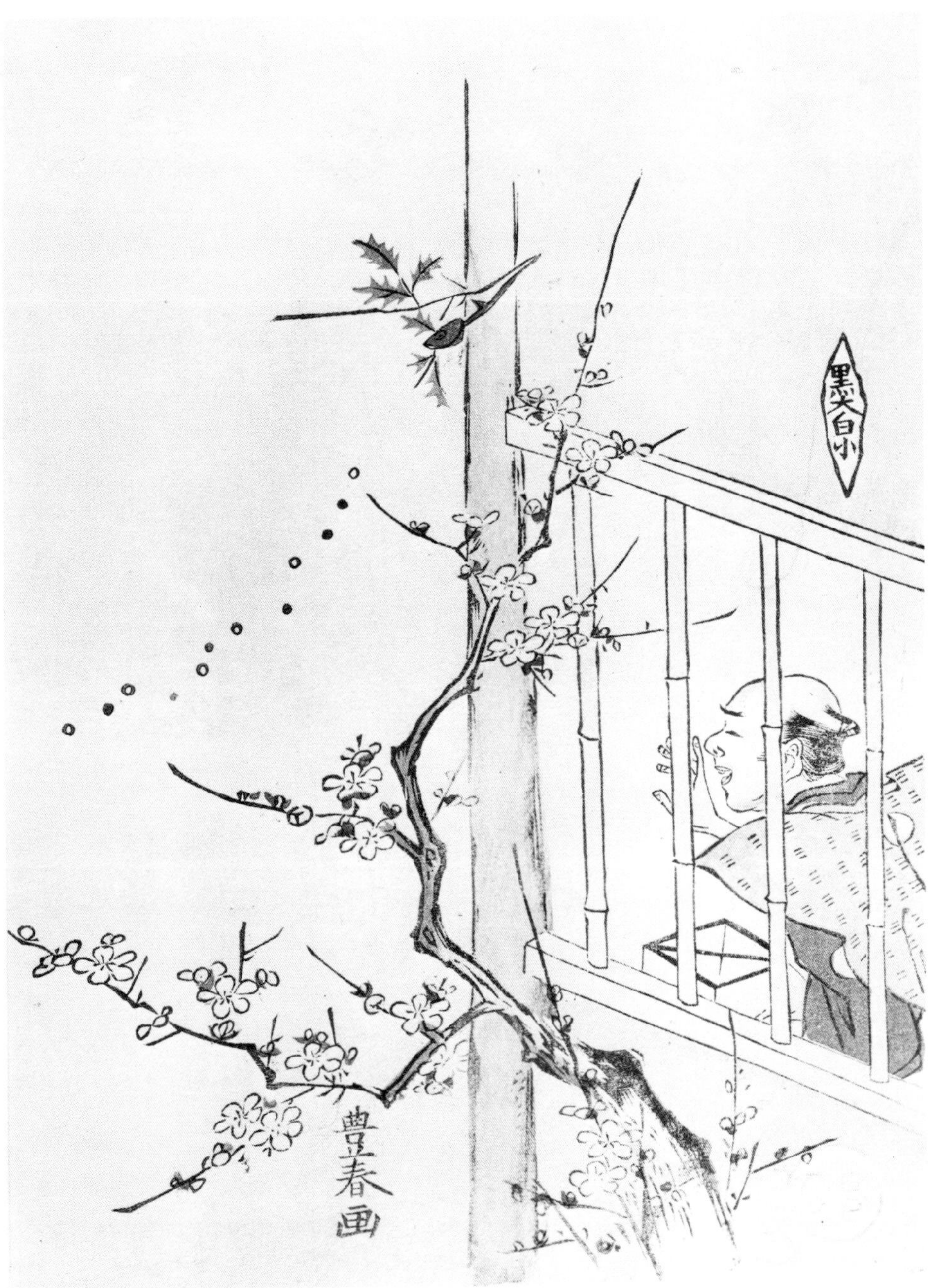

83

Man throwing beans to exorcise devils
1774
17.2 × 12.1 cm
signed Toyoharu ga
Beatty 2222

Bean throwing was a popular ritual performed at *setsubun*, the vernal equinox, to purify one's house. A member of the family would throw beans from the doorways crying: "Devils out, fortune in." Many woodblock prints of the subject show legendary historical figures throwing the beans and devils cowering from the onslaught. In Toyoharu's print, the head of the household is dressed in ceremonial robes. He is standing at the entrance to his house holding the wooden box that contains the beans. A plum tree blossoms beside the window and a decoration of a sardine head and holly leaves hangs on the post. This is a picture calendar for 1774. The inscription at the right says tht the black beans indicate the long months and the white beans the short months in the year. The sequence of long months reads, from top to bottom, 2, 3, 5, 7, 9 and 11.

Unsigned surimono

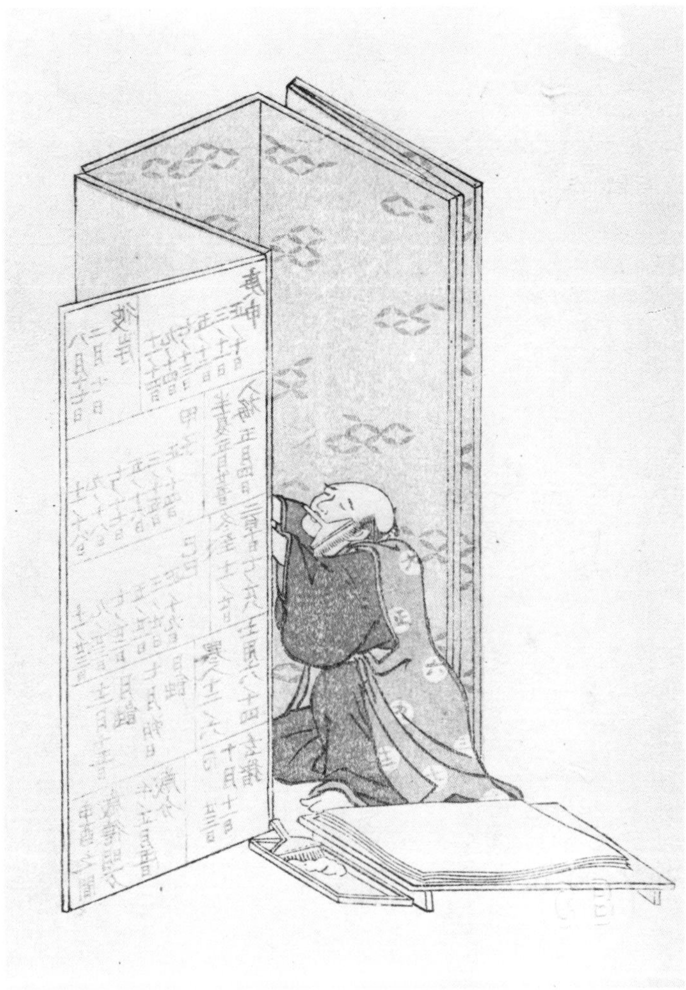

84

Mounter applying backing paper to a folding
screen
1785
13.7 × 9.4 cm
Beatty 2213

This is one of the most ingenious and charm-
ing of the early picture calendars. The Japanese folding screen was a wooden frame over
which several layers of laminated paper were
stretched as cushioning. Scrap paper was
often used to build up these layers and each
panel was usually covered by a picture on the
front and decorative paper on the back. The
mounter is kneeling by the screen; the circles
on his over-robe contain the character *dai*,
which means "large" or "long," and the numbers for the long months of 1785: 1, 3, 6, 7,
9, 10 and 12. On the floor beside him is a
wooden tray with sheets of gray backing paper arranged with their uncolored sides up.
The trough at the side of the tray contains
paste and a paste brush. The mounter has
applied paste to the back of one of the sheets
and carefully positions it on the screen panel;
when it is in place, he will set it with strokes
of the dry brush he holds in his mouth. The
unfinished panel facing the viewer is covered
with writing that looks like pages from an
outdated printed almanac. The writing is gray
because the sheets have been pasted on to the
screen face down and we are looking at the
back of the pages, with the writing showing
through in reverse. These sheets are a miniature almanac for 1785. The Japanese calendar
was organized on cycles of sixty days and
sixty years, counted by the regular combinations of two sets of calendrical signs. Three of
these recurring combinations were particularly
important in Japanese astrology and their
dates throughout the year are given on the
three largest panels. The other panels give the
exact dates of the two solstices and the begin-
nings of other important seasonal divisions of
the year.

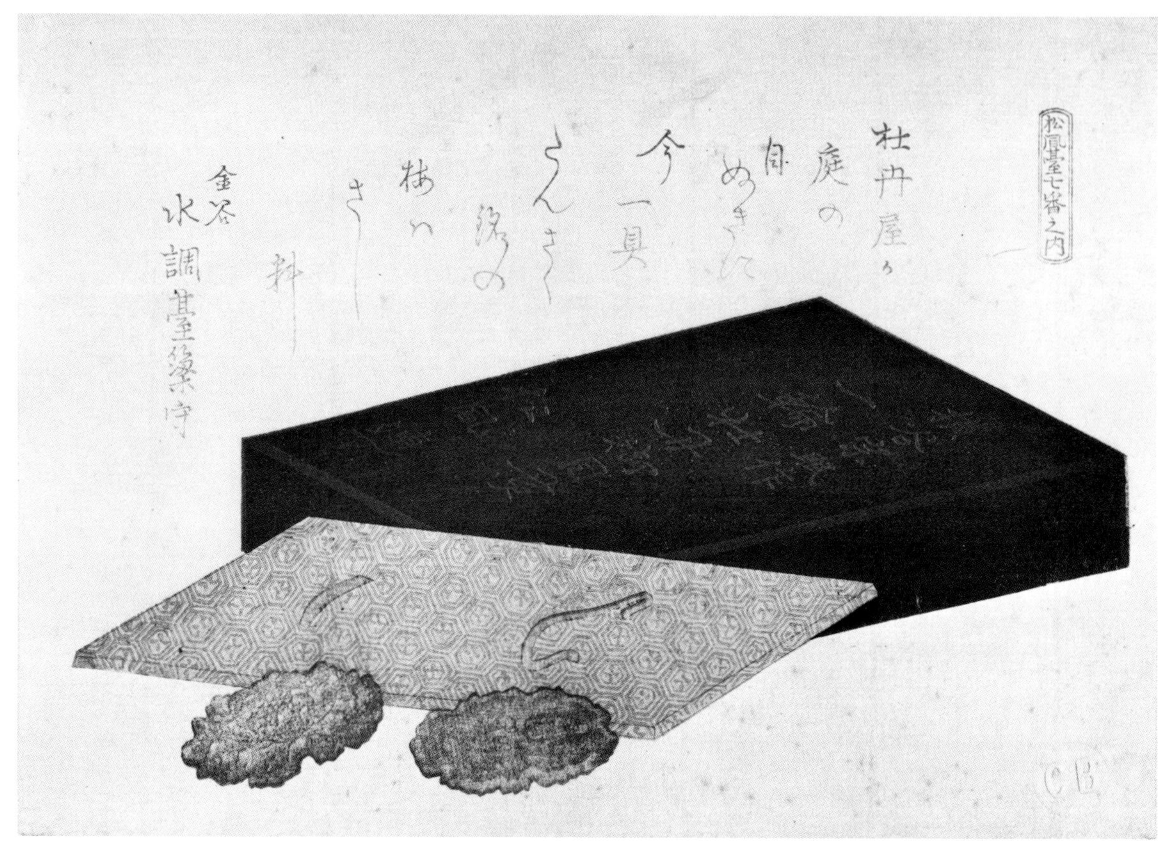

85

Black lacquer box with two gold sword-hilt
ornaments
series Seven Pictures for Shōfūdai
1810s
14.1 × 19.1 cm
Solf; Beatty 1040

The gold inscription carved on the cover of
the lacquer box says that it contains *menuki*,
sword-hilt ornaments, in the shape of single
peonies. They were made by Yokotani
Sōmin, a member of the Shōfū Circle, the
poetry group lead by Shōfūdai. *Botanya*, "The
Peony," was the name of a commercial establishment, or its proprieter, perhaps the person
who commissioned the sword fittings in the
picture. The long vertical signatures on sword
hilts reminded the poet of the narrow poem
slips that were often hung on the branches of
blossoming plum trees.

*Botanya ga niwa no menuki ni ima ichigu
tanzakumei no ume wa sashiryō*

"Peonies are the hilt ornaments of the garden
of Botanya; the plum tree with a signature on
a poem slip is the sword"
    Suichōdai Yanamori of Kanaya

Yabu Chōsui
active 1830–64

Painter, illustrator and calligrapher; son of the
painter and calligrapher Yabu Kakudō.

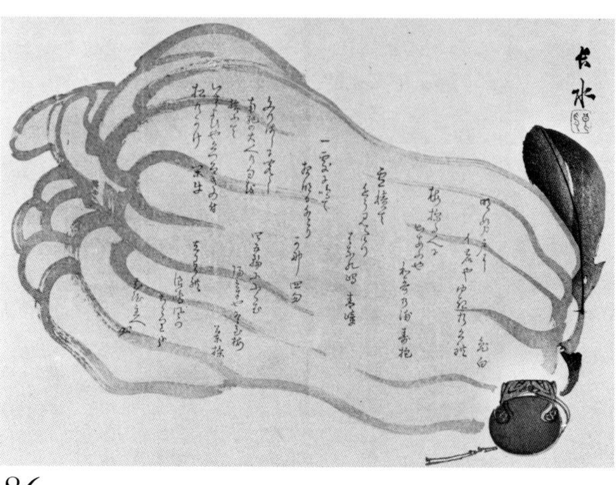

86
Gourd and toy bell
late 1850s or early 1860s
signed Chōsui
seal Ryō in

Gikei
active 1863
Possibly Takamatsu Gikei

A haiku poet and calligrapher active in
the 1810s, who originally worked in the
style of Gekkyo.

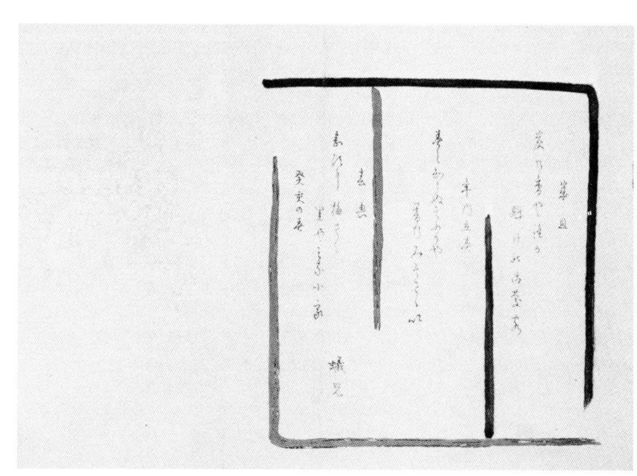

87
Abstract design in red and green
1863
signed Gikei

Gikei designed the pattern to separate his
three haiku, which are titled "New Year,"
"The Beginning of Spring" and "Spring Entertainment." The engraving reproduces the
rough strokes of the poet's brush.

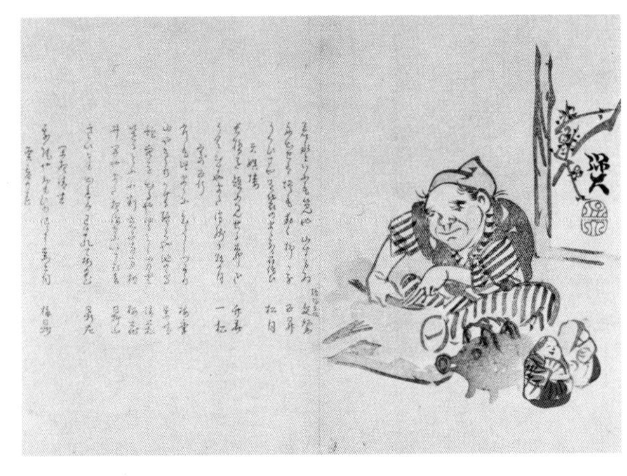

Satō Hodai

active 1830s–early 1860s

Possibly the leader of the Shōgōsha poetry group,
using the poetry name of Eminoya (q.v.).

88
Doll maker fashioning a boar of *papier-maché*
1863
signed Hodai
seal Hodai

Hodai's picture was published in 1863, a Boar
Year.

Kisui

active *c.* 1880s

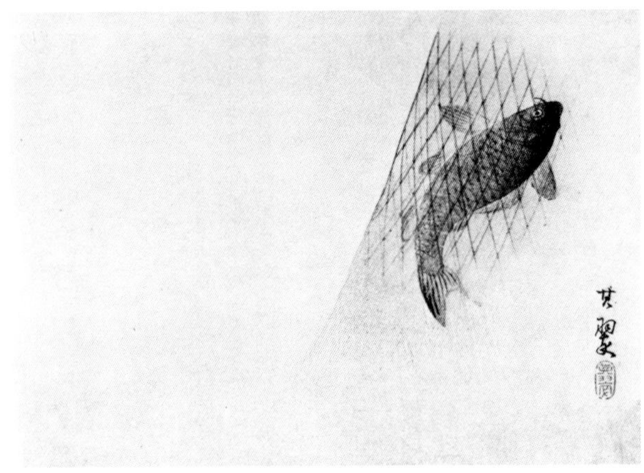

89
Fish in net
last quarter nineteenth century
signed Kisui
seal Kisui
19.1 × 26.3 cm
Beatty 1001

The fish is caught in the net which is being
lifted from the blue water at the bottom of the
print. This was probably not a privately commissioned picture, but it is included here because of its similarity in style. It is not from
one of the four albums that contain the majority of the Shijō surimono in the collection.

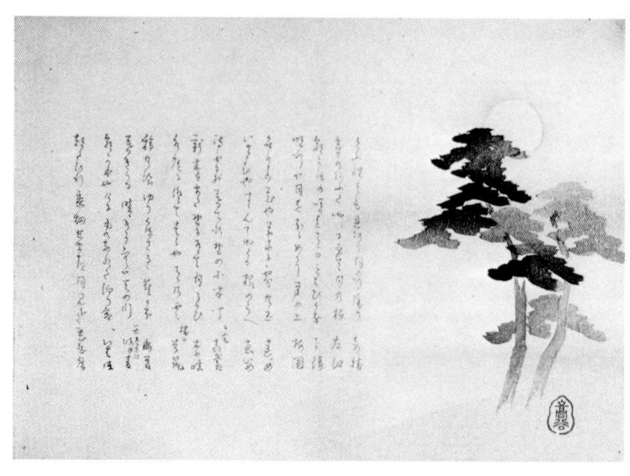

Kō Sūkoku II
1799–1876

The son of Kō Sūkei and the adopted
son of Kō Sūkoku I, this artist began
his career with the name Sūsui; he
moved from Edo to Ōsaka in 1849.

90
Moon and pine trees
late 1850s or early 1860s
seal Sūkoku

The poems are about the moon.

Shibata Zeshin
active 1807–91

The son of an Edo tobacconist, he
studied lacquer making at the age of
eleven, and painting with Suzuki
Nanrei at the age of sixteen. He later
studied painting with Okamoto
Toyohiko, literature with Kawara Keiju
and Rai Sanyō, haiku poetry and the
tea ceremony; one of the most
important painters and lacquer artists of
the late nineteenth century.

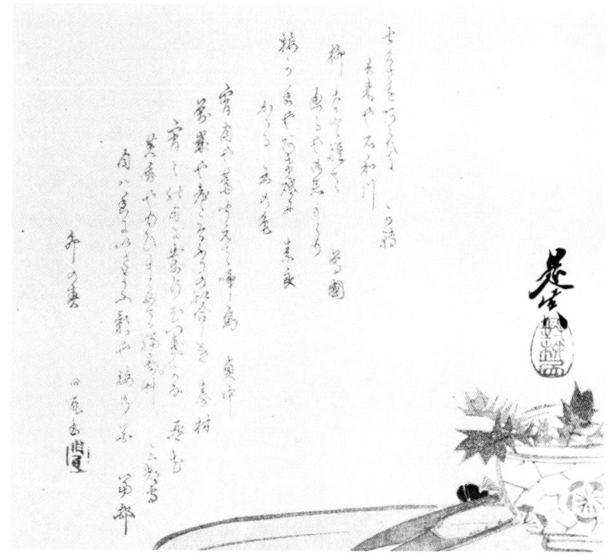

91
Tray with scissors and leaves in porcelain
bowl
perhaps 1855
20.2 × 18.3 cm
signed Zeshin
seal Tairyūkyo
Beatty 998

The picture is dated "Spring, Rabbit Year,"
the first poem mentions the Seven Spring
Herbs. The signature of the calligrapher
Kyūga appears on the left, followed by his
seal. This print is not from one of the four
albums that contain the majority of the Shijō
surimono in the collection.

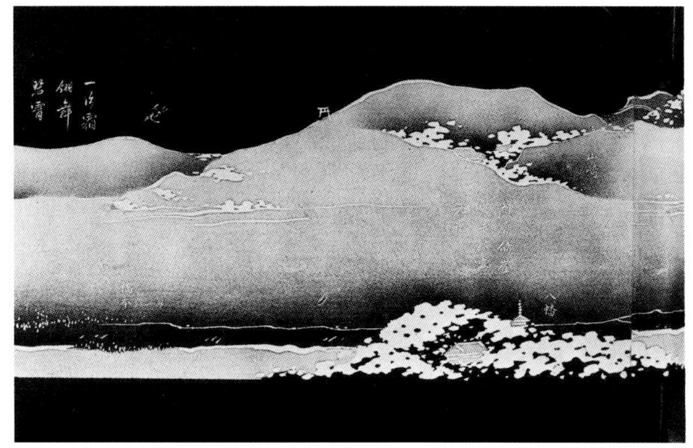
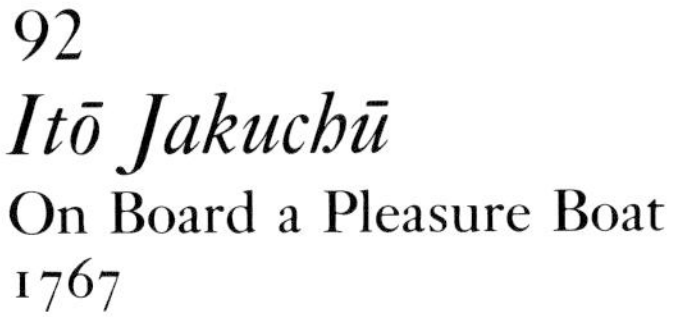
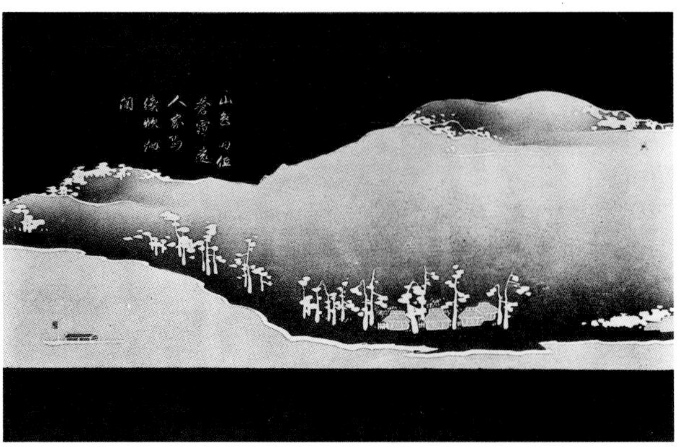

92

Itō Jakuchū

On Board a Pleasure Boat
1767

Handscroll, complete; 28.4 cm × 1147.6 cm;
brocade cover with original title slip engraved
in reserve, sealed Tōbeian. A continuous
landscape engraved and printed in *ishizuri*
style, that is to say in imitation of a stone
rubbing, with views along the Yodo River
near Ōsaka.

Inside the brocade cover a sheet of pink
paper 23.9 cm in length is followed by the
title in large characters on a single sheet of
50.9 cm length. The rest of the scroll is
printed on sheets of 14.7, 24.5 and 24.7 cm
length, carefully pieced together.

The following places are identified along
the river: Fushimizu kuchi, Yodo Castle,
Yamazaki, Yawata, Hashimoto, Takahama,
Maeshima, Otsuka, Makigata, Mishima,
Torikai, Hitotsuya, Tatsudō(?), Nagara,
Nijibashi ("Rainbow Bridge").

The scroll is signed Jakuchū ga, sealed Tō
Jokin in and Keiwa, and ends with a closing
note by the calligrapher Taishin describing
the circumstances under which he and Jakuchū
traveled together down the Yodo River to
Osaka in the spring of 1767. Only two other
examples of the scroll seem to be known; one
is now in the Rijksmuseum, Amsterdam, and
is reproduced in its entirety in Tsuji, *Jakuchū*,
pl. 75; the other is in the New York Public
Library. According to the Odin catalogue, the
box for the present example was inscribed
Yodogawa no zu, "Picture of the Yodo River."
The present box bears a handwritten title,
Jakuchū tōbeiō jōkyōshu, as well as the name of a
Japanese collector, Ashinoya shujin. The
scroll was sold to the dealer Hachette for 8200
francs at the Odin book sale in 1928, one of
the highest prices in the sale.

provenance Ashinoya shujin, Odin, Hachette
accession no CBL MS 93

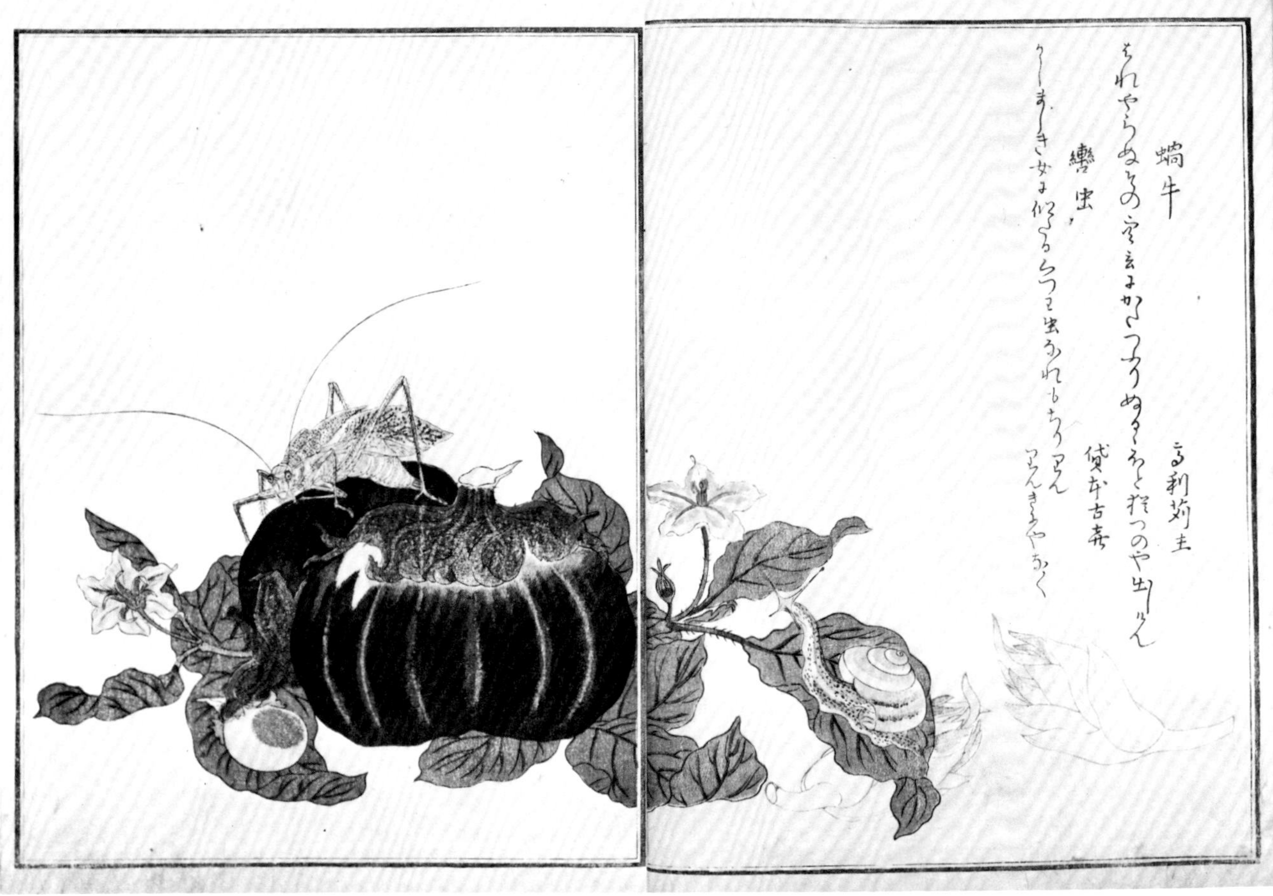

Kitagawa Utamaro
1753–1806, active from 1775

Utamaro's family probably came from Tochigi Prefecture. As a child he lived with the painter Toriyama Sekien and studied under him, using the art name Toyoaki. In the 1780s he lived for some time with the publisher Tsutaya Jūzaburō. Around 1782, he took the name Utamaro and in the next quarter century designed over 1200 single-sheet prints, over ninety illustrated books and albums, and a few surimono; he also produced a number of paintings, although the authenticity of many paintings attributed to him is in dispute. He specialized in pictures of women and was pàrticularly interested in distinguishing character and personality types. From around 1797 he developed an interest in women's relationships with men and children. About 1791 he simplified the character *uta* in his signature and around the spring of 1794 changed the last character in his signature on woodblock prints from *ga* to *hitsu*.

93

A Picture Book of Selected Insects or The Insect Book
1788

Two volumes, complete; 27.2 × 18.5 cm; original tan covers with geometric brown design and embossed cloth pattern; original red-patterned title slip. Twenty sheets, fifteen of them numbered, with fifteen color illustrations of insects, some of them printed with embossing and mica. Each picture is accompanied by kyōka verses about the insects depicted. The first two sheets of the first volume are both numbered "one."

VOLUME ONE

1a-1a (sic) Three-page preface by Yadoya Meshimori

1b-2a *Hachi, kemushi:* three wasps and hairy caterpillar on arrowroot plant

2b-3a *Umaoimushi, mukade;* grasshopper (*Locusta plantaris*) and centipede on aconite plant (*kabutogiku* or *torikabuto*)

3b-4a *Kera, hasamimushi;* mole cricket and earwig (*Dermaptera*) on bamboo shoot

4b-5a *Chō, tombo;* butterflies and dragonfly with poppies (*see illustration*)

5b-6a *Abu, imomushi;* horsefly on bindweed (*hirugao*) and white caterpillar on taro plant (*satoimo; Colocasia antiquorum*)

6b-7a *Matsumushi, hotaru;* cricket (*Calyptryphus marmoratus*) and fireflies on polygonum (*tade*) and reed (*yoshi; Phragmites communis*)

7b-(8a) *Batta, kamakiri;* grasshopper on bean pod (*sasage; Vagna sinensis*) and mantis on melon (*makuwa*)

(8b-9a) *Higurashi, kumo;* cicada and spider on corn

VOLUME TWO

1a Blank border without text

1b-2a *Akatombo, inago;* red dragonfly and locust by platycodon grandiflora (*kikyō*) and pinks (*nadeshiko*)

2b-3a *Hebi, tokage;* snake and lizard by *hotarugusa* bush (*Bupleurum sachalinense*)

3b-4a *Minomushi, kabutomushi;* basketworm and helmet beetle (*Xylotrupes dichtomus*) on bush clover (*hagi*) and *giboshi* plant (stone-leek flower or plantain lily; *Hosta undulata*)

4b-5a *Katatsuburi, kutsuwamushi;* snail and noisy cricket (*Mecapoda elongata*) on eggplant (*see illustration*)

5b-6a *Kirigirisu, semi;* katydid (*Platyphyllum concavum*) and cicada on gourd plant (*hechima; Luffa aegyptiaca*)

6b-7a *Mimizu, kōrogi;* earthworm and black cricket on creeping saxifrage (*Saxifraga sarmentosa*)

7b-(8a) *Kaeru, koganemushi;* frogs and gold bug by lotus

(8b) Colophon

    editor Yadoya Meshimori
    artist Kitagawa Utamaro
    publisher Tsutaya Jūzaburō, Kōshodō, Tōriaburachō
    date 1/1788

(9a-b) Two-page postscript by Toriyama Sekien, sealed Toriyama Toyofusa, dated Winter 1787

(10a) Advertisement of publications by Tsutaya Jūzaburō, Tōto, Motomachisuji Kitae, 8-chōme, Tōriaburachō, including: *Kokon kyōkabukuro, Azumaburi kyōka bunko, Kyōka saizōshū, Yomo no aka, Kyōka kei, Kyōshisen genkai, Ehon musha abumi* (illustrated by Kitao Shigemasa), *Ehon kotoba no hana* (illustrated by Kitagawa Utamaro), *Ehon sukiyagama* (illustrated by Kitagawa Utamaro), *Ehon momochidori* (illustrated by Kitao Shigemasa). The last two books are listed as soon to appear.

accession no CBL MS 75

A one-volume edition of the *Insect Book* is known; an example is in the New York Public Library (Sorimachi, 1968, 461). The book was frequently reprinted. As late as 1824, Philipp Frank van Siebold was given a copy of a two-volume edition, reprinted by Nishimura Yohachi in 8/1823. This example, in the Rijksmuseum voor Volkenkunde, Leiden, contains a new color frontispiece and advertisements for Utamaro's *Bird, Insect* and *Shell Books,* and for two works by Hokusai: *Imayō sekkin hinagata,* 3 vols (1822–23) and the large single-sheet print of *One hundred bridges,* which must have been first published around this date.

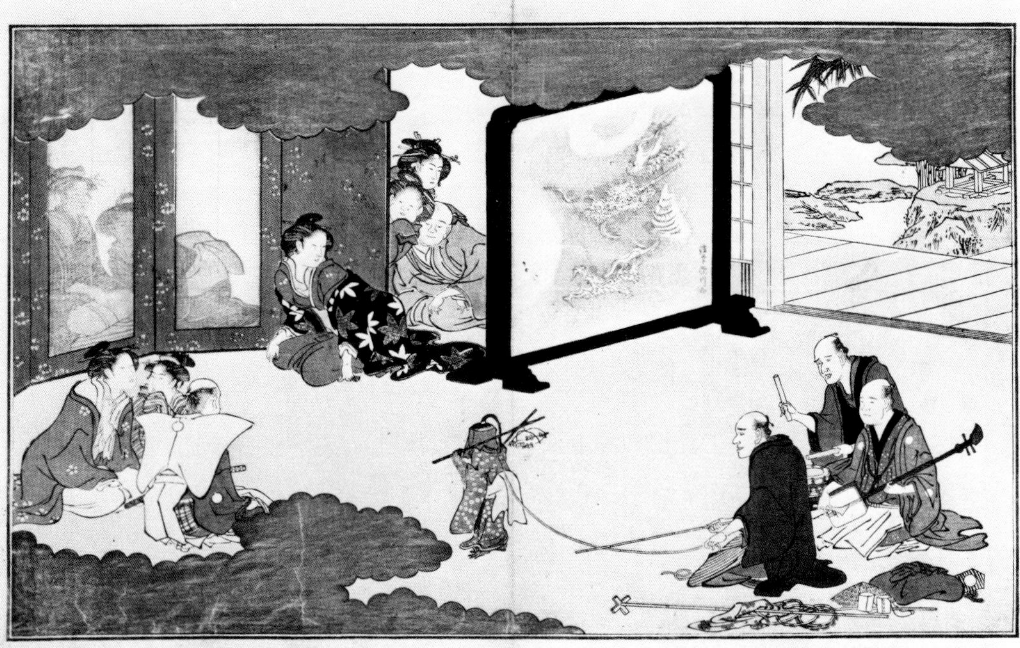

94

Verse for Ebisu
1/1789
One-volume album, complete; 25.6 ×
19.0 cm; original dark blue covers with hand-
painted gold decoration of cloud bands, pine
trees and grasses; original title slip on buff
paper, attached at left. Twelve unnumbered
sheets with five color illustrations, alternating
with pages of text.

1 Preface by Shikatsube Magao

2 Presentation of a black horse to the emperor
on the seventh day of the New Year; drawn
in Tosa style

3 Twelve kyōka verses, the first by Ki no
Sadamaru

4 *Manzai* dancers performing before a wealthy
household at New Year; drawn in the style of
Hishikawa Moronobu

5 Twelve kyōka verses, the first by Tsumuri
no Hikaru

6 Samurai carrying a child through the snow
at the New Year; apparently drawn in the
style of Suzuki Harunobu

7 Twelve kyōka verses, the first by Ichi no
Nakazumi

8 Lion dancers performing before a house at
the New Year; apparently drawn in the style
of Torii Kiyonaga

9 Twelve kyōka verses, the first by Ōya Urazumi

10 Monkey leader performing in a noble
household at the New Year (*see illustration*)

11 Twelve kyōka verses, the first by Kubo
Shumman

12 Postscript by Yadoya Meshimori, lacking
date; and colophon, giving the names of the
artist Kitagawa Utamaro (sealed Bokuen no in)
and the publisher Tsutaya Jūzaburō, Tōto,
Tōriaburachō

provenance Hayashi (seal at end of preface)
accession no CBL MS 70

The earliest examples of the book have the
date 1/1789 (*tori no hatsuharu*) on the final
page, after the postscript by Meshimori. Two
examples of the first edition are presently
known: one in the National Diet Library,
Tōkyō; the other in the Heinz Kaempfer collection, The Hague. For a discussion of the
book, advancing the idea that Utamaro was
consciously recapitulating the history of
ukiyo-e in his illustrations, see Keyes "Envi-
sioning the Past: Utamaro's album *Waka
Ebisu*." The last plate, of the monkey leader,
was adapted into a long surimono, signed
Utamaro hitsu, that was published around the
mid 1790s.

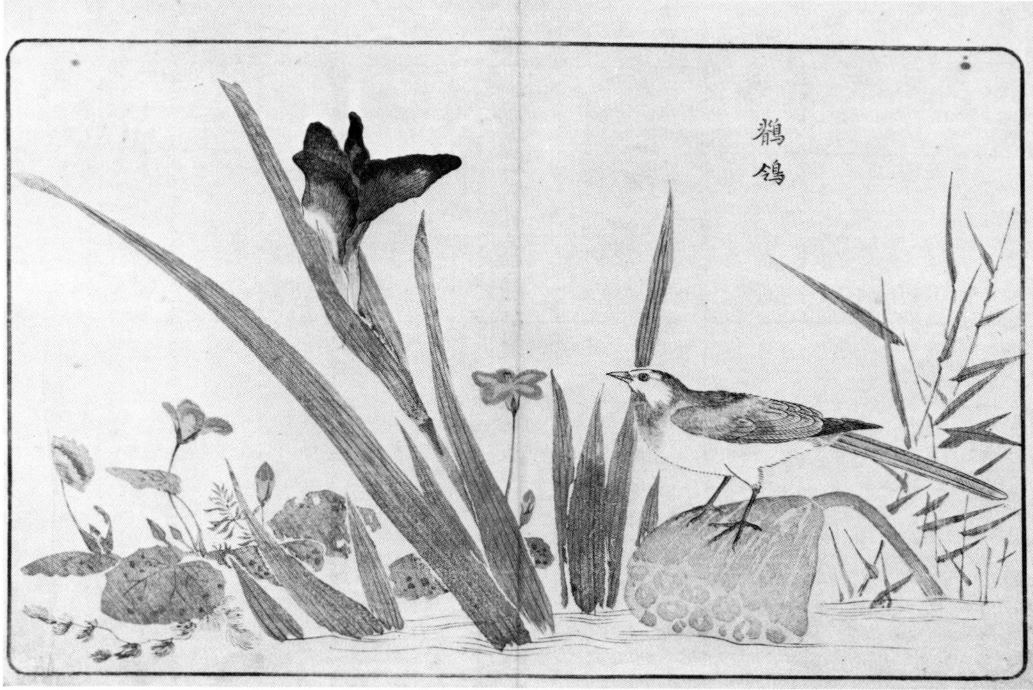

95

Kitao Masayoshi

A Compendium of Pictures of Birds Imported
from Overseas
2/1789

One-volume album, lacking colophon but
otherwise complete; 25.6 × 18.8 cm; original
dark blue covers; original buff title slip
mounted at center. Seventeen unnumbered
sheets, including twelve color illustrations, title page, preface and foreword.

1 Title page with inscription *Raikin zui,* "A
Compendium of Pictures of Birds," collected
by Fei Qinghu and Cheng Chichang of
Nanjing, published by Rokuyūsha

2 Preface in Chinese by Yushan Guan
Yingwen (Uzan Seki Eibun) of Shandung,
dated 9/1790 (*kansei ninen jōshō emmo heigetsu
kanoe inu ne [zame] zuki*); seals, Guan Yingwen
yin, another unread; calligraphy written by
Gungyokudō Teng Yuanyi (Tō Gengi), sealed
Gungyokudō sanjin

3–4 Foreword in Japanese explaining the circumstances under which the birds were
brought to Japan by Chinese and Dutch sea
captains. The pictures in the present volume
are said to be reduced facsimiles of paintings
by Kiyō Ishōsai Shusen, a Chinese artist who
produced more than one hundred pictures of

birds, and of foreigners and their ships. The
birds came to Japan from China and Indonesia
in 1788. Shusen's manuscript was seen by the
publisher Gungyokudō when it was brought
to Edo in 1789

5 Table of contents, with the birds' names
given in Japanese phonetic script and Chinese

6 *Nankinjin zu,* "Picture of Chinese"

7 *Jutaichō;* magpies on pine

8 *Gabichō;* bunting and cherry tree

9 *Kōri;* bush warbler and peonies

10 *Sekirei;* wagtail, iris and lotus (*see illustration*)

11 *Hakukan;* silver pheasants

12 *Chikukei;* quail and bamboo

13 *Hakutōō;* gray starling (*mukudori*) in loquat
tree

14 *Jūshimai;* finches and maple

15 *Yōkin;* falcon and camellia

16 *Shako;* partridges by cascade

17 *Chineesen op surroonden van Nankin,*
"Chinese from the vicinity of Nanking"

accession no CBL MS 32

This book is one of the masterpieces of Japanese book illustration; it was republished in

1793 with the title *Kaihaku raikin zui setsu*, according to KSM (*Raikin zue* according to Binyon & Sexton), either with an additional volume of explanatory text, or with the explanatory text in this example issued under separate covers as a second volume. At a later date the album seems to have been reissued again, this time with the signature Keisai added to each plate. Most individual impressions in public and private collections seem to be from this edition. According to a note in the Happer catalogue (Sotheby's, 26 April 1909, lot 398), the Chinese preface states that the two pictures of Chinese men were included in the work because "they were the importers of the birds and animals, and their likenesses would doubtless interest those who, not having been at Nagasaki, know nothing of foreigners." Two incomplete copies of an early edition of the book have been recorded: the De Goncourt copy (De Goncourt (1891), p. 184), which lacked the two pictures of the Chinese men, and the Kington Baker copy, lacking five of the birds.

The colophon at the end of the example in the British Museum, the only other example of the first edition of the book presently known, gives the following information:

artist Drawn from life by Kiyō Ishōsai Shusen; collected by Guan Yingwen; copied by Keisai Kitao Masayoshi
engraver Shumpūdo Ryūko
publisher Gungyokudō Matsumoto Zembei (who may also have been the calligrapher of the Chinese preface)
date 2/1789 (*kansei 1 tsuchinoto tori*)

There are also advertisements for second and third supplements that never appeared.

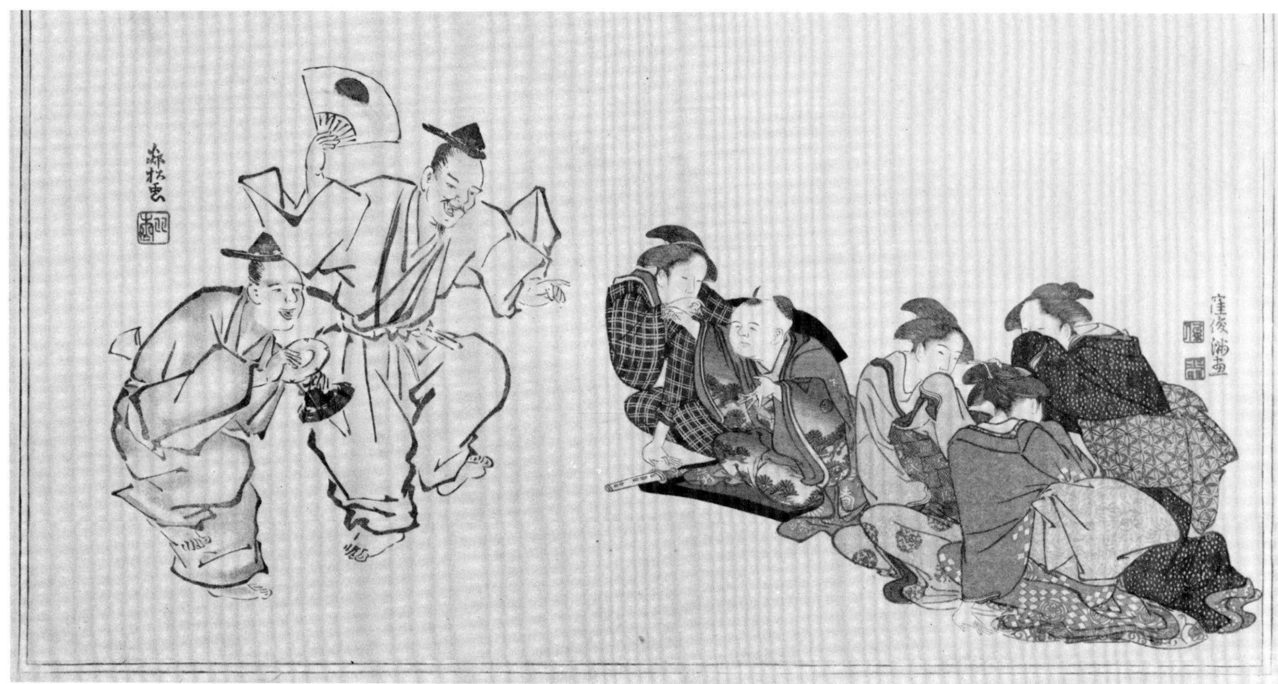

96

Suzuki Rinshō, Kitao Shigemasa, Kubo Shumman, Tsutsumi Tōrin and Kitagawa Utamaro

Colors of Spring
spring 1794

One-volume album, complete; 25.7 ×
18.8 cm; original dark blue covers, hand-
painted in gold with horizontal bands, pine
trees and grasses; original green title slip attached at left. Sixteen unnumbered sheets
with seven color illustrations.

1 Preface by Sōyōan (Tsumuri no Hikaru)
with seal of the Yomo Group, dated 1/1794
(kansei 6)

2 Calligraphy by Hajintei, seven kyōka
verses, the first by Fude no Yoshikasa

3 Mt Fuji from a bridge by Edo Castle,
sealed Unzan (another name of the artist
Tōrin)

4 Momotarō with demons, signed Rinshō ga,
with two illegible seals

5 Dancing child accompanied by two musi-
cians, signed Kitao Kōsuisai ga, sealed Kōsui
(Kōsuisai is another name of the artist
Shigemasa)

6 Old man holding a bare stick like a flute,
signed Tōrin hitsu, sealed Tōrin

7 Women and child watching *manzai* dancers.
The women are signed Kubo Shumman ga,
sealed Shumman; the dancers, signed Rinshō
ga, sealed Rinshō(?) (*see illustration*)

8 Peasants by bridge, signed Shōsadō Kubo
Shumman ga, sealed Shumman

9 Mirror polisher and court lady, signed
Utamaro ga; silver mica on mirror, lacquer on
workman's cap

10–16 Seven sheets of kyōka verse, the first
by Rakusuian Atsumaru; the last with eight
verses and the colophon:

calligrapher Kakei Ina Sadataka
    publisher Tsutaya Jūzaburō, Tōto, Tōriabur-
        achō Minami gawa
provenance Duret, Bing
accession no CBL MS

In most poetry anthologies published in the
1790s, the illustrations alternate with text.
However, the order of illustrations and verse
in an example of the book in the G. Pulverer
collection, Cologne, is identical to that described here. Inaba Kakei, also the calligrapher of two other albums in the collection,
died in 12/1800 (February 1801).

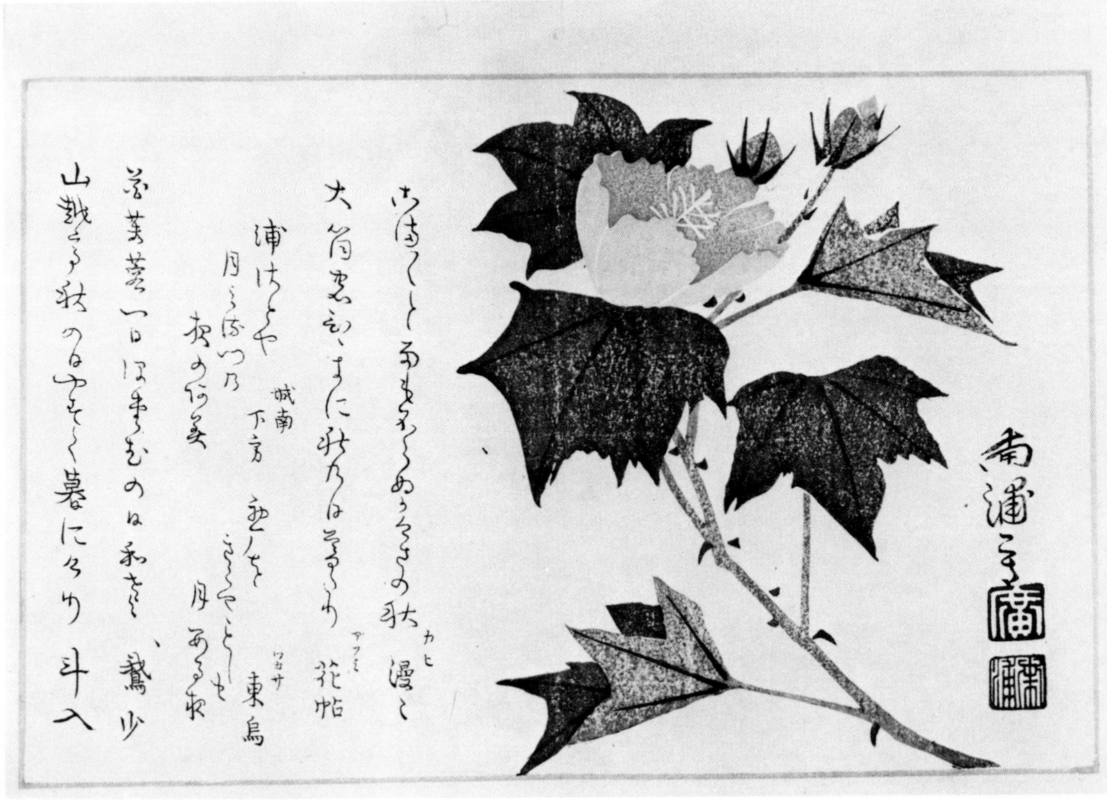

97

Hyakkajō

Album of One Hundred Flowers
1801
One-volume album, complete; 18.5 ×
12.6 cm; original yellow covers; original blue
title slip attached at center. Twenty unnumbered sheets with eighteen color illustrations
accompanied by haiku verse.

1 Preface by Gankōsha Kinsui, dated 12/1800
(January 1801)

2 Iris, signed Akaura Sekisō(?)

3 Gourd flower, signed Hakuyū

4 Peony(?) signed Shiga

5 Bush clover, signed Bumpō

6 *Kikyō (Platycodon grandiflora)*, signed Soken,
sealed Yamaguchi Sai

7 Red berries, signed Donga, sealed Donga

8 Blue flower, signed Kakutei

9 *Ominaeshi (Patrinia scabiosaefolia)*, signed
Genshō

10 Vine, signed Nangaku

11 Asters, signed Kunkei

12 Cricket and vegetable, signed Shira[kawa]
Shizan, sealed Keiko

13 Pink flowers, signed Araura Kanshi

14 Mallow, signed Nampō, sealed Kō(or
Hiro), Nampō (*see illustration*)

15 Pampas grass, signed Kofū

16 Chrysanthemums, signed Chikudō

17 Begonia, signed Hōkyō Sōen

18 Adonis, signed Tōbi

19 Cherry branch, signed Geppō

20 Postscript, signed Kajō(?) and a colophon:

date	autumn 1800
publisher	Kikusha Tahei, Kyōto, Sanjōdori Teramachi nishi
advertisements	one for *Hyakkajō*, volume two, and another for *Tamasudare*, nei- ther of which is recorded in KSM
provenance	Duret, Odin
accession no	CBL MS 76

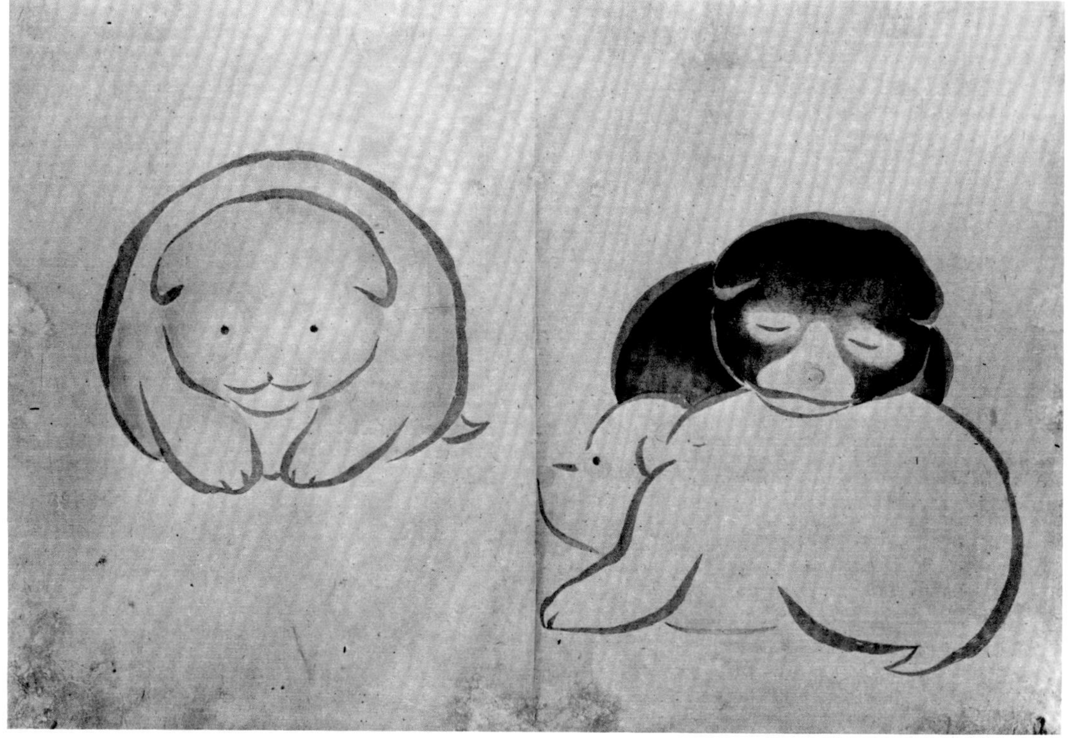

98

Nakamura Hōchū

An Album of Pictures by Kōrin
1802
Two-volume album, incomplete; 26.8 ×
19.0 cm; original(?) yellow paper covers; original buff title slips. Twenty-five unnumbered
sheets of thin paper with twenty-five illustrations with block-printed and hand-painted
color.

VOLUME ONE

1 Three turtles, sealed Ryūryoku

2 Three cranes, sealed Kakō

3 Six immortal poets

4 Plum branch, sealed Kakō

5 Peonies, sealed Ryūryoku

6 Two Taoist immortals, Tekka and Gama

7 Dandelions and blue flowers, sealed
Ryūryoku

8 Three puppies (*see illustration*)

9 Group in boat

10 Hollyhock, sealed Ryūryoku

11 Three rats, sealed Ryūryoku

12 Seven sages of the bamboo grove

VOLUME TWO

13 Musicians and Nō dancer

14 Morning glory and red flower

15 Jō and Uba by pine tree

16 Two doves, three sparrows

17 Blind man's buff

18 Four deer, sealed Kakō *see illustration*

19 Noblemen on bridge

20 Chrysanthemums, sealed Kakō

21 Descending geese and wave, sealed Kakō

22 Three women of Ōhara

23 Plovers and waves, gray background,
sealed Kakō

24 Daikoku, Ebisu and shrine dancer

25 Mt Fuji, sealed Kakō

provenance Odin
accession no CBL MS 22

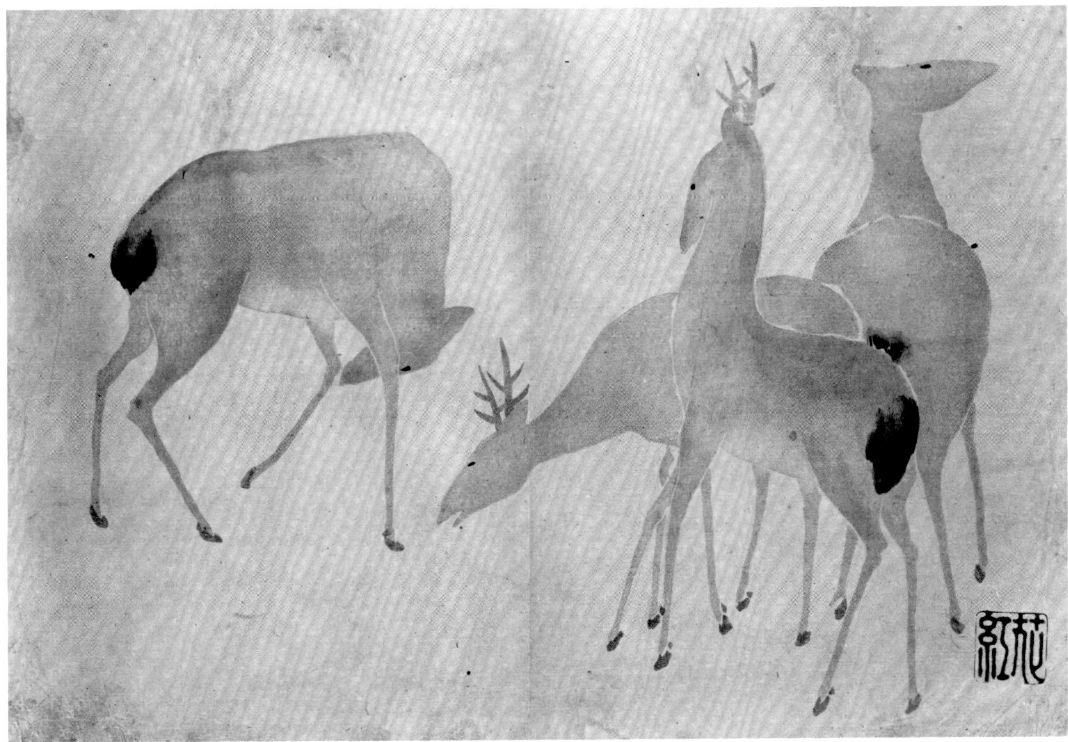

The book is titled *An Album of Pictures by Kōrin*, the early eighteenth-century artist who founded the Rimpa style of painting, but the pictures were actually designed by Hōchū, an artist who played an important role in the revival of Rimpa painting and decoration in the early nineteenth century. An advertisement for the book in the colophon of the 1826 edition clearly identifies Hōchū as its artist and Kakō, the name that appears on a hand-stamped square seal on several pictures in the original edition, is one of Hōchū's *gō*, or secondary art names.

There are two distinct editions of *Kōrin gafu* and individual examples show considerable variation. The original edition was published by Ōmiya Yohei of Nihombashidōri in the Eastern Capital (Edo). It contained twenty-six illustrations, a preface, a postscript and a colophon bearing the name of the printer Matsuda Shinsuke and the date 1802 (*kyōwa mizunoe inu no toshi*). A complete example of the first edition, with yellow covers, is in the colleciton of Huguette Beres, Paris. An example in the collection of Robert Ravicz, Los Angeles, also has yellow covers, preface, postscript and colophon, but lacks one picture of a man leading a horse. The example in the Chester Beatty Library lacks this picture and the printed text.

The book was reprinted in Edo by Izumiya Shōbei in 1826 (Bunsei 9). This edition has blue covers and was printed on normal Japanese paper, without the hand-coloring and hand-stamped seals that characterize the first edition. The book was reprinted after 1826; many examples with blue covers lack the date and the publisher's advertisements. The keyblocks for the 1802 and 1826 editions are apparently the same; the color blocks appear to differ, although this may merely reflect the different techniques of printing in the two editions.

The book was copied in the late nineteenth or early twentieth century. The copies have yellow covers and the date 1802, but bear the names of the publisher Kinkadō Shūkoku (or Morikuro) and the printer Tanhankan. The keyblocks and color blocks for the copy are entirely different from those used in the first edition, and were printed on heavy paper without the hand-coloring and hand-stamped seals used in 1802.

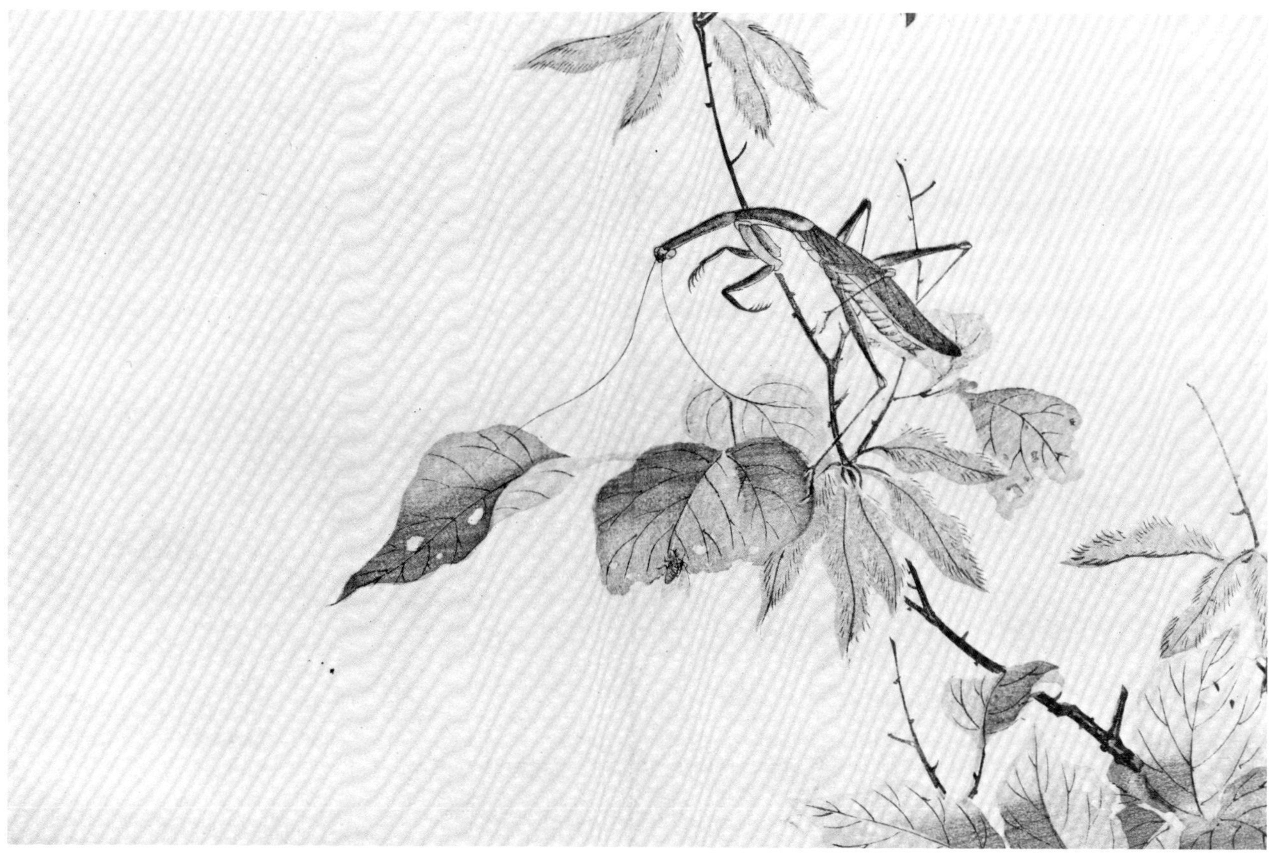

99

Mori Shunkei

Things Creeping Under Hand
1820
One-volume album, complete; 20.9 ×
14.2 cm; blue silk cover with original micaed
title slip attached at left. Twenty-five unnumbered sheets with twelve color illustrations
and eleven calligraphic specimens.

1 Preface, signed Shōhitsu, dated 7/1820
(Bunsei 3); seals, Shōhitsu and another unread. Engraver: Tani Seikō, sealed Edo

2 Grasshopper and rice plant

3 Calligraphy by Genkichi

4 Corn, spider, beetle

5 Calligraphy by Chikusō

6 Wasp and cicada on lotus

7 Calligraphy by Shōchiku (with same seals
as author of preface)

8 Snail, caterpillar, insects

9 Calligraphy by Chikusō

10 Red dragonfly and caterpillar on plant (not
included in reprint)

11 Calligraphy by Genkichi, undeciphered
signature (Chōsui?)

12 Fireflies and insect on grass

13 Calligraphy by Shōchiku

14 Insects and pinks

15 Calligraphy by Chikusō

16 Grasshopper and squash flowers

17 Calligraphy by Genkichi

18 Mantis and fly on vine (*see illustration*)

19 Calligraphy by Chikusō

20 Cricket and frog

21 Calligraphy by Shōchiku

22 Grasshopper and bee

23 Calligraphy by Genkichi

24 Butterflies, signed Mori Shunkei, dated
spring/summer 1820

Engraver and printer: Tōbu Tani Seikō hori
narabi suri, sealed Hori, another seal unread.
This picture was not included in the later
edition of the book, nor in the reprint

25 Calligraphy by Shōchiku

provenance Duret
accession no CBL MS 77

Another example of the first edition of the book formerly owned by Henri Vever and now in the Heinz Kaempfer collection, The Hague, is one centimeter taller than either of the examples in the Chester Beatty Library, both of which seem to have been trimmed, possibly at the time of rebinding. A blank sheet precedes the preface in the Kaempfer example. The pictures in this edition are on Chinese-style paper; the printing employs mica on some sheets and is particularly refined. The book was probably inspired by Utamaro's *Ehon mushi erami*, "The Insect Book" (see cat. no. 93).

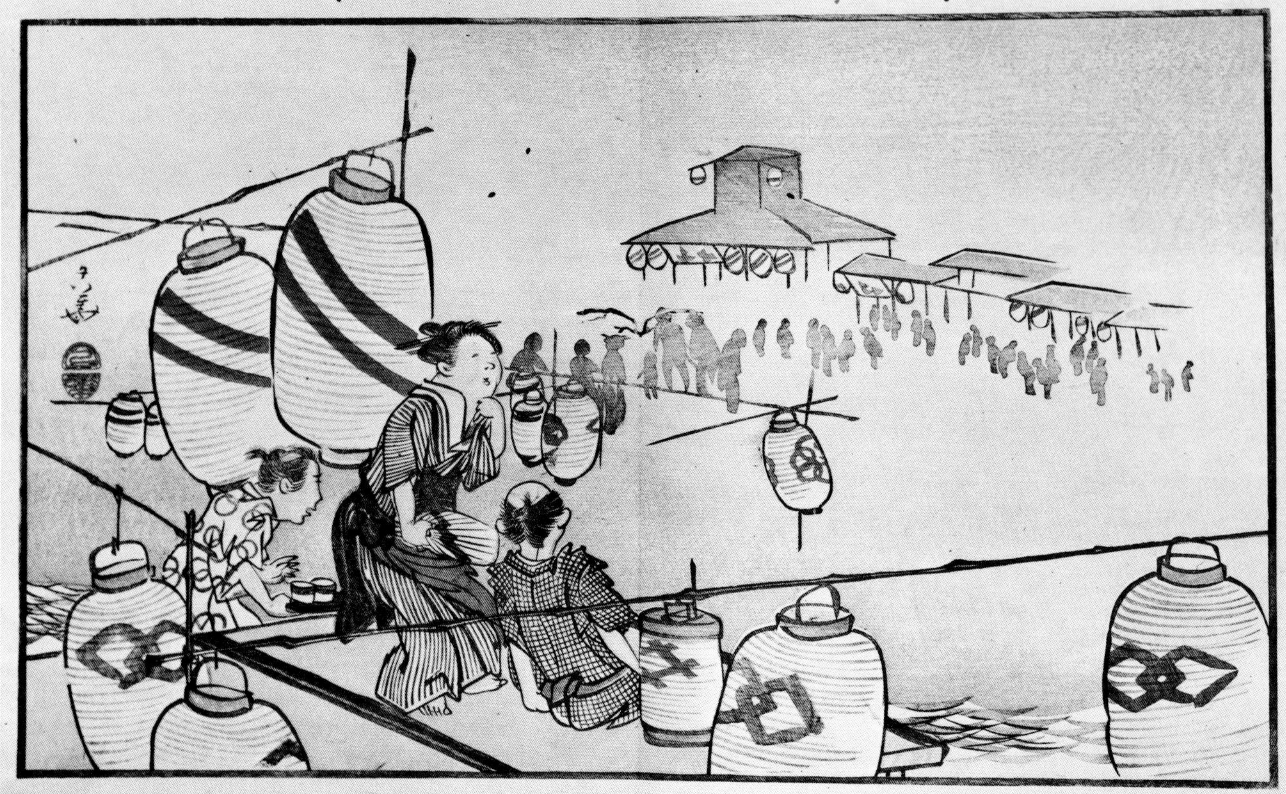

100

Ōhara Donshū and Tanaka Nikka

Early to Dawn
1837
One-volume album, complete; 24.7 ×
18.6 cm; original green paper covers with pol-
ished geometric floral designs; original buff
title slip attached at center. Ten unnumbered
sheets with two color illustrations.

1 Frontispiece with flight of sanderlings and
preface, signed Kōkōan (or Rōrōan?), dated
summer 1837

2 Revellers and passers-by beside river at
Arashiyama, signed Donshū

3–5 Three sheets of haiku verse, the first
signed Baishitsu

6 Evening by the Kamo River near Shijō in
Kyōto, signed Nikka, sealed Nikka (*see illustration*)

7–9 Three pages of haiku verse

10 Postscript by Toshū explaining that the
book was published to celebrate the erection
of a small shrine to house the portrait of the
master-founder of haiku poetry. On the same
page with the text is a block-printed picture of
a flight of sanderlings, continued from the
frontispiece.

publisher(?) Kishundō
accession no CBL MS 20

The two pictures in this album were originally published in a larger verse anthology,
Kakusei chō, "Cranes' Voices," in 1828
(Mitchell, p. 332). The example of the album
in the Ryerson collection contains nine sheets;
Toda gives the name of the compiler of the
anthology as Kitamuraan of Kyōto.